_To Abla_

_Dickensian magic_

_to you!_

"Only think of that excellent Dickens
playing the _conjurer_ for one whole hour –
the _best_ conjurer I ever saw"

_Ian Keable_

# Charles Dickens Magician

## CONJURING IN LIFE, LETTERS AND LITERATURE

## Ian Keable

www.iankeable.co.uk

First published 2014

ISBN 978-0-9557353-2-5

Cover Design by Lucy Byatt

Printed by Berfort's Information Press

*Dedicated to my mother Gilian Mary Keable-Elliott (1930-2011).
She had a great love of Dickens, but sadly died before she discovered
I shared it too.*

# Contents

# CONTENT

# Introduction

Michael Slater, in his book *Charles Dickens*, commented that part of the problem with Dickens's *American Notes*, written in 1842 after he had returned from a tour of the US, was that 'there seems to have been some confusion in his mind about his target audience'. I have rather a similar problem with this book.

Am I writing for those who know nothing about magic but are intrigued to discover that Dickens was an amateur conjurer? Or am I writing for those primarily interested in magic history and who have come across references to Dickens's conjuring before and are keen to learn more? Or am I writing for Dickensian aficionados who know plenty about Dickens and want to discover if his quirky hobby has any bearing on his personality and novels?

The answer is that I am writing for all three; and in order to tackle the problem of appealing to everybody, I have opted for a slightly unusual format. Whilst there are conventional chapters, after each there follows what I have called a 'chapter supplement'; most of which are considerably greater in length than the chapter itself.

There are six chapters in the book which can be read on their own without any reference to the supplements. Chapter One sets the scene for Dickens becoming a conjurer. It is framed around the only depiction of a conjurer in any of Dickens's novels or short stories. It shows how the type of conjurer that Dickens eventually became was very different from the fictional character he described.

Chapter Two looks at the conjurer who inspired Dickens to take up magic, Dickens's first and subsequent shows, where they were performed and how they were reported in contemporary letters and later memoirs. Dickens's span as an actual conjurer was short, only seven years, from the age of thirty, when he had just begun *Martin Chuzzlewit*, through to thirty-seven, when he was making a start on

*David Copperfield.*

Chapter Three concentrates on the show that defines Dickens's image as a conjurer, a performance he did on the Isle of Wight. With the help of his own playbill, his tricks are detailed and an analysis is made of how he succeeded as a conjurer. Consideration is given as to why he might have stopped performing.

Chapter Four scrutinises the performances of a couple of conjurers it is known Dickens saw. One of them made a huge impression on Dickens with a new type of magic which he had never come across before. He is someone who, because of Dickens's thorough report, deserves far greater attention than he has received to date.

Chapters Five and Six are rather more discursive and answer the question which was put to me by the distinguished Dickensian expert, Michael Hollington, at a Dickens Conference I attended in Hungary in November 2012. He asked if I thought that 'Dickensians' had neglected the impact of Dickens's conjuring on the man and his writings. I said back then it was probably 'no'; and I still think that is, by and large, the answer. However on reading these two chapters, maybe some will disagree: I will be delighted if they do.

## Why Chapter Supplement?

The incorporation of lengthy chapter supplements contravenes conventional writing formats. The reason is dictated by the existence of a huge number of books and journals that are only readily available to magicians, either because they are highly specialised in subject matter or because they reveal the secrets of tricks. Many of these writings were never intended to be read by anyone outside the magic community – even if they contain information and original research that might be of interest to non-magicians.

It so happens that Dickens falls into this cross-fertilisation category; magic historians are interested in him because he was a famous person who was a conjurer. And some of what they have found out about him could have a bearing on assessing the man and his writing more generally. But it is necessary to delve deeply into material that often has no relevance or interest to non-magicians in order to perhaps discover some jewel that might excite the lovers of Dickens.

The six main chapters are the result of this digging; and alone should be sufficient to more than satiate the knowledge of most readers about Dickens and conjuring. But I considered it would be unfair on my predecessors if I did not also show how I reached those conclusions from the massive amount of research done by them – hence the presence of the supplements.

Under various headings they cover additional topics: some of those expand on matters touched upon already in a chapter; whilst others look at new, subsidiary areas. A handful of these subject matters may be deemed a digression, but it is hoped they provide their own entertaining diversion, however peripheral they might be. They are all self-contained which allows the reader to pick and choose.

Included in them is a fair amount of space devoted to tackling perceived errors when it comes to Dickens and conjuring: the majority of these do relate to mistakes in books and journals primarily accessed by magicians. However occasionally there is an element of error-creep into more mainstream books.

Many of these inaccuracies occurred long ago (although there is one recent book, *Charles Dickens: Conjurer, Mesmerist and Showman* by Trevor Dawson, which has a revisionist assessment of Dickens – arguing that he took up conjuring much earlier than was previously thought; that he saw, and knew, many more conjurers than was previously acknowledged; and that he wrote much more about conjuring than was previously recognised) and have been carried forward from one writer to the next. It is for that reason it has been thought preferable to go into what some might perceive as overzealous forensic detail in order, not just to correct mistakes, but also to track down, where possible, their original provenance. Because of the nature of this exercise, there are numerous notes throughout the supplements.

I accept that an attempt to prove that some things written in relatively obscure publications about Dickens are questionable – when most readers would be unaware that they had ever been postulated – might seem a little redundant. However I trust that these excursive investigations, as well as throwing up some interesting facts in their wake (not to mention the occasional hilarious blooper) will involve some twists and turns in getting at the truth which, in themselves, will intrigue.

One bit of housekeeping, slightly ironic in view of the title of this book, is that I have adopted the nomenclature, which was prevalent in Dickens's time, of always calling a 'magician' – the term used today – a 'conjurer'. I have also spelt conjurer with 'er' at the end, rather than an 'or'; although Dickens switches between the two, conjurer was the more popular spelling in his two weekly journals. When quoting directly, though, I have kept the spelling as was used originally. I have also gone with Dickens's, rather than Dickens', mainly because that is the punctuation followed by the prestigious *The Dickensian* journal.

I think Dickensians would be amazed at the huge number of publications devoted to magic history; and similarly magicians would be surprised at the vast amount of literature analysing Dickens's life and works. It is rare that such seemingly unrelated subject matters intersect. This book has been written with the belief that somehow these two unlikely bedfellows can successfully procreate; and bring to life a 'Dickensian Conjurer' that is worthwhile and engaging. If, in the process, it adds a small fraction of knowledge to two of my great loves, then I will be happy with my task.

# Cast of Characters

**Anderson, John Henry** (1814-74) The most famous British conjurer of the mid-Victorian era, known as the Northern Wizard or Great Wizard of the North. CD repeated his catch-phrase and copied many of his tricks.

**Carlyle, Jane** (1801-66) Married to social historian and essayist Thomas Carlyle and huge admirer of CD's magic. She wrote that he could earn a full-time living from conjuring if he wished.

**Chorley, Henry** (1808-72) Bachelor friend of CD who also saw Alfred de Caston perform. It was thanks to his Journals that the French conjurer was identified as the man who had fooled CD.

**Coutts, Angela Burdett** (1814-1906) Generous benefactor and extremely wealthy woman. CD advised her in her charitable donations and wrote to her about his successes as a conjurer.

**De Caston, Alfred** (1822-82) French conjurer who CD saw in Boulogne in 1854. De Caston's mind reading skills so impressed CD that he called him 'a perfectly original genius'.

**Dickens, Catherine** (1815-79) Like many an amateur magician's wife she appeared to play no part in CD's conjuring.

**Dickens, Charley** (1837-96) The oldest son of CD. CD's first conjuring show was performed on his sixth birthday, held on Twelfth Night on 6th January, 1843; and conjuring at his birthday party became a regular event.

**Dickens, Fred** (1820-68) Younger brother of CD who turned out to be as wayward as his father. He was asked by CD to try and find a conjurer's outfit for himself and John Forster.

**Dickens, Mamie** (1838-96) Wrote in later memoires about her father's prowess as a conjurer, particularly recalling the Bonus Genius trick and the production of a pudding from a hat.

**Döbler, Ludwig** (1801-64) Name spelt variously Doebler, Dobler. Austrian conjurer who influenced CD to take up magic when he saw him in July 1842; he was cited several times in CD's letters.

**Felton, Cornelius** (1807-62) American friend to whom CD first informed he had taken up conjuring in a letter in December 1842. He accompanied CD to see the French conjurer, Robert-Houdin.

**Forster, John** (1812-76) Great friend and first biographer. Together they bought CD's first set of magic props. It was in his biography that the playbill for CD's show on the Isle of Wight was reproduced.

**Khia Khan Khruse** (dates unknown) Also spelt Kia. He left behind some intriguing playbills and inspired Rhia Rhama Rhoos, the name under which CD performed on the Isle of Wight.

**Leech, John** (1817-64) Leading cartoonist for *Punch* for many years. Another man who acted as CD's assistant in his shows. Was 'cured' by CD's mesmerism when he was hit by a wave in 1849.

**Macready, Catherine** (1805-52) Wife of the great actor William, known as Nina. It was at her birthday party in 1843 that both CD, and Jane Carlyle, wrote so enthusiastically about his conjuring.

**Mitton, Thomas** (1812-1878) CD's solicitor and recipient of letters about his conjuring.

**Ramo Samee** (d. 1849) Indian conjurer and juggler who came to England in 1815. The only real-life conjurer that CD stated by name in any of his articles; and that was five years after he had died.

**Robert-Houdin, Jean Eugène** (1805-1871) Easily the most prominent French conjurer of the nineteenth century whose memoirs were reviewed in *Household Words*. CD saw him perform in May 1853.

**Stanfield, Clarkson** (1793-1867) Acclaimed marine painter who played CD's assistant in his first conjuring show. CD named him Ivory for this role.

**Stodare, Colonel** (1831-1866) CD attended his show in 1865 where he performed the sensational Sphinx illusion. CD wrote his suggested explanation of the trick to his daughter Mamie.

**Watson, Richard** (1800-18520 and wife **Lavinia** (1816-88) It was at their home in Rockingham Castle in Leicester that CD did his last ever known conjuring show in November 1849. Also performed some tricks for them in Lausanne in 1846.

# Dickens's Life and Conjuring Timeline

| Year | Key Events in Dickens's Life | Conjuring Landmarks |
|------|------------------------------|---------------------|
| 1812 | Born on 7th February in Portsmouth. | |
| 1815 | | Ramo Samee and Khia Khan Khruse arrived in England from India. |
| 1817 | Moved to Chatham in Kent. | |
| 1819 | | Last performance in London of Munito the Learned Dog. |
| 1822 | Sept: Moved to Camden in London. | CD saw street conjurers according to 1854 article in *Household Words*. |
| 1824 | Worked for 6 months in shoe-blacking factory. | |
| 1825 | Attended Wellington House Academy for two years. | |
| 1827 | Joined Ellis & Blackmore as solicitor's clerk; went to the theatre almost every night. | |
| 1828 | | Theatre conjuring on the rise. Signor Blitz & Jules de Rovère had residencies in London theatres. |
| 1829 | Shorthand writer for law courts & Parliament. | |
| 1833 | First literary work published. | |
| 1834 | Engaged as parliamentary reporter by the *Morning Chronicle*. | |

| 1836 | *Sketches by Boz* published. *Pickwick Papers* in serial form. Married Catherine Hogarth. Became freelance writer. | CD wrote about thimble-rigging in Greenwich Fair chapter in *Sketches by Boz*. |
| 1837 | *Pickwick Papers* published. | Jan: George Sutton at the New Strand Theatre. |
| 1838 | *Oliver Twist* published. Sept: First visit to Isle of Wight staying at Groves's Needles Hotel, Alum Bay | Dec: Ramo Samee appeared on same bill as theatrical bootleg production of *Nicholas Nickleby*. |
| 1839 | *Nicholas Nickleby* published. | Thimble-rigging depicted in *Nicholas Nickleby*. |
| 1840 | April: Weekly periodical, *Master Humphrey's Clock*, began – it serialised *The Old Curiosity Shop*. | Feb: John Henry Anderson first performed in London. |
| 1841 | *The Old Curiosity Shop* published. *Barnaby Rudge* published. | CD's only portrayal of a fictional conjurer, Sweet William, in *The Old Curiosity Shop*. Feb: Joseph Jacobs at the New Strand Theatre. |
| 1842 | Jan-June: first American tour. *American Notes* published. | July: CD saw Ludwig Döbler perform. Dec: CD confirmed he had bought the stock in trade of a conjurer. |
| 1843 | *A Christmas Carol* published. | Jan: CD's first proper conjuring show on Twelfth Night. Dec: Jane Carlyle praised CD's magic at Nina Macready's birthday. |

| | | |
|---|---|---|
| 1844 | *Martin Chuzzlewit* published. July: First visit to France. | Jan: CD's second conjuring show on Twelfth Night. July: Ludwig Döbler second season in London. |
| 1845 | Sept: Produced and acted in Ben Jonson's *Every Man in His Humour*. | |
| 1846 | Jun-Nov: Resided in Lausanne, Switzerland. Nov: In Paris for three months. | July: CD entertained Mr & Mrs Watson in Lausanne with tricks. |
| 1848 | *Dombey and Son* published. | May: Robert-Houdin first performed in London. |
| 1849 | July: Family holiday at Winterbourne House in Bonchurch on Isle of Wight. Oct: Left Bonchurch. | Jan: CD's third conjuring show on Twelfth Night. Aug/Sept: CD performed as Rhia Rhama Rhoos in Bonchurch. Nov: CD's final known conjuring show at Rockingham Castle. |
| 1850 | *Household Words* founded. *David Copperfield* published. | |
| 1853 | *Bleak House* published. First public reading, for charity, from *A Christmas Carol*. | May: CD saw Robert-Houdin perform at Sadler's Wells in his final London appearance. |
| 1854 | *Hard Times* published. | Sept: CD saw Alfred de Caston in Boulogne in France. Nov: Ramo Samee mentioned in article in *Household Words*. |

| | | |
|---|---|---|
| 1855 | Lived in Paris for several months. | |
| 1857 | Aug: Met actress Ellen Ternan. | |
| 1858 | Separated from wife Catherine. First public reading for his own benefit. | |
| 1859 | *All the Year Round* founded. *A Tale of Two Cities* published. | April: Review of Robert-Houdin's 'Memoirs' appeared in *Household Words*. |
| 1861 | *Great Expectations* published. | |
| 1862 | | French conjurer Henri Robin at Egyptian Hall: CD attended a séance with him. Dec: first performance of Pepper's Ghost alongside CD's *The Haunted Man*. |
| 1865 | *Our Mutual Friend* published. | Nov: CD saw Colonel Stodare perform the Sphinx illusion; wrote to daughter with explanation of trick. |
| 1867 | Nov: second American tour began. | March: Anderson & CD perform in Dublin. |
| 1870 | Mar: last public reading. Died on 9th June. Uncompleted *The Mystery of Edwin Drood* published. | |
| 1874 | Third volume of John Forster's *The Life of Charles Dickens* published. | The Bonchurch playbill and CD's admiration of Alfred de Caston first made known. |

# CHAPTER ONE

# The Observer

## Dickens's Fictional Conjurer

There is only one conjurer in any of Charles Dickens's novels or short stories; a surprising revelation given his interest in magic and the couple of thousand fictional characters he must have penned over his life time of writing. Even more striking is that Dickens wrote the portrait before he took up conjuring himself. However the conjurer he depicted proves to be extremely informative about Dickens's attitude towards magic at the time – a point of view that was probably shared by many of his readers.

*The Old Curiosity Shop* was Dickens's fourth novel. It followed *The Pickwick Papers*, *Oliver Twist* and *Nicholas Nickleby* which had already established him, before he was aged thirty, as one of the leading writers of his day. Dickens's original intention was that it was to be a short story; one of those recounted by the eponymous narrator in the weekly periodical *Master Humphrey's Clock*. Dickens soon discovered his public wanted something more substantial, so he expanded it into a full-length book, which was serialised weekly between April 1840 and February1841. By the end of the run, Dickens was selling 100,000 copies of each issue.

The singular conjurer made his appearance at the start of Chapter 19, which would have been written around June 1840. He arrived at the Jolly Sandboys inn, alongside the 'proprietor of a giant, and a little lady without legs or arms' called Vuffin, where Little Nell and her grandfather were staying. He was described by Dickens as 'a silent gentleman who earned his living by showing tricks upon the cards'. Possible 'tricks upon the cards' he might have performed are given in some contemporary reports.

One nineteenth century street entertainer demonstrated his ability by 'telling a named card by throwing a pack in the air and catching the card on a sword point'. This is known as the Card Stab and is still a popular stage trick, although it rarely, perhaps unsurprisingly given the need for a dangerous weapon, features on the street. A more detailed description of another trick involved a selected card vanishing from a pack and ending up in the bag in which the busker collected his takings.

The phrase 'tricks upon the cards' sounds outmoded. Nowadays 'card tricks' would be substituted. There is of course, with Dickens, as in the analysis of any writer, a danger of reading far more into a few words than were intended by the author. But knowing Dickens did have a choice – 'card trick' was in common usage at the time – why would he go for the more archaic expression? Admittedly it gives a better rhythm to the sentence; more significantly it was representative of the type of performer who would have used this wording in describing his own repertoire.

In *The Old Curiosity Shop* Dickens was not portraying a theatrical conjurer, a recognisable stereotype that came of age in the Victorian era; instead he was depicting a seasoned street entertainer whose roots could be traced back to the eighteenth century and earlier. Dickens's characterisation is noteworthy as it reflected all that he disapproved of in a conjurer; with no hint of the type of conjurer he would later try to emulate.

Dickens became a successful amateur conjurer, not just because he had the character profile which attracted him towards such a hobby, but also because he was around at a time when conjuring started to become acceptable to the middle-classes and, equally importantly, when the type of magic in fashion suited his circumstances. It needs to be appreciated how fortunate it was that the prevailing zeitgeist resulted in a style of conjuring which appealed to, and was practical for, Dickens.

To understand why this is so, a distinction has to be made

between two genres – 'street' and 'theatre' conjuring; the former, as already hinted at, had a decisive influence on Dickens's portrayal of his fictional conjurer; the latter is crucial in explaining his personal journey to becoming a performer.

## Theatre Conjuring

There was very little conjuring in theatres at the end of the eighteenth century. It was not considered the type of entertainment suitable for the middle-classes to attend on a large scale. This was partly due to the perceived social status of the majority of conjurers, which was often not much higher than that of the vagrant. Thomas Frost in *The Lives of the Conjurors*, wrote that conjurers in this period 'could not hope to obtain audiences large enough to fill Covent Garden theatre, or even the smallest temple of the dramatic Muses which the metropolis then contained'. Their choice of venue was limited to hiring their own room and fitting it up with a stage, chairs and basic lighting.

Despite the gradual increase in theatrical conjuring through the early years of the nineteenth century, the general consensus was that the quality of magic was not commensurately evolving. One can partly understand this from the conditions in which the performers were working. If you did not have the benefit of a proper stage, with wings, trap doors and special lighting to assist you, it was hard to produce spectacular magic. It did not help either that in the same period supernatural ghost shows and phantasmagorical exhibitions, created by optical devices such as magic lanterns, seemed to 'out-magic' conjurers when it came to producing startling illusions and drawing in audiences.

It was around 1827 that Dickens began to visit the theatre on a regular basis. This was when he had joined a firm of solicitors called Ellis and Blackmore at the age of fifteen. He later wrote: 'I went to some theatre every night, with a very few exceptions, for at least three years: really studying the bills first, and going to where there was the best acting: and always to see Mathews whenever he played.' Dickens was genuinely thinking of becoming an actor up to 1832 – even indulging in some minor theatrical parts. His inspiration was Charles Mathews, well-known for his comic impersonations and someone Dickens would model himself on when it came to his public readings.

In the 1820s a new style of magic performing emerged that attracted theatre-goers. These were conjurers who performed predominantly with apparatus, exhibiting on stage a dazzling display of paraphernalia to intrigue their audience. It will be seen in the next chapter that it was one specific 'apparatus-type' conjurer Dickens saw in 1842 who inspired him to take up conjuring. But there were many others whom Dickens might have seen, similarly involved in this vogue of 'prop' conjuring, from the late 1820s onwards.

The popularity of this type of magic suited the amateur well. It meant they did not have to spend an excessive amount of time practising, as the magic prop did the majority of work for them. This did not imply that somehow they would emerge overnight as good conjurers – other talents were required. But what it offered was a lower entry skill-set; and that certainly suited Dickens. This ability to call yourself a conjurer, without having to master sleight of hand, was a new phenomenon, and very different from the magic of the street conjurer that Dickens had seen in his youth.

## Street Conjuring

Street conjurers have been documented since medieval times – performing at street corners, open spaces and in metropolitan and provincial fairs. The most famous location was Bartholomew Fair in London which began in 1133, changing over the years to an event that lasted between one day and two weeks; it eventually ceased in 1855. The meaning of 'street conjurer' was not restricted solely to someone who works outside – many of them performed their tricks in bars and taverns. Rather it referred to an itinerant way of life, earning a living primarily by busking, as opposed to charging a ticket admission price or an agreed fee for a one-off show.

As the conjurer was continuously travelling, and had to carry all his belongings with him, he (women street conjurers were rare) was restricted in the size and quantity of his magic props. He performed his tricks with everyday objects, such as cups and balls, pieces of rope, a pack of cards and some coins. What these tricks had in common was that they required manual dexterity combined with strong misdirection (the ability to make the audience look somewhere other than where the sleight of hand is taking place) to carry them off. These skills could not be mastered overnight; they depended upon not only many hours of practice but also time spent in front of audiences, learning from mistakes and experiencing the trauma of tricks going wrong.

Such a life was far from easy in Victorian times. A street conjurer interviewed by Henry Mayhew in the 1840s, later reproduced in *London Labour and the London Poor*, said: 'I have sometimes walked my twenty miles a-day, and busked at every parlour I came to...and come home with only 1s 6d in my pocket.' In London there was immense competition with other forms of street entertainers and street sellers generally. Many conjurers doubled up as jugglers, hoping that combining skills might generate more takings.

It is unclear if Dickens saw any theatre conjurers prior to 1842 but he did see street conjurers. In 1854, in his weekly journal *Household Words*, Dickens contributed an article called 'An Unsettled Neighbourhood', which was based upon his memories of living in Bayham Street, Camden Town, an area of London he moved to aged ten. Here he wrote: 'As to Punches, they knew better than to do anything but squeak and drum in the neighbourhood, unless a collection was made in advance – which never succeeded. Conjurors and strong men strayed among us, at long intervals; but, I never saw the donkey go up once.'

'Punches' was a reference to Punch and Judy shows, whilst the 'donkey' going up related to a stunt performed by strong-men of holding up a donkey attached to a pole. Conjurers competed with these entertainers. Later on, in the same paragraph, Dickens wrote about a young man 'practising Ramo Samee with three potatoes'. Ramo Samee was a well-known juggler, as well as a conjurer, so Dickens was using the name as a metaphor for juggling.

Ramo Samee (see Plates 1 and 2) was one of the few who made the transition from street conjuring to theatre conjuring, so would have been someone Dickens admired. But generally, in addition to the fact that they would have reminded him about a period of life he did not like to talk about, it can be seen why neither the life-style nor the skill-set of the street conjurer would have appealed to Dickens. Those reasons are well summarised by a conjurer who spoke to Mayhew about one of his contemporary street entertainers. He said he was perhaps 'the best hand at the cups and balls of any man in England' (in other words, extremely skilled) but he was also 'a very uneducated man'.

This was worlds apart from the eventual conjuring of Dickens, with his reliance on apparatus magic, performing to his cultivated friends and family.

## Sweet William

With the distinction made between the new form of theatre conjuring that attracted Dickens, and the old form of street conjuring that held no such allurement, it is opportune to return to Dickens's conjurer in *The Old Curiosity Shop*. Only the start of his initial description was given earlier. In full, Dickens wrote that he was 'a silent gentleman who earned his living by showing tricks upon the cards, and who had rather deranged the natural expression of his countenance by putting small leaden lozenges into his eyes and bringing them out at his mouth, which was one of his professional accomplishments'.

Leaving aside the expression 'tricks upon the cards', already covered earlier, the rest of the sentence also suggests Dickens was portraying a street conjurer; in particular the poor man's distasteful facial features which is reminiscent of an actual street conjurer who was described by Mayhew as having a 'sallow complexion'. His disreputable appearance resulted from his multiple rendition of a classic street trick; shoving lozenges into your eyes would have been an excellent way of attracting the attention of people bustling along a busy road or causing a stir in a parlour.

A similar stunt can be found in the first book in English which revealed how magic tricks were done, Reginald Scot's 1584 *The Discoverie of Witchcraft*. It explained how you could 'thrust a peece of lead into one eie, and to drive it about (with a sticke) betweene the skin and flesh of the forehead, untill it be brought to the other eie, and there thrust out'. Dickens's conjurer, whilst pretending to place the lead lozenges into his eyes, would have pushed them under his eye lids; it would have been other pieces of lead, which were already inside his mouth that he would have supposedly regurgitated – thereby creating the impression they had passed through the inside of his head.

Despite his tiny walk-on part in *The Old Curiosity Shop*, Dickens wrote that the conjurer's name 'probably as a pleasant satire upon his ugliness, was called Sweet William'. Sweet William was a reference to a character in a 1720 ballad written by John Gay, best known for *The Beggar's Opera*, called 'Sweet William's Farewell to Black-eyed Susan'. The ironic contrast between the clearly handsome Sweet William of the ballad, and the conjurer who had 'deranged the natural expression of his countenance', would have been understood by his readers.

Sweet William made a further brief appearance in *The Old Curiosity Shop*, with Dickens continuing to emphasise the slightly unsavoury nature of his character. The other guests at the inn seemed to be deliberately avoiding his company as 'the silent gentleman sat in a warm corner, swallowing, or seeming to swallow, sixpennyworth of halfpence for practice, balancing a feather upon his nose, and rehearsing other feats of dexterity of that kind, without paying any regard whatever to the company, who in their turn left him utterly unnoticed'.

Even these small details of how Sweet William was passing the time pick up on what one would anticipate from a street conjurer doubling up as a juggler. One of those interviewed by Mayhew described an incident where he 'apparently swallowed' a pickwick (a pickwick was an implement used to catch up and raise a short wick of an oil lamp); whilst a street juggler remarked that he used to balance the feathers of peacocks.

The unflattering portrait reinforces the standpoint that Dickens would have had towards street conjurers generally. Perhaps he had a similar image in mind in the first issue of *Master Humphrey's Clock*: this was published in April 1840, so predated his character Sweet William. The eponymous narrator related how suspicious his neighbours were of him when he first moved to a new house in London: 'I became the centre of a popular ferment, extending for half a mile round, and in one direction for a full mile. Various rumours were circulated to my prejudice. I was a spy, an infidel, a conjurer, a kidnapper of children, a refugee, a priest, a monster.'

For Dickens, a conjurer was apparently the equivalent of a 'kidnapper of children' and 'a monster' – although it is amusing to note that 'a priest' was also tacked onto this list of reprobates.

## Hustles and Cheating

Apart from the life-style of the street conjurer, there was an additional element of prejudice against them, which was that they were often associated with con games which tricked the public out of money. It has relevance to Dickens because he was clearly knowledgeable about such activities. And, although Dickens himself never made the connection, it has been argued that a familiarity with cheating presupposes that he was somehow a closet conjurer.

A hustle that Dickens knew plenty about was called thimble-rigging. Its direct association with conjuring was made clear by one street entertainer questioned in Mayhew's book, who, although he never practised it himself, was constantly asked how thimble-rigging was done.

Thimble-rigging, or 'Three Thimbles and a Pea', involved placing a pea under one of three thimbles, mixing them up and asking the punter to guess where the pea was. Needless to say the participant had no chance of winning; this was because the operator could steal the pea out of one thimble, and undetectably place it under another, whilst moving the thimbles around. In the unlikely event of somebody choosing the correct thimble, in the process of pushing it forward for the spectator to lift it up, the pea was surreptitiously removed (see Plate 3).

Dickens vividly described the game in action in a factual passage from 'Greenwich Fair' in *Sketches by Boz*, where a greenhorn was relieved of 'two bob and a bender', or two shillings and sixpence. Dickens clearly realised it was all a con, and also noted the presence of a confederate, who conveniently had 'unfortunately left his purse at home', to persuade the unsuspecting victim to make a bet. He 'strongly urges the stranger not to neglect such a golden opportunity' and 'the stranger of course loses'.

Dickens's commentary on this seamy side of hustling in no way suggested any desire to perform, or indeed any knowledge of, conjuring. He did not describe how the man with the thimbles was actually manipulating the pea. He has picked up on the fact that it was one of those games you cannot win; and the thimble-rigger had stooges to assist him. But that was something any observant person would have quickly realised if he was to watch the hustle in action for any length of time. And one thing definitely known about Dickens was that he was an unsurpassed observer and recorder of London life.

Another area where conjuring and cheating appears to go hand in hand is that of card-sharping; hence the expression that many a magician hears, 'I wouldn't want to play cards with you'. There is the, usually false, assumption that just because someone can manipulate a pack of cards whilst performing tricks, they are capable of fleecing you during a game of poker. Dickens was clearly familiar with card cheating and was knowledgeable enough to be able to detect it happening. When travelling to America in January 1842 he spotted a fellow passenger being fleeced by card-sharpers, and discreetly warned him from continuing to play.

He also wrote about the sadistic dwarf Quilp, in *The Old Curiosity Shop*, 'always cheating at cards'; however his description of how the villain cheated was rather generalised – he mentioned his having 'a close observance of the game, and a sleight-of-hand in counting and scoring'. Dickens did not display any particular inside knowledge of how a card expert might actually manipulate the cards to his advantage.

It can therefore be seen from Dickens's fictional and factual writings prior to 1842 that he was a keen observer of con games and card-cheating – but that was as far as it went. In the same way that he had not practised any actual conjuring, so he had not learnt any of the specific skills of the hustler or the card cheat. There is no reason to speculate that Dickens ever did indulge in such nefarious actions. But it is a different story as far as his interest in conjuring was concerned. The development of this will be primarily traced through a completely new, and revealing, source of writing: the letters of Dickens.

# Chapter One Supplement

## Tricks Upon the Cards and Card Tricks

The expression 'tricks upon the cards' was not coined by Dickens: its origins can be traced back to at least the seventeenth century. When the Italian nobleman, and Renaissance court conjurer, Hieronymus Scotto performed in front of Queen Elizabeth on 12th May 1602, a journalist wrote about 'an Italian at court that doth wonderful tricks upon the cards'.

A very similar phrase also appeared in Ben Jonson's 1610 play *The Alchemist* in which one of the characters said: 'I'll believe / That Alchemy is a pretty kind of game, / Somewhat like tricks o' the cards, to cheat a man / With charming.' It was another Jonson play, *Every Man in his Humour*, which was to revitalise Dickens's interest in acting in 1845.

By contrast, 'card tricks' is a comparatively recent term. One of the earliest references was in 1778 where there was a notice in the *Public Advertiser*. 'The droll performance of the little conjuring horse and learned dog, both of which exhibit card tricks equal to the best performance.' It gradually crept into usage; so in an 1838 playbill for John Henry Anderson it stated, after it had claimed he would make cards walk from the pack, 'He will conclude his Card Tricks with System of Gaming...'

'Card tricks' was still not in general circulation a few decades after 1841, the year *The Old Curiosity Shop* was published. Books on magic in the latter part of the nineteenth century went around the houses in not using these words, instead choosing to categorise them as 'Feats with Cards, 'Tricks with Cards', 'Tricks on Cards', 'Recreations with Cards' and 'Popular Tricks and Changes in Cards'. It was only in 1876 that it became the title of a book, *Cards and Card Tricks*. The following year it was given the official stamp of conjuring approval when Professor Hoffmann published *Card Tricks without Sleight of Hand*. Finally the far more evocative 'tricks upon the cards' was consigned to magic history.[1]

## Theatre Conjurers prior to 1842[2]

The first conjurer to hire a theatre was Guiseppe Pinetti, who came to London in the autumn of 1784 and had a winter season at the Little Theatre in Haymarket. However it was not until the 1820s, with the Swiss conjurer, Chalon, appearing at the St James's Theatre and then moving in the following year to the Adelphi, that theatre hiring by conjurers became more frequent. Chalon died in 1825 so Dickens was unlikely to have seen him; the same was true of Chalon's supposed nephew Girardelli, who performed in England

[1] [Dawes, Rich] No. 196: 'The Italian Court Conjurer Hieronymus Scotto', Vol. 87, October, 1993, p 151. *The Alchemist*, Ben Jonson, Act II, Scene III, cited in 'The Conjurer and His Art in Literature', TB Donovan [Magic Circular] Vol. 23, March, 1929, p. 89. *Public Advertiser*, Wednesday 2 December, 1778. The Anderson playbill is in [Houdini, Unmasking] p. 150. *Cards and Card Tricks*, HE Heather, 'The Bazaar' Office, London:, 1876; *Card Tricks without Sleight of Hand*, Professor Hoffmann, Frederick Warne, London, c. 1877.

[2] 'The social position of the professional conjurer was at this period [the end of the eighteenth century] even more dubious than that of the actor. The prejudice against his art and its professors which had been born of ignorance and superstition was dying out with the process of mental enlightenment; but he was ranked, in common with the juggler, the posture, and the tumbler, as a vagrant...He might be patronised by the upper classes, and even by the royal family; but he was not admitted into good society, or even regarded as a respectable character.' [Frost] pp.125-6. Frost went on to write that such conjurers 'hired a first-floor room of some house within a radius of half a mile from Charing Cross, fitted up his stage at one end, procured as many chairs as the room would hold, and lighted it with wax candles.' [Frost] pp. 127-8. For optical illusion shows, which for a period proved more popular than conjurers, see [During] pp. 102-3 and [Dawes, Great Illusionists] pp. 84-7.

in the same year.[3]

Girardelli is best known as the first 'to introduce in his bills and programmes that sonorous nomenclature which excites the imagination without conveying any suggestion even of its meaning.' That is, labelling tricks with nonsensical names such as 'The Mesmeric Couch', 'Magical Locomotion' or 'The Bottle of Bacchus'; an especially unfortunate legacy for the magic historian, as it means it is virtually impossible to work out what the trick actually was from the playbill alone. It was a stylistic form that Dickens was to parody in his own playbill at his performance in 1849 on the Isle of Wight.[4]

As theatre conjuring really began to take off in the late 1820s – the very time when Dickens began to regularly attend shows in London – there were a handful of conjurers whom he could have seen. One such was Jules de Rovère, a French conjurer who was the first to coin the phrase prestidigitateur (derived from the Italian 'presto', meaning quick, and 'digitus', a finger, or literally 'nimble-fingered') to describe himself. He appeared at the new Theatre Royal in the Haymarket for a week in October 1828. Another was a German called Signor Blitz who also was around in the same year when he gave some performances at the Coburg Theatre, later to become the Old Vic: his son, Antonio Blitz, did shows in England and Ireland between 1826 and 1834 but how often, and when, he appeared in London, is not known.[5]

---

[3] For references to Pinetti, Chalon and Girardelli, see [During] p. 94; [Clarke] p. 168 and [Frost] pp. 196 & 200.

[4] Quotation is from [Frost] p. 200. The 'nonsensical names' are taken from a John Henry Anderson playbill, at the Standard Theatre, Shoreditch, 1856. Reproduced in [Bayer] p. 103.

[5] The quotation in the main chapter about CD going to the theatre every night for three years was from [Forster, Vol. 2] Chapter 9. See also [Smith, Grahame] p. 96. The comparison between the acting of Matthews and

There are three conjurers[6] though who stand out as the most likely candidates for Dickens to have seen; this was because they appeared nearer the time when Dickens's interest in conjuring started developing, they had longer residencies at their respective venues and their performing profile, in terms of advertising and promotion, would have been that much greater. The first of these was George Sutton, who surfaced in 1837 at the Grand Saloon of the Colosseum in Regent's Park; but Dickens was more likely to have seen him the following year at his extended run at the New Strand Theatre from 22nd January until at least 16th February.

By all accounts Sutton was a better ventriloquist than a conjurer, but still performed an impressive display of tricks such as the inexhaustible bottle – in which different drinks were poured from the same receptacle – production of a shower of sweets from a paper shaped like a cornucopia and, perhaps his pièce de résistance, a trick in which a young lady disappeared and was afterwards served up in an enormous pie. This last illusion might have had an influence on Dickens's depiction of the vanish of the Ghost of Christmas Past in *A Christmas Carol*; this is considered in Chapter Six.[7]

---

Dickens's public readings was made in [Schlicke] pp. 234-41. For references to de Rovère and Blitz, see [Clarke] pp. 204 & 206-8.

[6] It was clear that Sidney Clarke had conjurers such as these in mind when he wrote that: 'A new school of conjurers arose who went in for display, sometimes in addition to – but too often in substitution for – skill. They piled their stages with gorgeous apparatus...and it was open to even the veriest duffer to set out as a conjurer with some prospect of success, if only he could purchase the requisite number of almost self-working "tricks" from a maker of apparatus.' [Clarke] p. 203

[7] Sutton was at the Grand Saloon of the Colosseum in Regent's Park on 25 March, 1837 and again on 8 May. He was also at the Lowther Rooms, King William Street from 24 April. Information is from [Dawes, Rich] No. 424: 'Mr George Sutton, "The Great Magician",' Vol. 108, March, 2014, p. 70., where Dawes wrote: 'In the nineteenth century many magicians sought to impress

Secondly, there was Joseph Jacobs who was in London, again at the New Strand Theatre, in February 1841 for at least two weeks and at Christmas in the same year. His February playbill boasted that the 'Stage is filled up with great Splendour; The Apparatus is Costly and Gorgeous'. Amongst his tricks were the Chinese Linking Rings (metal rings that link and unlink) and the production of a guinea pig.[8]

Finally, there was John Henry Anderson, whose name crops up quite a few times during the telling of Dickens's conjuring life. Anderson debuted in London at the New Strand Theatre from February to May 1840, and then performed at St James's Bazaar in June and July. He did another season the following year at the Adelphi Theatre from May to September. Anderson was well-known for his extensive advertising – no better illustrated than his claim that his self-imposed title of 'The Great Wizard of the North' was conferred on him by Sir Walter Scott, even though the timescale made it impossible – and, even more than Sutton and Jacobs, for his extravagant stage settings; as late as 1857 he was proclaiming that 'gorgeously superb apparatus will be used' in performing his repertoire.[9]

Anderson continuously amended his repertoire, but in the early

their audiences by filling their stages with a dazzling display of apparatus'.

[8] [Clarke] pp. 225-7. For the playbills of Jacobs in 1841, see [Price] p. 65 and [Houdini, Unmasking] p. 151.

[9] Anderson's actual dates were as follows. Mon 10 Feb - Sat 30 May, 1840: New Strand Theatre, London (His first London appearance; from the wording of advertisements, he may have taken a few days off w/c 13 April, prior to restarting on Easter Mon 20 April). Wed 10 June - Sat 11 July, 1840: St James's Bazaar, London. Mon 24 May - Sat 4 Sep, 1841: Adelphi Theatre, London (billed as the Wizard's '2nd appearance in the British Metropolis', thus counting the two successive London venues in 1840 as a single 'appearance'). Data from [Dawes, Anderson]. Apparatus quotation came from Anderson playbill in [Dawes, Great Illusionists] p. 109.

1840s performed such tricks as selected playing cards vanishing and reappearing in different drawers of a cabinet and the transportation of a ring from one casket to another, before being eventually found inside an orange. He also did tricks – like the production of a guinea pig, the revelation of a handkerchief in a bottle and the baking of a pudding in a top hat – that Dickens went on to do himself. The sheer amount of time that Anderson was in London in 1840 and 1841 (almost eight months) makes him the most likely of the three that Dickens would have seen.[10]

## Munito the Learned Dog

There is one rather unusual conjurer that it has been suggested Dickens saw which, if true, would constitute one of his earliest conjuring experiences. The conjurer was unusual because he was not human, he was canine – Munito the Learned Dog. Munito was owned by Signor Castelli and could 'read, write, cast accounts, play at dominos, distinguish colours, and perform tricks with cards'. He also 'adds, subtracts, and multiplies'. He arrived in England in May 1817 and was exhibited at Saville House in Leicester Square.[11]

Munito's supposed link to Dickens came about because he was mentioned in an article, 'Performing Animals', that was published in Dickens's weekly journal *All the Year Round* in 1867. The anonymous author wrote that he saw Munito 'forty-five years ago': this would be the year 1822 and therefore predated by several years any of the possible theatrical conjurers that Dickens might have

[10] For Anderson's tricks see [Frost] pp. 232-4 and [Clarke] p. 213.

[11] Information about Munito's exploits come from *The Literary Gazette*, 5 April, 1817, p. 170 (when Munito was in Paris – a month later he was performing in London) and an advertisement in the *Morning Chronicle*, 31 May, 1817: 'The exhibition will commence this day from two till four o'clock and will be repeated each succeeding day. Admission 3s each person.'

seen.[12]

It was Ricky Jay who first drew attention to the possibility of the meeting of two such eminent examples of their respective species. He wrote, in the first issue of *Jay's Journal of Anomalies*, a quarterly periodical that eventually totalled sixteen numbers, 'Such was the poodle's impact that forty-five years after witnessing his show Charles Dickens was able to recall Munito's repertoire'. Jay probably picked up the attribution of the piece to Dickens from Steven Tigner's article in his 'Charles Dickens In and About Magic' in the short-lived *The Journal of Magic History*. Tigner had written: 'We do not need to credit Grimaldi for rousing Dickens' interest in conjuring tricks, however, if an article in Dickens' journal, *All the Year Round*...may fairly be credited to him. It is on "Performing Animals".'[13]

In 'Performing Animals', the author was keen to work out how Munito did his tricks. He had to see the dog a second time before, as he wrote, 'the mystery was solved'. Having conjectured that the owner secretly added aniseed to the playing card he wanted his dog to sniff out (allegedly he had the spicy substance concealed in his pocket), 'after the performance' he gave its master his considered opinion, who 'did not deny the discovery of his principle'. This was all too much for Jay:

In the time-honoured tradition the amateur, thoroughly fooled...intuits a method which, although almost certainly incorrect...satisfies him. He now confronts the conjurer (unlike many of his present-day counterparts, Dickens had the courtesy to wait for the room to clear) and proudly announces his theory. The performer

---

[12] [AYR] Vol. XVII, No. 405, 26 January, 1867, pp. 105-6.

[13] *Jay's Journal of Anomalies* 'The Faithful Monetto & The Inimitable Dick' was first published in Vol. 1, No. 1 Spring, 1994. The journal was later turned into a book, with some additional notes. The extracts come from [Jay, Journal] pp. 4-5. See also [Tigner] p. 92.

smiles and says nothing. This the amateur interprets as a sign of assent.

The problem with all this righteous indignation is that Dickens never wrote the article. Admittedly it is one of those in *All The Year Round* that at present remains unattributed – which in itself almost certainly means it was not written by Dickens[14] – but there were other factors in play which rule out the possibility of him having seen Munito.

The major obstacle is that the author must have his timescale wrong. Munito only performed in London for a couple of years – his last traceable show was in June 1819. His trail after that is hard to follow but there is no evidence that he returned again to England. Part of the reason he left might be explained by a playbill of the year of his departure that showed the cost of seeing Munito was now one shilling, whereas previously it had been three. Clearly the Learned Dog no longer had the pulling power of old and it was time to find pastures new.[15]

In June 1819 Dickens was seven years old; he was living in Chatham in Kent. It is utterly implausible to imagine that Dickens

---

[14] For further discussion on attribution of articles, see 'Articles from *Household Words* and *All the Year Round*', Chapter Six Supplement.

[15] Last show in England was from an advertisement in *The Morning Post* 19 June, 1819. Munito's exploits in Europe were noted in 'Antoine Castelli and His Physical Amusements', William Kalush [Gibecière] Winter, 2010, Vol. 5, No. 1, p. 150. [Dawson] p. 143 agreed that Munito left England in June, 1819 and 'toured Europe'. For cost of entry to see Munito, citation is a playbill in [Dawes, Rich] No. 123: '"Bobby", The Only Handcuff King Dog in the World', Vol. 80, May, 1986, p. 85, which stated 'Admittance one shilling'. Although this playbill was undated, the venue of No. 1 Leicester Square matched the same venue in advertisements in the *Morning Chronicle* and *The Morning Post* for June, 1819. Compare note 11 above, where the admission price, in May, 1817, was three shillings.

somehow made a trip to London, not once but twice; and that furthermore, at that tender age, he confronted the Italian owner with his considered opinion as to how Munito did his tricks. The confident conclusion is that Dickens never wrote the article 'Performing Animals' and never saw Munito. So Dickens's impugned social graces and powers of detection on this occasion remain unsullied.[16]

## Life of the Street Conjurer

Some indication of the diversity of street performers in Victorian London was given by Mayhew in his pioneering *London Labour and the London Poor*. Leaving aside conjurers, there were strong men; acrobats; jugglers; tumblers; sword-swallowers; fire-eaters; puppet-show operators, featuring both puppets on strings and Punch and Judy; shows of extraordinary persons such as giants, dwarfs, Albinos, spotted boys and pig-faced ladies; shows of extraordinary animals like pigs with six legs or horses with two heads; artists doing profile cuts and draughtsmen in coloured chalks; peep-shows; wax-work shows; fortune-telling apparatus; flea-circuses; owners of trained animals with monkey organists, dancing bears and sapient dogs; dancers; street actors; musicians, whether bands or individuals playing the guitar, harp, hurdy-gurdy, bagpipes; singers of glees, ballads, comic songs and psalms

---

[16] [Dawson] p. 144 was still convinced that CD wrote the article and therefore categorically stated, without any evidence and in contradiction to his own findings (see note 15 above), that Munito must have been in London in 1822 ('Munito must have performed in London around that time'). CD arrived in London in September 1822 and this period coincided with his years of impoverishment; a time when his family certainly could not afford the one shilling fee to see Munito (or two shillings, as he supposedly saw him twice). To put that into perspective, when CD was working at the blacking factory in 1824, he was earning around six or seven shillings a week: [Ackroyd] p. 84.

improvisation; and proprietors of street games. And this is before you take into account the myriad street sellers and costermongers.[17]

In Volume 3 of the same work, Mayhew interviewed a number of street performers, research which he conducted in the 1840s, two of whom were conjurers. If the lives of the conjurers he questioned were not as depressing as the street clown ('His story was more pathetic than comic and proved that the life of the clown is, perhaps, the most wretched of all existence.'), or as exacting on the body as the Street Fire-King or Salamander ('He was a tall, gaunt man with an absent-looking face, and so pale that his dark eyes looked positively wild. I could not help thinking as I looked at his bony form, that fire was not the most nutritious food in the world.'), overall it did not appear to be an especially pleasant way of making a living, with the constant travelling and the daily uncertainty of how much you might earn.

In Chapter One a street conjurer was quoted: 'I have sometimes walked my twenty miles a-day and busked at every parlour I came to, (for I never enter tap-rooms,) and come home with only 1s 6d in my pocket.' The mention of the tap-rooms was omitted but the Victorian distinction between the 'parlour' and the 'tap-room' would seem to be akin to the modern-day 'saloon' and 'public' bar in a pub.

You can tell why the street conjurer wisely discriminated

---

[17] For early references to street conjurers, see [Clarke] p. 119. [During] p. 110 wrote that 'Significantly, Henry Mayhew does not mention conjurers in his exhaustive survey of London street performers.' This is not so. Under his list of 'street performers' Mayhew included 'conjurors' [Mayhew, Vol. 1] p. 4, as well as other performers, pp. 5-6. Quotations in this and the next section have been taken from [Mayhew, Vol. 3], where the following were interviewed: 'The Street Juggler', pp. 104–107; 'The Street Conjurer', pp. 107-110; 'Statement of Another Street Conjurer', pp. 110-113; 'The Street-Fire King, or Salamander', pp. 113-117 and 'Street Clown', pp. 119–121.

between the two when you read this description in an anonymously written book published in 1840.

> In the parlour of a public-house, properly kept, frequently assemble some of the most pleasant company...most of the frequenters drink moderately, and it is a rare thing to see a drunken man in the parlour. The tap-room is not so well conducted. Here collect the working men, male servants in and out of place, hackney-coachmen, omnibus cads, &c. These frequenters drink far more in proportion than those of the parlour. Many leave the place in a reeling attitude.[18]

The first street conjurer interviewed by Mayhew began his testimony with rather a telling statement: 'I call myself a wizard as well; but that's only the polite term for a conjurer': an acceptance that the street conjurer was not an admired profession. Hal. Lewis, in 1840, wrote about a street conjurer that he had observed; it was even more downbeat than the testimony of those speaking to Mayhew.

> The faded finery of the tawdry little jacket or vest – the soiled white "tights" and the muddy high-low boots – and the sallow complexion of the loud-voice performer – are all sad, very sad! He looks like a "soiled remnant" of the scattered company of the once-splendid Richardson, the emperor of showmen; and when we recal to mind the annual display which feasted our devouring eyes at the Fair of St. Bartholomew, we sigh to think of the sorrowful changes relentless Time hath sought. The familiar tricks – the repetition of oft repeated jokes (as threadbare as the speaker) – bring fresh to our pondering mind those happy days when 'trifle light as air' were wont to tickle us to laughter.
> How has he fallen from his "high estate"! We – not uncharitably but reasonably – conclude, from his appearance, that half his time is perhaps passed in the public streets, and the other half wasted in the

---

[18] [Servant] p. 14.

public-houses.[19]

The reference to the 'Fair of St. Bartholomew' is apt. It was contended by Paul Schlicke in his book *Dickens and Popular Entertainment* that the decline in the fortunes of the street entertainer was partly due to the gradual collapse of this annual festival, as it represented their most important source of guaranteed financial reward.

Bartholomew Fair had begun in the twelfth century and was at its height from the time of the Restoration through to the middle of the eighteenth century. By the 1830s it was in freefall as the authorities, unhappy with the unseemly behaviour of many of the visitors, raised taxes and ground rents for the participating showmen; although the official line was that social mobility meant the general public were changing their recreational habits. The final blow was the introduction, in 1840, of an order that banned 'theatrical representation' from the fair; it limped on for a few more years before permanently closing in 1855.[20]

Simon During, in *Modern Enchantments*, looking more specifically at street conjurers, saw their fall in earning capacity as a combination of the prohibition in 1826 of lotteries that many conjurers benefited from, together with increased competition from theatrical conjurers.[21] Either way the heyday of the itinerant street performer was long over by the time Dickens was writing *The Old Curiosity Shop*. He reflected this in his characterisation not only of Sweet William but also other travelling show folk depicted in some

[19] [Lewis] p. 274. Richardson was a late seventeenth century showman, so the author is rather unfairly going back over 150 years to make the comparison; however there was a regular Richardson's theatre in Bartholomew Fair, named after him – so that might be to what he was referring: [Clarke] p. 115.

[20] [Schlicke] pp. 91- 4.

[21] [During] p. 98.

of his other novels.

For instance, in *Our Mutual Friend*, Dickens described 'a little Fair' in a village where there was a 'vicious spectacle' of 'A Fat Lady, perhaps in part sustained upon postponed pork, her professional associate being a Learned Pig, displayed her life-size picture in a low dress as she appeared when presented at Court, several yards round'. Whilst in *Great Expectations* Pip expressed his dread of Magwitch with the metaphor that he was surveying him 'with the air of an Exhibitor', reminiscent here of Mr Vuffin, the 'proprietor of a giant, and a little lady without legs or arms' who had accompanied Sweet William into the Jolly Sandboys inn.[22]

In an article in *Household Words* entitled 'Things Departed', GA Sala wrote that 'whole hosts of street arts and street artists are among things departed'; a thesis supported by the observation made by one of Mayhew's interviewed conjurers that there 'are very few conjurers out busking now. I don't know above four'. That was probably an under-exaggeration; but it gives an idea of the meagre living from this profession at the time Dickens was describing his own conjurer Sweet William.[23]

## Tricks of the Street Conjurer

There are few sources of the actual tricks performed by street entertainers in Victorian times; newspapers, like today, concentrated on reporting the repertoire of theatre conjurers. But there can be found the occasional contemporary mention. One such was the street conjurer described in the section above by Hal. Lewis. His appearance may well have fallen from a 'high estate' but once he got out a 'pack of dirty cards' and started to perform, he was transformed.

---

[22] *Great Expectations*, Chapter 40; *Our Mutual Friend*, Book the Fourth, Chapter 6.
[23] 'Things Departed' [HW] Vol. IV. No. 95, 17 Jan, 1852, pp. 397-401.

The conjurer paraded around the circle, requesting one of his audience to draw a card "anywhere, no matter which," as he said. A boy took a card. "Look at it", said he, "you'll remember it? Now place it in the pack, take it in your own hands, and shuffle it. There don't be afraid, mix 'em well together. Now you sure it's there"?

He asked the boy to name the card – the Jack of Clubs. The conjurer displayed 'the cards one by one upon the ground, the identical card was found – wanting.' The conjurer said he would give a penny to anybody who could find the missing card as 'the pack will be spoiled without it'.

And taking up the leathern bag for the reward, he suddenly drew out, instead of the penny, the missing card! This delusion was so well executed that there was a general murmur of applause.[24]

One of Mayhew's conjurers, as well as performing the Card Stab with a sword ('telling a named card by throwing a pack in the air and catching the card on a sword point'), was also able to tell 'people's thoughts by the cards'. He was skilled with other props. He passed a three inch square die through a borrowed hat; secretly exchanged a sovereign, supposedly held in somebody's hand, for a farthing; and cut a piece of tape in two and restored it. He also performed the trick known as the Bonus Genius: 'I'd pull out my cards and card-boxes and the bonus genius or the wooden doll, and then I'd spread a nice clean cloth (which I always carried with me) on the table and then I'd go to work.' The Bonus Genius crops up later as it was a trick that Dickens did – one of the few from his repertoire which required an element of sleight of hand ability.

---

[24] [Lewis] pp. 274-7. According to Hal. Lewis, the 'implements' of the conjurer he described, who also doubled up as a juggler, were 'an old rusty sword, some balls, a dish or plate, a pack of dirty cards and some broad-bladed knives'.

# CHAPTER ONE SUPPLEMENT

Conjurers often doubled up as jugglers and vice versa. So the street juggler, whom Mayhew interviewed, said:

> After the juggling I generally has to do conjuring. I does what they call the 'piles of mags', that is putting four halfpence on a boy's cap and making them disappear when I say "Presto, fly!" Then there's the empty cups and making 'taters come under 'em or there's bringing a cabbage into an empty hat. There's also making a shilling pass from a gentleman's hand into a nest of boxes, and such-like tricks.

A 'mag' was slang for a half-penny. A number of them could be vanished by secretly substituting a specially constructed gimmick, of a riveted stack of half-pennies, in place of the loose coins. The successful execution of the empty cups (balls appearing and disappearing from three cups, and ending up with a potato under each) and the production of a cabbage from a borrowed hat, required the highest level of a conjurer's ability. The nest of boxes was another trick that Dickens performed – although he probably would have relied more on apparatus in his version.

Another performer, again displaying great dexterity and verve, was witnessed by Charles Smith, in a book published in 1857. In this mini, half-an-hour, street-show there were three entertainers working as a team; an acrobat, juggler and conjurer. The unnamed conjurer was the final act.

> He flourishes an old silk hand kerchief, holding it at one corner, and drawing it through his left hand, fast clenched, a dozen times in a minute. "What will you have, ladies and gentlemen?" he asks. "Did you say eggs?" - and incontinently the passage of the handkerchief through his clenched hand is stopped by three or four eggs in succession, which are carefully taken out and laid on the drum. "Did you say a pint pot?" – and immediately the silk, which an instant before was waving loose in the air, is seen to contain a pewter pot, which also is taken out and bid with the eggs. "Did you say rabbit-pie?" – and the next moment a live rabbit is struggling in the folds of

the handkerchief, and has to be let loose. "Did you say some thing to drink, sir? Certainly, sir. Here, you little boy with the speckled face – come here, sir. Hold that funnel to your chin, sir." Then seizing an ale-glass, the wizard works the boy's elbow as though it were the handle of a pump, draws off a glass of ale from the spout of the funnel, and drinks it to the health of the company.[25]

Later it will be seen how very few of Dickens's conjuring tricks were in contemporary conjuring books – which is significant in the context of determining how Dickens learnt his magic. In contrast, nearly all the tricks of the street conjurers can be found in books dating back at least one hundred years. It was because the tricks had been around for such a long time, and endlessly repeated, that writers accumulated the necessary information to reveal the methods. The corollary was that the street conjurer's routines hardly changed: indeed they still remain broadly the same today – easily the most popular trick of the twenty-first century street conjurer is the Cups and Balls.

Of the tricks performed by the various street conjurers referred to in this section, the following can be found in the 1722 first edition of *The Whole Art of Legerdemain or Hocus Pocus in Perfection* by Henry Dean. There is the Cups and Balls ('How to pass the Balls through the Cups'); drawing a drink from the boy's elbow ('To show the Trick with a Funnel'); the wooden doll trick ("Bonus Genius, or Hiccius Doccius') producing the eggs and live rabbit ('How to shew the Hen and Egg-bag, and out of an empty Bag to bring out about an Hundred Eggs, and afterwards to bring out a living Hen'); telling people's thoughts by the cards ('How to tell what Card any Man thinketh on'); cutting and restoring the tape ('To cut a Lace asunder in the middle, and to make it whole again'); and the pile of mags ('How to command seven Half-pence through

[25] [Smith, Charles] p. 8.

a Table').[26]

It would have been quite a challenge to learn how to do any of these tricks from the write-up in such books as Dean's alone. Only the bare bones of the technique required were given; and you really would have had to be taught by someone else, or at least seen another conjurer perform, before fully understanding the methodology. As one of Mayhew's street conjurers perceptively said, admittedly in self-justification of making money from his teachings, 'it doesn't matter so much showing how these tricks are done, because they depend upon the quickness and dexterity of handling. You may know how an artist paints a picture, but you mayn't be able to paint one yourself.'[27]

## Ramo Samee

Ramo Samee is a name that sends magic historians into paroxysms of excitement when it comes to Dickens. Perhaps because he was the only actual conjurer[28] that Dickens mentioned in any of his

---

[26] [Dean] pp. 8, 26, 28, 30, 52, 84 & 90.

[27] The distinction between apparatus magic and sleight of hand magic has been emphasised in understanding CD becoming a conjurer. It is sometimes confused by non-magicians. Take, for instance, this passage from Peter Ackroyd's *Dickens* where he attempted to sum up CD's ability as a conjurer; but in doing so conflated two different tools of the magician's armoury as if they were synonymous. 'Experts in such matters, on examining all the available evidence, incline to the belief that Dickens was no more than a competent magician, relying upon *simple mechanical tricks* of illusion, but that he was an unparalleled "patterer" as he talked his way through the various *sleights of hand.*' [Ackroyd] p. 414 - my italics. For a comprehensive understanding of what constitutes sleight of hand for conjuring purposes, [Sachs, 2nd] is recommended: this has been reprinted by Dover Magic Books.

[28] In reality Ramo Samee, although he did conjuring in his act, was primarily

novels, short stories or articles; although by the time Dickens came to give him his name check, Ramo Samee was dead. The Indian entertainer turned up in Dickens's article 'An Unsettled Neighbourhood' where young Slaughter, who managed the Greengrocer, used to lurk in 'the Coal Department, practising Ramo Samee with three potatoes'. The *Household Words* piece was written in 1854 but Dickens was reminiscing about his old neighbourhood when he lived in Camden in London. This would have been in 1822 when Dickens was ten years old.[29]

Ramo Samee came over from India in 1815 with a troupe of fellow artists. But from the start he was considered the 'chief of the Indian jugglers'. Having turned solo, he became famous in his own right, performing in England until at least 1846. His repertoire included such feats as swallowing a stone as big as an egg, juggling four brass balls the size of an orange, building a canopy with his tongue on the top of his nose and tossing a twenty-four pounder cannon ball with his feet over his head.

He was clearly a popular performer before 1822. He had the distinction, if that is the right word, of appearing in the guise of a mechanical toy in a show by a certain Mr Schmidt in 1821. Named Ramo Sammee (the double 'm' presumably to avoid any confusion with the real Ramo Samee), the public were informed that 'This amusing little Figure will correctly inform the Company the Time by any Person's Watch; he will also decipher Writing, and answer any Questions proposed to him'.

In December, 1826 he was in pantomime and the reviewer from *The Times* wrote about 'the extraordinary performances of the well-known Ramo Samee'. Another review, from the same paper, dated 2nd February, 1830, stated, 'it is impossible to enumerate all the

considered to be a juggler.

[29] [HW] Vol. X, No. 242, 11 Nov, 1854, pp. 289-292. See [Slater, Journalism] p. 241 for dating of the article's contents.

entertainments provided for the evening; but it is only justice to mention that the clever juggler, Ramo Samee, exerted himself with his usual success'. *The Times* recorded other appearances in 1841 and 1844.[30]

His fame is marked by a name check in a satirical article in *Punch* magazine in 1842 called 'Parliamentary Comforts – Card Legislation': 'We confess that card legislation may admit of cheating; we own that if a RAMO SAMEE...were to be returned to Parliament by the constituency frequenting the Coburg Theatre, and were base enough...to attempt to force or to hide a card for party purposes, he might occasionally succeed.'[31]

He died in 1849 but that did not prevent his name being used in a genuine Parliamentary debate some three years later.

> Since the lamented demise of Ramo Samee, a gentleman unequalled for dexterity of hand and facility of legerdemain, who would either cut himself a hand of trumps or swallow a broadsword, he had known no one with so many ingenious devices and such an inordinate capacity of swallow as the right honourable gentleman the creator of his party. He called upon the house not to be deluded by this great state conjurer [cheers & laughter] but to do what was wise and just.[32]

Finally, to demonstrate his celebrity status, it is of note that two of

---

[30] Information about Ramo Samee's arrival in England and his repertoire comes from [Clarke] p. 395 and [Dawes, Great Illusionists] p. 133. There is a playbill of the mechanical toy, Ramo Sammee, in [Houdini, Unmasking] p. 182. *The Times* appearances are for 27 Dec, 1826; 2 Feb, 1830; 28 August, 1841 ('There was also Ramo Samee, the Indian juggler...') and 11 Sept, 1844.

[31] *Punch*, Vol. 2, 1842, p. 250.

[32] His year of death: [Whaley, Who's Who] p. 265. Mr B Osboure, House of Commons, *The Times*, 26 Nov, 1852 reporting on a debate held the day before.

the street performers interviewed by Mayhew in *London Labour and the London Poor*, referred to him. This was the Street Juggler:

> I dare say I've been juggling 40 years for I was between 14 and 15 when I begun and I'm 55 now. I remember Ramo Samee and all the first process of the art. He was the first as ever I knew and very good indeed; there was no other to oppose him...One night I went to the theatre, and there I saw Ramo Samee doing his juggling and in a minute I forgot all about tumbling, and only wanted to do as he did.

The Street-Fire King, or Salamander, was also influenced by Ramo Samee; he talked about a trick which was 'one of Ramo Samee's which he used to perform in public houses and tap-rooms and make a deal of money out of it'.

There is little doubt then that Ramo Samee was in England in 1822. Trevor Dawson, in his 2012 book, *Charles Dickens: Conjurer, Mesmerist and Showman,* assumed, because his name turned up in the 'An Unsettled Neighbourhood' article, that Dickens 'was very familiar with Ramo Samee...He performed mainly in London and therefore it is probable that Dickens saw his show probably several times, as a young boy at the age of ten, probably at the famous Vauxhall Gardens where Ramo performed magic and sword swallowing in 1822'. Dawson hypothesised from this that Dickens's 'conjuring interest therefore, as far as research so far reveals, dates back to around 1822'.[33]

There is plenty of speculative guesswork here that it is impossible to prove one way or the other. However one aspect is certain: whatever Dawson might have thought, it cannot be inferred from Dickens's mention of Ramo Samee by name in an article he wrote in 1854 that he therefore must have seen him in 1822. As has been shown, Ramo Samee was still well remembered several years after

[33] [Dawson] pp. 18-19 & 24.

his death; he certainly would have been familiar enough for Dickens's educated readers to know what he meant by, and to whom he was referring, when he wrote 'practising Ramo Samee with three potatoes'. Neither Dickens, nor his readers, needed to have seen Ramo Samee to make, and understand, the reference.

Just to add to the confusion, for many years magic historians had assumed Dickens definitely saw Ramo Samee in 1838. The supposition that he did was put first forward by an article which appeared in The Dickensian in October 1921, when JSP Grove found that a playbill of Nicholas Nickleby at the Hull Theatre Royal on 28th December, 1838 also included 'the celebrated East Indian Ramo Samee'.[34]

This Hull production was called Nicholas Nickleby; or, Doings at Do-The-Boys Hall, and was dramatised by Edward Stirling. It was one of at least twenty-five theatrical productions that appeared before Nicholas Nickleby had been completed – some indeed were put on before one third of the novel was finished. By 1850 a staggering two hundred and forty dramatisations of Dickens's works had been staged, of which nearly twenty-five per cent were plays adapted from Nicholas Nickleby – the vast majority of them unsanctioned by Dickens.[35]

Grove, when he wrote his article, was unaware of all these unauthorised adaptations, and therefore made the not unreasonable assumption that 'Dickens and the juggler [Ramo Samee] were on the stage together' in Hull. From this Grove made two other suppositions. Firstly, that Dickens recalled having seen Ramo Samee

---

[34] 'Ramo Samee and the Three Potatoes', JSP Grove [Dickensian] Vol. 17, No. 4, Oct, 1921, pp. 211-4.

[35] [Bolton] p. 3 & pp. 154-8. The justification for this particular production was set out in the text to Edward Stirling's dramatisation: it was claimed that the play would not prejudice 'the real end of this eventful history' but rather add to the novel's suspense.

in 1838 when he wrote his 1854 article, 'unless Ramo continued juggling in later years'. And secondly, 'one thinks' that seeing Ramo Samee in 1838 'must have helped' Dickens blossoming 'into being a conjurer'.

Frank Staff, in an article in *The Magic Circular* in 1929 upped the stakes rather more when he implied that Dickens was not just on the stage with Ramo Samee but actually one of the actors in the production – he wrote that Dickens was 'in the caste [sic], at the Theatre Royal, Hull, in 1838' and 'it is safe to state that Ramo and Dickens were performing at the same theatre'. However he was more circumspect about whether Dickens had had his interest in conjuring stimulated by Ramo Samee: 'it may be that Ramo was responsible for Dickens' interest in magic.'[36]

JB Findlay, in *Charles Dickens and his Magic*, published in 1962, reworded Grove's conjecture rather more emphatically.

> In the last month of 1838, Charles Dickens was in Hull, where he was appearing with his own play *Nicholas Nickleby*. Amongst the other attractions on the bill was Ramo Samee. This show ran from the 26th December, 1838 to the 4th January, 1839. During this period Dickens seems to have become imbued with a desire to know more about magic.

It was with reference to the Grove original article, and the subsequent Findlay booklet, that Edwin Dawes agreed that it was 'plausibly argued that Dickens interest in conjuring was aroused' by this duel billing.[37]

Trevor Dawson wrote, 'according to Grove, Dickens first became interested in conjuring in 1838 at the age of 26'. This was a little

---

[36] 'Charles Dickens and Magic', Frank Staff [Magic Circular] Vol. 23, April 1929, p. 107.

[37] [Findlay] p. 6; [Dawes, Great Illusionists] p. 131.

unfair because, as can be seen from the quotation above from his original article, Grove was not so unequivocal. Nevertheless all credit to Dawson for proving that Dickens could not have seen Ramo Samee in late December, 1838 in Hull. As his letters over Christmas and the New Year made clear, Dickens was in London. Dawson cited Michael Slater to show this.[38]

Ironically, however, Dawson directed his ire against Grove – calling it an 'ill-researched article' that arrived at 'a totally erroneous conclusion' – not for his mistake in thinking that Dickens saw Ramo Samee in 1838; but in having the effrontery to believe that Dickens could possibly have been inspired to take up conjuring so late in his life. He put this down to the fact that 'Grove made no attempt to date the *Household Words*, "three potatoes article", which if investigated would have undermined his conclusion'. As can be seen in the final section of this supplement, Dawson is convinced it was 1822 that was the relevant 'road to Damascus' year of Dickens becoming a conjurer.[39]

It is always tempting fate to attack another historian for an 'ill-researched article', particularly when you make statements such as Ramo Samee 'performed in England from December 1815 to 1838'. This was not so: as was shown above, there is plenty of evidence that

[38] [Slater, Dickens] p. 127, cited in [Dawson] pp. 20-4. Slater had consulted the letters in [Pilgrim, Vol. 1] to verify where CD was. Dawson wrote: 'The myth of Dickens in Hull in 1838 was perpetuated by Findlay, Warlock and a host of other historians to the present day.' Warlock had written about CD 'seeing Rama [sic] Samee at Hull' in 'Magic and Charles Dickens', Peter Warlock [Magic Circular] Vol. 79, December 1985, pp. 478-9. Findlay did indeed refer to Grove, but of course this was many years before the letters of Dickens were readily available for Grove's allegation to be easily disproved. And, given that Findlay's booklet was generally well researched, one cannot really blame later historians, such as Peter Warlock and Eddie Dawes, for similarly relying on him.

[39] [Dawson] p. 21.

Ramo Samee was performing several years later after 1838, possibly to at least 1846.[40]

Furthermore, Dawson wrote that Dickens 'would be very familiar with [Ramo Samee's] act, even to the extent of having a knowledge of the cups and balls trick for which Ramo Samee was well known, otherwise he would not have made the comment about 'young slaughter' [sic] practising with three potatoes. The feature of the Ramo Samee cups and balls routine was that the balls changed colour at command.'[41]

Dawson had assumed that 'practising Ramo Samee with three potatoes' was a reference to the Cups and Balls trick of producing three potatoes from the cups. No records exist that Ramo Samee performed this trick. In fact he was much better known for his juggling skills – and this was clearly what Dickens was referring to.

## Derivation of the name Sweet William

The brief appearance of the conjurer Sweet William in *The Old Curiosity Shop* has failed to be picked up by many magic historians, some of them concluding that Dickens did not refer to any conjurers at all in his fictional writing.[42]

---

[40] [Dawson] p. 18. Dawson probably took Ramo Samee's last appearance in England from [Whaley, Who's Who] p. 265. *The Times* had him performing on 11 Sept, 1844, whilst Houdini in [Houdini, Conjurers' Monthly] Vol. 1, No. 3, November, 1906, pp. 72-3 stated that his latest programme for Ramo Samee was dated 9 February, 1846 for a solo performance at the Garrick Theatre, London.

[41] [Dawson] p. 19 had misread some wording in *Annals of Conjuring* where Sidney Clarke listed some of the 'tricks of these Indians' – a troupe of four with Ramo Samee as one of the performers. These 'included the Cups and Balls, the ball which changed its colour at command, changing the colour of sand, juggling...' [Clarke] p. 395.

[42] 'It is surely strange, given his magical interests and knowledge, that among

The name Sweet William was probably taken from the ballad of *Sweet William's Farewell to Black-eyed Susan,* written by John Gay in 1720. John Gay is best known for his satirical musical *The Beggar's Opera.* Dickens showed his familiarity with the ballad in *The Pickwick Papers.* One character urges another to 'Go on, Jemmy...like black-eyed Susan – all in the Downs.' Gay's ballad began with the line: 'All in the Downs the fleet was moor'd'. In it, the beautiful black-eyed Susan has to say a tearful farewell to her sailor lover, before he sets sail on his ship.[43]

The use of a 'ballad name' for his conjurer by Dickens was almost certainly intentional. The singing and selling of ballads in the streets was still very popular in the nineteenth century and street ballad-singers would have jostled alongside conjurers competing for attention. In 'The Streets – Night' in *Sketches by Boz,* Dickens wrote about 'a wretched woman...attempting to sing some popular ballad, in the hope of wringing a few pence from the compassionate passer-by'.[44]

the hundreds of characters in Dickens' novels, not one is a magician'. [Tigner] p. 109. 'It is interesting that the only character in Dickens's work remotely connected with the art of magic is Fagin.' [Williams] p. 20. Dawson would seem to be the first magic historian to draw attention to Sweet William [Dawson] p. 63; but only quoted his initial mention and did not give it any significance. He wrote, erroneously, that Sweet William's expertise is 'not referred to later in the story'.

[43] *The Pickwick Papers,* Chapter 3. The link between the Sweet William ballad and *The Pickwick Papers* extract was made in 'Letters to the Editor', [Dickensian] Vol. 19, No. 3, 1 Jul, 1923, p. 156. The first verse of John Gay's *Sweet William's Farewell to Black-eyed Susan,* 1720, was as follows: 'All in the Downs the fleet was moor'd, / The streamers waving in the wind, / When black-eyed Susan came aboard, / 'Oh! Where shall I my true love find! / Tell me, ye jovial sailors, tell me true, / If my Sweet William sails among the crew.'

[44] A coincidental connection between ballad singing and 'tricks upon the cards' was made in an 18th century magazine where the writer seamlessly segued

Dickens might have had his memory jostled with regard to Sweet William by a theatrical spin-off, written in 1829 by Douglas Jerrold, called *Black-Eyed Susan; or 'All in the Downs'*. The play revolved around 'William' (not 'Sweet William'), a sailor, returning to find his wife Susan has been harassed by various unsavoury characters. The play was a great success and has been continuously revived right through to this century. Dickens was friendly with Jerrold from 1836 and would have known his work. It is possible that the reference in *The Pickwick Papers* could have been to the Jerrold play, rather than the ballad, as William was not mentioned in the extract. However the conjurer's name clearly related to the ballad, not the play.

There is one more intriguing link of the conjurer's name to the Jerrold play: the connection being the conjurer John Henry Anderson whom Dickens almost certainly saw at some point. Anderson was a frustrated actor; although never a particularly good one. An Irish manager remarked about his portrayal of Romeo, 'Ye've brought bad acting, sur, to the greatest height of perfection'. His favourite theatrical role was *Rob Roy*, but he also played the part of William in *Black-Eyed Susan*, usually at the last night of a magical run. His first documented performance was not until 1849, long after Dickens had written *The Old Curiosity Shop*; but nevertheless it provides a neat circular match to the name through some inspired serendipity by Dickens.[45]

from the 'scandalous practice' of singing ballads to gentry allowing 'their daughters, to frequent the Kitchen', which inevitably leads to 'kissing...dancing...and to show Tricks upon the cards.' 'A view of the Weekly Essays and Disputes in this Month. Of Ballads, Ballad-singing etc', *The London Magazine*, March, 1735.

[45] The bad acting anecdote is related in [Dawes, Great Illusionists] p. 108. The first documented performance of Anderson playing the part of William is on 27 Feb, 1849 in a one-off benefit production of the play at the Theatre Royal,

# CHAPTER ONE SUPPLEMENT

## Thimble-Rigging from *Sketches by Boz*

Dickens was very conversant with thimble-rigging. It was assumed that street conjurers had a knowledge of it – as evidenced by the conjurer interviewed in Mayhew's *London Labour and the London Poor* who, although he never practised it, was constantly asked by his audience how thimble-rigging was done. But it does not follow from this, as Dawson inferred, that because 'Dickens was well informed on thimble rigging...that he had by now a good knowledge of conjuring'.[46]

Indeed reading Dickens's description one is struck by the absence of the machinations of how the thimble-riggers practised their deception. It is instructive to compare Dickens's passage reporting some of them at work at Greenwich Fair with that, immediately following, of Mayhew's street conjurer.

> Pedestrians linger in groups at the roadside, unable to resist the allurements of the stout proprietress of the "Jack-in-the-box, three shies a penny," or the more splendid offers of the man with three thimbles and a pea on a little round board, who astonishes the bewildered crowd with some such address as, "Here's the sort o' game to make you laugh seven years arter you're dead, and turn ev'ry air on your ed gray vith delight! Three thimbles and vun little pea –

---

Birmingham: [Dawes, Anderson].

[46] [Dawson] p. 28. Heathcote Williams made a related claim to this thimble-rigger at work. He wrote that 'all the writers on the subject seem to have overlooked' this 'most obvious candidate' as being the reason that CD was inspired to take up conjuring: [Williams] p. 18. Williams called him a 'street magician' - which he was not. Simon During failed to pick up this error by Williams when he stated that in 1836 Dickens 'recorded the rote patter of a French' magician at 'Bartholomew Fair', [During] p. 98. It is not known why During thought he might have been French; he has also confused Bartholomew Fair with Greenwich Fair.

with a vun, two, three, and a two, three, vun: catch him who can, look on, keep your eyes open, and niver say die! niver mind the change, and the expense: all fair and above board: them as don't play can't vin, and luck attend the ryal sportsman! Bet any gen'lm'n any sum of money, from harf-a-crown up to a suverin, as he doesn't name the thimble as kivers the pea!"

Here some greenhorn whispers his friend that he distinctly saw the pea roll under the middle thimble – an impression which is immediately confirmed by a gentleman in top-boots, who is standing by, and who, in a low tone, regrets his own inability to bet, in consequence of having unfortunately left his purse at home, but strongly urges the stranger not to neglect such a golden opportunity. The 'plant' is successful, the bet is made, the stranger of course loses: and the gentleman with the thimbles consoles him, as he pockets the money, with an assurance that it's "all the fortin of war! this time I vin, next time you vin: niver mind the loss of two bob and a bender! Do it up in a small parcel, and break out in a fresh place. Here's the sort o' game," &c. – and the eloquent harangue, with such variations as the speaker's exuberant fancy suggests, is again repeated to the gaping crowd, reinforced by the accession of several new-comers.[47]

Contrast this with the language, the vernacular and the detailed description of the workings, of the street conjurer in Mayhew: he clearly knew the hustle intimately.

This is the way it's done. They have three thimbles, and they put a pea under two of 'em, so that there's only one without the pea. The man then begins moving them about and saying, "Out of this one into that one," and so on, and winds up by offering to "lay anything, from a shilling to a pound," that nobody can tell which thimble the pea is under. Then he turns round to the crowd, and pretends to be pushing them back, and whilst he's saying, "Come, gentlemen, stand more backwarder," one of the confederates, who is called 'a button,'

---

[47] 'Greenwich Fair', Chapter 12, *Sketches by Boz*.

lifts up one of the thimbles with a pea under it, and laughs to those around, as much as to say, "We've found it out."

He shows the pea two or three times, and the last time he does so, he removes it, either by taking it up under his forefinger nail or between his thumb and finger. It wants a great deal of practice to do this nicely, so as not to be found out. When the man turns to the table again the button says, "I'll bet you a couple of sovereigns I know where the pea is. Will any gentleman go me halves?" Then, if there's any hesitation, the man at the table will pretend to be nervous and offer to move the thimbles again, but the button will seize him by the arm, and shout as if he was in a passion, "No, no, none of that! It was a fair bet, and you shan't touch 'em." He'll then again ask if anybody will go him halves, and there's usually somebody flat enough to join him. Then the stranger is asked to lift up the thimble, so that he shouldn't suspect anything, and of course there's no pea there. He is naturally staggered a bit, and another confederate standing by will say calmly, "I knew you was wrong; here's the pea;" and he lifts up the thimble with the second pea under it. If nobody will go shares in the 'button's' bet, then he lifts up the thimble and replaces the pea as he does so, and of course wins the stake, and he takes good care to say as he pockets the sovereign, "I knew it was there; what a fool you was not to stand in." The second time they repeat the trick there's sure to be somebody lose his money.

## Thimble-Rigging from *Nicholas Nickleby*

Dickens was renowned for incorporating what he wrote in factual articles into his fiction later on. This is illustrated in Chapter 50 of *Nicholas Nickleby*. Dickens described the scene at a horse racing track which was reminiscent of that depicted in the *Sketches by Boz* article: an unfortunate is deprived of his money by some thimble-riggers.

Here, a little knot gathered round a pea and thimble table to watch the plucking of some unhappy greenhorn; and there, another proprietor with his confederates in various disguises – one man in spectacles; another, with an eyeglass and a stylish hat; a third, dressed as a farmer well to do in the world, with his top-coat over his arm and his flash notes in a large leathern pocket-book; and all with heavy-handled whips to represent most innocent country fellows who had trotted there on horseback – sought, by loud and noisy talk and pretended play, to entrap some unwary customer, while the gentlemen confederates (of more villainous aspect still, in clean linen and good clothes), betrayed their close interest in the concern by the anxious furtive glance they cast on all new comers.

## Roulette from *Nicholas Nickleby*

Other, more legitimate, means of taking money from the unwary were clearly a feature of the race track. Dickens's ability to recall not just a description, but also the patois, of a sideshow croupier operating a roulette wheel was evocatively captured a little later in the same chapter as above in *Nicholas Nickleby*. Dickens called it a 'rouge-et-noir table', or a red and black table, rather than roulette: which made sense as, of course, gamblers principally staked their money on either red or black, although there were numerous other number permutations which could result in wins.[48]

> The other presided over the ROUGE-ET-NOIR table. He was probably some ten years younger, and was a plump, paunchy, sturdy-looking fellow, with his under-lip a little pursed, from a habit of counting money inwardly as he paid it, but with no decidedly bad expression in his face, which was rather an honest and jolly one than otherwise. He wore no coat, the weather being hot, and stood behind the table with a huge mound of crowns and half-crowns before him, and a cash-box for notes. This game was constantly playing. Perhaps

[48] There is actually a game with cards called Rouge et Noir, but the rolling of a ball that CD described, almost certainly meant he was referring to roulette; devised in France in the eighteenth century, it spread all over Europe in the nineteenth century.

twenty people would be staking at the same time. This man had to roll the ball, to watch the stakes as they were laid down, to gather them off the colour which lost, to pay those who won, to do it all with the utmost dispatch, to roll the ball again, and to keep this game perpetually alive. He did it all with a rapidity absolutely marvellous; never hesitating, never making a mistake, never stopping, and never ceasing to repeat such unconnected phrases as the following, which, partly from habit, and partly to have something appropriate and business-like to say, he constantly poured out with the same monotonous emphasis, and in nearly the same order, all day long:-

'Rooge-a-nore from Paris! Gentlemen, make your game and back your own opinions – any time while the ball rolls – rooge-a-nore from Paris, gentlemen, it's a French game, gentlemen, I brought it over myself, I did indeed! – Rooge-a-nore from Paris – black wins – black – stop a minute, sir, and I'll pay you, directly – two there, half a pound there, three there – and one there – gentlemen, the ball's a rolling – any time, sir, while the ball rolls! – The beauty of this game is, that you can double your stakes or put down your money, gentlemen, any time while the ball rolls – black again – black wins – I never saw such a thing – I never did, in all my life, upon my word I never did; if any gentleman had been backing the black in the last five minutes he must have won five-and-forty pound in four rolls of the ball, he must indeed. Gentlemen, we've port, sherry, cigars, and most excellent champagne. Here, wai-ter, bring a bottle of champagne, and let's have a dozen or fifteen cigars here – and let's be comfortable, gentlemen – and bring some clean glasses – any time while the ball rolls! – I lost one hundred and thirty-seven pound yesterday, gentlemen, at one roll of the ball, I did indeed! – how do you do, sir?" (recognising some knowing gentleman without any halt or change of voice, and giving a wink so slight that it seems an accident), "will you take a glass of sherry, sir? – here, wai-ter! bring a clean glass, and hand the sherry to this gentleman – and hand it round, will you, waiter? – this is the rooge-a-nore from Paris, gentlemen – any time while the ball rolls! – gentlemen, make your game, and back your own opinions – it's the rooge-a-nore from Paris – quite a new game, I brought it over myself, I did indeed – gentlemen, the ball's a-rolling!'

Just because Dickens brought alive the shenanigans of thimble-rigging, and other gambling activities, it should not be thought that he somehow endorsed them. Dickens wrote about the fair in Hyde Park that took place during the Queen's Coronation in 1838, where he expressed his support of the absence of these hustlers.

> This part of the amusements of the people, on the occasion of the Coronation, is particularly worthy of notice, not only as being a very pleasant and agreeable scene, but as affording a strong and additional proof, if proof were necessary, that the many are at least as capable of decent enjoyment as the few. There were no thimble-rig men, who are plentiful at race-courses, as at Epsom, where only *gold* can be staked; no gambling tents, roulette tables, hazard booths, or dice shops.[49]

## Warning a Fellow Passenger of Card Cheating

In January, 1842 Dickens took his first trip to America; this was essentially a mixture of a holiday and a promotional tour. During the journey over on the ship, he spotted a fellow passenger playing with some card cheats. Dickens never referred to the incident but the grateful recipient of his warning, Joseph Debar, a French-born American artist and government official, whose claim to fame lies in designing the official seal and coat of arms for the state of West Virginia, later wrote about it.

> For pastime only – for I have never played anything but whist or e'carte' before – I took part in a game of vingt-et-un[50] in the saloon,

---

49 *Examiner*, 1 July, 1838 p. 403. Attributed to CD in [Pilgrim, Vol. 1] p. 408.

50 Vingt-et-un, or twenty one, is another term for blackjack. The game which CD depicted Quilp as cheating at in *The Old Curiosity Shop* was cribbage: the pegs are placed in a 'cribbage board' for scoring. Dickens wrote that Quilp had among 'his various eccentric habits ... a humorous one of always cheating at cards, which rendered necessary on his part, not only a close observance of

supposing the company respectable and the risk slight. The fascinations of the game, however, and the stimulating example of an American gentleman at my elbow, carried me beyond my soundings.

I lost nearly fifty dollars the first day and half as much the next – almost a catastrophe for a young commercial traveler on a moderate salary. Hoping to retrieve my luck, I next morning again ventured to the shrine of the fickle goddess and had recovered half my losses, when, a change of dealer or banker occurring, I felt a soft but significant touch upon my right shoulder, and looking around beheld a pair of large and wonderfully eloquent eyes beckoning me to come away.

Comprehending the situation, I quietly arose under some pretext and took a walk on deck, where Mr. Dickens made his appearance an hour after, apparently unconscious of my presence. Seeing me approach him, he waived the formality of my expressions of gratitude with a sweeping gesture, merely inquiring whether I meant to play again in that company.

Upon my unhesitating reply in the negative his satisfaction was unequivocal, and with a brief injunction of secrecy regarding his intervention he gently bowed himself away. Subsequent developments in the case of another victim of nearly my age revealed the fact that certain passengers, rising importers of New York City, whose banking proved so disastrous to some of their clients, were confederates playing into each other's hands by such tricks as may readily be surmised by persons familiar with the game.[51]

the game, and a sleight-of-hand in counting and scoring, but also involved the constant correction, by looks, and frowns, and kicks under the table, of Richard Swiveller, who being bewildered by the rapidity with which his cards were told, and the rate at which the pegs travelled down the board, could not be prevented from sometimes expressing his surprise and incredulity.'

[51] [Debar] 'Reminiscence of Charles Dickens' first visit to America by a fellow passenger', J. H. Diss Debar; *Joseph Hubert Diss Debar Collection Ms79-191.2*, West Virginia Archives & History. Cited in [Ackroyd] p. 359 – although he named the passenger as Pierre Morand.

## Interest in Conjuring prior to 1842

Many magic historians have assumed that Dickens's curiosity in conjuring was first properly aroused by seeing Ramo Samee appear on the same bill as the bootleg production of *Nicholas Nickleby* in 1838. Thanks to Dawson, it is now known that Dickens never attended that performance – so this supposedly earlier inspiration source can now be discounted; although Dawson went on to argue that Dickens first became enamoured by conjuring sixteen year prior to that in 1822.[52]

However Dawson also made an even more radical revisionist viewpoint; that not only had Dickens a great deal of interest in conjuring prior to 1842 but he had even started performing. There were two specific references which Dawson cited to support his argument that Dickens had more hands-on experience than was previously known about.

The first was that Dickens attended a dinner, prior to 1837, with Samuel Rogers and later 'he reported to a friend: "I especially liked the way Mr Rogers entertained the children and grownups on Twelfth Night' with his skilful conjuring tricks".' Dawson wrote: 'Dickens must have been sufficiently knowledgeable [about conjuring] to make this judgement.' He also assumed that this dinner must have taken place in 1836 or earlier, as Dickens 'was not then to know that his first born...would be born on Twelfth Night, 1837'.

There was no source for the citation, even though there was a footnote reference which went astray. Nevertheless Dawson clearly thought it was of particular significance because he went on to write that 'clearly this event made a strong impression upon him [Dickens] such that subsequently as his children grew older the celebration of Twelfth Night with games and conjuring became a

---

[52] All this was addressed in the section on 'Ramo Samee' above.

family ritual. It is rather a pity that no further record of Samuel Rogers's conjuring abilities has yet to come to light'.[53]

Leaving aside the fallacious link, (similar to Dawson's supposed connection of a knowledge of thimble-rigging and conjuring), between the capacity to admire somebody's skills at conjuring and the ability to conjure yourself, there is a more fundamental problem with the quotation. Dickens did not actually meet Samuel Rogers until 1839; and therefore could not have witnessed any performance of his prior to that year. This is confirmed by the *Pilgrim Letters* ('CD first met him [Rogers], in 1839') and also by Claire Tomalin and Michael Slater in their respective books *Charles Dickens A Life* and *Charles Dickens.*[54]

If Dickens did indeed make the remark about Rogers's prowess to a friend, either he was not referring to Samuel Rogers, but a different Rogers; or he said it in 1839 or later. However, until that is resolved, the quotation, and the assumptions Dawson made from it, can safely be ignored.

The second extract that Dawson cited is more potent as it suggested directly that Dickens was conjuring before 1842; to be precise in 1835, when he was aged twenty-three. 'Dickens fascinated them all [a reference to the Hogarth family, whilst he was courting their daughter, later his wife, Catherine] with his vitality, his charm, his knack for mimicry, recitations and practical joking. One evening he entered by a window dressed as a sailor, and danced a hornpipe before the startled family: and he was never at a loss when it came to parlour tricks and entertainment.' Dawson wrote: 'This may be the first mention of a conjuring performance, but clearly from the

---

[53] [Dawson] pp. 28-9.

[54] [Pilgrim Vol. 1] p. 602 n. 1. Tomalin wrote in her Cast List about Rogers that he 'from 1839, knew, admired, entertained D': [Tomalin] p. xxxv. Slater noted an entry in Dickens's diary on 15 Sept, 1839 when 'the famous elderly banker-poet Samuel Rogers had called': [Slater, Dickens] p. 135.

comment he had been performing for family and friends for years.'

The actual quotation, though, was not from a primary source. It came from a book written in 1979 called *Dickens A Life*. The book had no references in it and it is quite clear that the 'parlour tricks' comment was a throwaway remark made by the writers who knew that Dickens at some point performed conjuring in his life. The story about Dickens dressing up as a sailor and dancing a hornpipe is well documented which adds to the confusion; if you run a 'true story' alongside a 'false allegation', the latter is more likely to fly by the reader. And this is what has happened here.[55]

A final possible piece of evidence that Dickens was exposed to conjuring as a youngster rather surprisingly appeared in Peter Ackroyd's *Dickens*. He wrote that Dickens's father, John Dickens, might well have tried to recreate the atmosphere of his youth by introducing into his own home 'conjurings, dances, recitations, charades, forfeits, blind-man's-buffs, and card games like Pope Joan or Speculation.' However the reference to 'conjurings' was clearly speculative on Ackroyd's part; he was just going through a list of Victorian pastimes to make his point.[56]

---

[55] [Mackenzie] pp. 31-2 cited in [Dawson] p. 26.

[56] [Ackroyd] p. 36. Ackroyd seemed to echo a letter written by CD to Cornelius Felton on 2 January, 1844 when he wrote about a party that took place over the New Year: 'such dinings, such dancings, such conjurings, such blindman's-buffings...' [Pilgrim Vol. 4] pp. 2-3.

# CHAPTER TWO

# The Conjurer

## Ludwig Döbler

Sometime between the 18th and 25th July, 1842, Dickens turned down a dinner invitation to Lady Holland on the excuse that he 'had engaged to carry a whole bevy of young people to see the conjurer tonight'. This was some two years after Dickens had portrayed the conjurer Sweet William in *The Old Curiosity Shop*. Since then, he had written *Barnaby Rudge*, one of his least read books, based on the Gordon Riots of 1780. At the time of this theatrical outing he was, having just returned from a six month trip to the US, writing the travelogue *American Notes*. He had a fine bright face, long dark hair, clean-shaven and was thirty years old.

As so often happened when Dickens mentioned a specific conjurer, he failed to name him; and it was only because of a letter he sent two years later on the 26th April, 1844, that it is known for certain whom he had gone to see:

Mr. Charles Dickens presents his compliments to M. Döbler, and very much regrets that being already engaged for tomorrow, he cannot avail himself of the box which M. Döbler has so kindly sent him through Mr Schloss [Döbler's Manager]. But if M. Döbler should have another opportunity of conferring a similar favor on Mr. Dickens, it will give Mr. D. great pleasure to accept it.

Mr. Dickens begs to add, that he had the pleasure of seeing M. Döbler at the Saint James's Theatre on the last occasion of M. Döbler's being in London; and that he was much astonished and delighted by his magical performances.

Döbler only appeared in London twice and the initial occasion, which was from early April through to the 25th July 1842, coincided with the date of Dickens's first letter: so there is no doubt that 'the conjurer' Dickens saw was indeed 'M. Döbler'.

Ludwig Döbler (see Plates 4 and 5) was considered to be the best of the apparatus conjurers who flourished in the period from the 1820s to the 1840s, mainly because he had, as one magic historian noted, a 'real genius for artistic presentation'. He was born in Vienna and, remarkably, did not speak any English, or, as *The Times* put it in their review of his act on 16th April, 1842, 'If there be a drawback to his natural qualifications to please, those who visit his exhibition, it is that he is a foreigner, and, not being acquainted with our native tongue, is obliged to address his explanations in his own vernacular German'. He got around this rather fundamental handicap by 'so fine a zest and such excellent gesticulations, that no one can fail to discover the meaning he really intends to convey'. As well as speaking the language, Döbler also wore the German costume of a student of the fifteenth century.

His opening trick was sensational. Contemporary reports stated that when the curtain opened 'two hundred wax candles' stood unlighted on 'the cabalistic implements and vessels'. Döbler entered, discharged a pistol and 'they burst simultaneously into illumination'. A couple more tricks give a flavour of what else Dickens would have seen. 'A kettle is elevated on brackets...and a number of dead pigeons are deposited therein with a sufficient quantity of water to cook them; and after fire is supplied by means of a spirit-lamp the lid is raised to take out the birds, when lo and behold out issue a flight of live pigeons.'

Later in the programme Döbler borrowed eight or ten handkerchiefs, put them in a basket and poured water on them. A washerwoman was then produced from an empty basket and proceeded to scrub them. 'At the discharge of a pistol, another box, previously empty, is opened, and there appear the handkerchiefs washed and ironed in a first-rate condition, and ready for use.'

The reviews of Döbler's act were uniformly complimentary. *The Times* concluded that 'the entertainment is excellent of its kind, and well worth the attention of the admirers of "natural magic".' *The Morning Post* wrote: 'The great secret of all these tricks is substitution; but he [Döbler] manages it so cleverly, that he really deserves great praise and encouragement.'

Could it have been Döbler that persuaded Dickens to try his hand at conjuring? He certainly ticked all the boxes. Döbler was young (he was apparently forty when Dickens saw him but looked younger), elegantly dressed, reportedly 'pleasing in manner, prepossessing in appearance', performed delightful magic to an enthusiastic audience in a packed theatre: a far cry indeed from the rough, demanding world of the street entertainer. And with his orchestral music and chivalrous distribution of flowers, which he pulled out of a hat to give to women, Döbler allegedly 'courted a more solidly middle-class audience' than his contemporaries.

It is easy to imagine Dickens wanting to replicate his feats after watching such a show; particularly perhaps after seeing the amazement on the faces of the youngsters he brought with him. Dickens was an innate showman (as is known from both his acting and public readings) and an enthusiastic host at the parties he loved to give. Conjuring provided the perfect vehicle for entertaining his friends and family of all ages.

That Döbler was a particular favourite of Dickens is clear from some subsequent letters he wrote. Two months after taking up magic he wrote to his friend and solicitor, Thomas Mitton, stating that a trick he was working on was 'better than the Northern Wizard and as good as Doebler' (see Plate 8). The Northern Wizard (or Great Wizard of the North) referred to the conjurer John Henry Anderson, a contemporary of Döbler, whom Dickens almost certainly saw at some stage (see Plates 6 and 7). At the end of 1843 he boasted to the philanthropist Angela Burdett Coutts that he had 'made a tremendous hit with a conjuring apparatus, which includes some of Doëbler's best tricks'. Dickens never suffered from false modesty and it was natural to compare himself favourably to the person who had influenced him in taking up his new endeavour.

The timescale of seeing the German conjurer and then going on to perform his first magic show reinforces the likelihood that Döbler was his main inspiration. That was a period of six months – plenty of time to buy some tricks, rehearse them and put together a show; provided the type of magic that Dickens did was predominantly apparatus based and did not rely on mastering sleight of hand.

## First Conjuring Show

The first indication that Dickens's interest was piqued by the thought of conjuring after seeing Döbler, can be seen in a letter he wrote on 16th September, 1842. 'At the Isle of Thanet races yesterday I saw- oh! who shall say what an immense amount of character in the way of inconceivable villainy and blackguardism! I even got some new wrinkles in the way of showmen, conjurors, pea-and-thimblers, and trampers generally.'

A tramper was another word for a tramp – someone who travelled aimlessly about on foot, doing odd jobs or begging for a living; so once again not the most flattering of pools in which to include conjurers. But there is a hint here that Dickens was studying these dubious characters so he could apply some of their skills – their 'wrinkles' – for conjuring purposes; rather than solely for a future writing project.

Three months after that letter, there was positive confirmation, in the form of another communication, that he had actually taken up conjuring. On 31st December, 1842 he wrote a long letter to his great friend Cornelius Felton – Professor of Greek, later President of Harvard – whom he had first met earlier that year in America (see Plate 21). In it he included a reference to *Martin Chuzzlewit* which he was writing at the time ('I have been hard at work on my new book, of which the first number has just appeared'). This was to be his next novel after *Barnaby Rudge*, and he would be concentrating on it right through to the summer of the following year. Later on in the letter Dickens wrote as follows:

> The actuary of the National Debt couldn't calculate the number of children who are coming here on Twelfth Night, in honor of Charley's birthday, for which occasion I have provided a Magic Lantern and divers other tremendous engines of that nature. But the best of it, is, that Forster and I have purchased between us the entire stock in trade of a conjurer, the practice and display whereof is entrusted to me. And oh my dear eyes, Felton, if you could see me conjuring the company's watches into impossible tea caddies, and causing pieces of money to fly, and burning pocket handkerchiefs without hurting 'em, – and practising in my own room, without anybody to admire – you would never forget it as long as you live. In those tricks which require a confederate I am assisted (by reason of his imperturbable good humour) by Stanfield, who always does his part exactly the wrong way: to the unspeakable delight of all beholders. We come out on a small scale tonight, at Forster's, where we see the Old Year out and the New One in. Particulars of Success shall be forwarded in my next.

Forster was John Forster, Dickens's literary adviser and editor, his best friend over the longest period and his first biographer (see Plate 17). When Dickens died he touchingly said: 'The duties of life remain while life remains, but for me the joy of it is gone forever more'. Quite why Forster was inveigled into contributing to the purchase of Dickens's magic props is never made clear. He did become Dickens's 'confederate', or assistant, in later shows but, on this occasion – the individual changed, presumably depending on who was available – it was Clarkson Stanfield. He was another close friend of Dickens and a scene painter and marine artist by profession.

Everything about this letter, apart perhaps from one phrase, suggests that Dickens was about to perform his first magic show. There is the inference that the purchase of the props was relatively recent (if he had bought them before he went to America, surely he would have told Felton about it on his visit over there); there is his emphasis on telling Felton about his practising, rather than an actual performance; and then there is the statement that 'we come out on a small scale tonight' – a clear indication that this was to be his debut performance, a preamble to the main event six days later of the show on his son's birthday.

The only slight oddity is that Dickens wrote that his confederate 'always does his part exactly the wrong way: to the unspeakable delight of all beholders'. This could imply that they had done some previous shows. However a far more likely interpretation is that Dickens and Stanfield have been practising their tricks on anybody who happened to be around – in anticipation of their more formal show. This is a necessity for any conjurer building up the confidence to do a first public performance. It is known from the enormous amount of preparation that Dickens did for his acting and public readings, how much store he put on rehearsing thoroughly. And conjuring, which often involves audience participation and the borrowing of props to get the most out of the tricks, requires that some of the run-throughs (clearly not all, as Dickens refers to 'practising in my own room, without anybody to admire') would need to be done on passing friends and relatives.

What is certain is that the New Year's Eve 'small scale' performance was a success, as the Twelfth Night show on 6th January, 1843, his eldest son's sixth birthday, went ahead. It is suspected that Dickens's conjuring was a complete surprise for the guests. In sending out the invitations there was no hint of an intended magic show. Felton, who lived in America, was not going to be there, so it was fine for him to be informed – in any event his letter would not have reached him until the party was long over.

The earliest invitation known about was to Frank Stone, a Manchester-born artist, who received one on 28th December, 1842. Dickens seemed to be anticipating his magic:

> All manner of childish entertainments are coming off here on
> Twelfth Night, in honour of my eldest son attaining the tremendous
> age of six years. It has occurred to me that a few older boys and girls
> (all of whom you know) might protract the festivities on their own
> account, and make a merry evening of it. Come and try – as early as
> between 7 and 8.

Clearly Frank Stone did not respond because Dickens wrote a
follow up letter on 2nd January, 1843: 'Did you get a letter I wrote to
you t'other day, and forwarded per Post, touching the next Twelfth
Night as ever comes? If 'yes', well and good. If 'no', learn that you
are expected here, *early* on that Evening.' It looked like Dickens was
not going to accept a refusal.

Another guest was Leigh Hunt, an editor and essayist who was
later to be cruelly satirised as Harold Skimpole in *Bleak House*. He
was also the author of a rather lovely poem called *Jenny Kissed Me*,
inspired, it was said, by Jane Carlyle, the wife of Thomas Carlyle,
who later was to sing Dickens's praises as a conjurer. He was asked,
with a wonderful turn of phrase, on 3rd January, 1843:

> Next Friday – Twelfth Night – is the Anniversary of my Son and
> Heir's birthday; on which occasion, a Magic Lantern and divers other
> engines are going to be let off on these premises.
>
> I have asked some children of a larger growth (all of whom you
> know) to come and make merry on their own account. If you be well
> enough to join us, and will do so by half past seven, you will give my
> Wife and myself great pleasure, and (I think I may predict) Leigh
> Hunt no pain.

And this to Frederick Marryat, a naval officer turned author, on the
same day: 'Friday next – twelfth night – is the anniversary of my son
and heir's birthday; on which occasion I am going to let off a magic
lantern and other strong engines.'

If there was a conspiracy of silence about Dickens's intended
conjuring show, his wife, Catherine, was clearly part of it. She asked

some other friends to arrive about seven. 'We meet at that early hour, as Charles is going to exhibit a magic lantern for the amusement of the children.' Perhaps the 'magic lantern' was a decoy for the magic show. All this secrecy certainly suggests a debut.

Yet another indication that this was Dickens's first performance is seen in a letter he wrote a month later, dated 3rd February, 1843, to Clarkson Stanfield. In it he displayed all the enthusiasm of a neophyte conjurer; the pleasure at another booking combined with the realisation that he needed to make some changes to his repertoire. The letter was written on a Friday, with the forthcoming show on the Monday; so, in another nod to the busy amateur, he was not giving himself much time to rehearse with his assistant.

My Dear Stanfield

Landseer [Charles Landseer, an artist] has spread such exciting reports of the conjurations we performed on Twelfth Night, that I have been fain to promise Mrs. Norton they shall come off for the behoof of her boys on Monday.

I have some new tricks, and some improvements on the old, which require an exact knowledge on the part of Ivory. And as I hear you are going to Mrs. Norton's on Monday, will you be here at 5 – not later – that we may have time to go over them? Do you dine at Ainsworth's [William Harrison Ainsworth, a novelist] tomorrow? In the event of such extraordinary good luck, will you come here *tomorrow* at 5?

A word in answer.

Ivory was Stanfield's on-stage name when he acted as assistant to Dickens's conjurer. The editors of Dickens's letters postulate that Ivory 'was the name of an actual conjuror's assistant – but not of any well-known conjuror'. This is unlikely. This was not Dickens's way with names: he much preferred finding one that was apposite to the character – as was seen with Sweet William – rather than appropriating a genuine name of someone in the same profession. Much more probable is that Dickens was thinking about a magic wand, an implement often used to 'assist' the conjurer. These were, to quote the famous nineteenth century French conjurer Robert-Houdin, 'generally a small ebony rod, with a rounded *ivory* tip at each end' [my italics].

It is also noteworthy that a slave with the name of Ivory appeared in Chapter 17 of Dickens's *American Notes*, which were published in October 1842 – a few months before his first conjuring show. Dickens listed numerous extracts from American papers from the South advertising the escape of slaves, with a reward given for anyone who found them. This was one such: 'Ran away, a negro man, named Ivory. Has a small piece cut out of the top of each ear.' Even though Dickens violently opposed slavery, the name – and Ivory's situation as a 'forced assistant' – might have stuck in his mind.

## Subsequent Shows

Nothing more was heard about the show for Mrs Norton's boys; and there was a gap of a year before there was a mention of another conjuring performance. The occasion was a birthday party for Nina Macready (her husband, the actor William Charles Macready, was touring America at the time) held on 26th December, 1843. Dickens wrote the day after to the philanthropist Angela Burdett Coutts:

Charley is in great force, and, with his sisters, desires his hearty love. They all went, with us, last night to a juvenile party at Mrs Macreadys, and came out very strong – especially Charley who called divers small boys by their Christian names (after the manner of a Young Nobleman on the Stage) and indulged in numerous phases of genteel dissipation. I have made a tremendous hit with a conjuring apparatus, which includes some of Doëbler's best tricks, and was more popular last evening after cooking a plum pudding in a hat, and producing a pocket handkerchief from a Wine Bottle, than ever I have been in my life. I shall hope to raise myself in your esteem by these means.

This was the first show where there was a credible third party witness to Dickens's abilities as a conjurer. Jane Carlyle, the wife of the social historian and essayist, Thomas Carlyle (perhaps the living writer whom Dickens most revered, making much use of Carlyle's three volume *The French Revolution: A History* for his *A Tale of Two Cities*), wrote to her cousin about the same party.

> Dickens and Forster above all exerted themselves till the perspiration was pouring down and they seemed *drunk* with their efforts! Only think of that excellent Dickens playing the *conjuror* for one whole hour -- the *best* conjuror I ever saw -- (and I have paid money to see several) -- and Forster acting as his servant. This part of the entertainment concluded with a plum pudding made out of raw flour, raw eggs -- all the raw usual ingredients -- boiled in a gentleman's hat -- and tumbled out reeking -- all in one minute before the eyes of the astonished children, and astonished grown people! that trick -- and his other of changing ladies' pocket handkerchiefs into comfits -- and a box full of bran into a box full of -- a live-guinea-pig! -- would enable him to make a handsome subsistence let the book-seller trade go as it please -- !

In case anybody might suspect Jane Carlyle was a little gushing in her praise of Dickens, this is her writing about him in another setting. When Dickens played the part of Bobadil in a performance of the play *Every Man in His Humour* by Ben Jonson on 20th September, 1844, she wrote to her husband about the production: '...not one performer among them could be called good, and none that could be called absolutely *bad*...poor little Dickens, all painted in black and red, and affecting the voice of a man of six feet, would have been unrecognisable for the mother who bore him!'

Dickens himself was clearly still buzzing about his Boxing Day performance several days later as he wrote again to Cornelius Felton on 2nd January, 1844. 'Such dinings, such dancings, such conjurings, such blindman's-buffings, such theatre-goings, such kissings-out of old years and kissings-in of new ones, never took place in these parts before.'

And then, even more exuberantly, to the husband of the birthday girl, William Macready, the following day. It is perhaps this letter, more than any other that Dickens wrote about his own conjuring, that captures some of his brilliance as a writer. Running alongside his vivid description of the tricks he performed is the masterful repetitive theme of telling Macready what he, apparently, did not want to hear – how wonderful his wife was. Reading it now brings alive the fun everybody must have had who had been there that Boxing Day evening.

Oh that you had been in Clarence Terrace on Nina's birthday! Good God how we missed you, talked of you, drank your health, and wondered what you were doing! Perhaps you are Falkland [a reference to the jealous disposition of the character Faulkland in Sheridan's play *The Rivals*] enough (I swear I suspect you of it) to feel rather sore – just a little bit you know; the merest trifle in the world – on hearing that Mrs. Macready looked brilliant – blooming, young, and handsome; and that she danced a country dance with the writer hereof (Acres to your Falkland) in a thorough spirit of beaming good humour and enjoyment. Now you don't like to be told that?

Nor do you quite like to hear that Forster and I conjured bravely – that a hot plum pudding was produced from an empty saucepan, held over a blazing fire, kindled in Stanfield's hat, without damage to the lining – that a box of bran was changed into a live Guinea Pig, which ran between my God Child's feet, and was the cause of such a shrill uproar and clapping of hands that you might have heard it (and I daresay did) in America – that three half crowns being taken from Major Burns [James Burns, the son of the famous Scottish poet Robert Burns] and put into a tumbler-glass before his eyes did then and there give jingling answers unto questions asked of them by me, and knew where you were, and what you were doing; to the unspeakable admiration of the whole assembly. Neither do you quite like to be told that we are going to do it again, next Saturday, with the addition of Demoniacal dresses from a Masquerade shop. Nor, that Mrs Macready, for her gallant bearing always, and her best sort of best affection, is the best creature that I know. Never mind. No man shall gag me; and those are my opinions.

An interesting comparison is to be made in two of the above letters when it came to producing the hot plum pudding from the borrowed hat. The way Jane Carlyle described it was that all the 'raw ingredients' were poured into a hat and a pudding 'tumbled out reeking': this is of course was exactly how the audience were meant to remember the trick. However Dickens was rather more honest in his description. He wrote that the pudding was produced from an empty saucepan, 'kindled' in a hat; in other words the 'raw ingredients' were poured into a saucepan which was inside the hat. It is still an impressive trick – where did the ingredients go to? – where did the pudding come from? But not quite as impossible as the way Jane Carlyle recalled it.

It is also of note that the hat was borrowed from Stanfield, who had been Dickens's previous assistant in his show (this time it was John Forster); and therefore would have been privy to the secret. Although it was possible to produce the pudding from any hat, one assumes that Dickens was ensuring he had the best hat possible to guarantee the trick worked most effectively. This little attention to detail shows how careful Dickens was in his preparation; and that he was performing in a manner that befits a professional.

In his letter to Macready, Dickens was already planning his next performance: 'we are going to do it again, next Saturday, with the addition of Demoniacal dresses from a Masquerade shop'. Clearly he was unsuccessful at finding suitable attire himself so he sent a letter to his younger brother the day after, on 4th January, 1844, which was a Thursday.

Mr Dear Fred

Will you, and can you, make it convenient to go to the Lowther Rooms [in King William Street, Strand – masquerades were held there] for me, after the receipt of this; upon the following errand.

I want to hire for twelfth night, a Magician's dress – that is to say a black cloak with hieroglyphics on it – some kind of doublet to wear underneath – a grave black beard – and a high black sugar-loaf hat – and a wand with a snake on it, or some such thing. Forster wants a similar set of garments in fiery red. Anything between these and the dress of Mephistopheles will suit him, but it must be blazing red, or have a good deal of red in it. Also he wants a jolly mask – such as Wieland [after George Wieland, an actor and dancer, mainly in pantomime, who was a brilliant mime] would have if he were a grinning spirit. He must be able to see well out of it. Our legs we don't care for.

I have been to Nathan's [a masquerade and fancy-dress warehouse] myself, but they have not such things. The production of my card will materially assist you with the Lowther Vagabond, I dare say. But I want to know the cost, and must have the things sent up for inspection, that I may be quite sure they are of the right sort.

If you can effect this wonderful work, fifty people are expected to fall into fits.

Affectionately Always

Charles Dickens

PS Don't *leave* my card if you can't get the dresses. For they'll stick it up in the chimney glass of some whorehouse.

Apparently the final word of the 'PS' had been inked out by someone, so this is the best guess at it. If so, it was a funny joke, typical of what you might write to your younger brother. It is reminiscent of a comical exchange between Mr Noddy and Mr Gunter in Chapter 32 of *The Pickwick Papers*.

"I request that you'll favour me with your card, Sir," said Mr. Noddy. "I'll do nothing of the kind, Sir," replied Mr. Gunter. "Why not, Sir?" inquired Mr. Noddy. "Because you'll stick it up over your chimney-piece, and delude your visitors into the false belief that a gentleman has been to see you, Sir," replied Mr. Gunter.

Unfortunately nothing more is known about this Twelfth Night party and whether his brother found suitable dress to suit Dickens's requirements. Indeed it would be another five years before another conjuring show is referred to in any detail. In the meantime there was the briefest of extracts in a diary kept by Mrs Watson who, along with her husband, first met Dickens in Lausanne on 6th July, 1846. Dickens was staying in Switzerland whilst planning the writing of *Dombey and Son*. Ten days later the Watsons were invited to dinner and she recorded this in her diary: 'Dined with the Dickenses and passed an evening just as one would expect at the home of Boz. He was in extraordinary spirits and was very amusing: Tricks, Characters etc.'

Undoubtedly Dickens did other performances through the 1840s, not only on Twelfth Night, but also when his family were on holiday. His daughter, Mamie Dickens, in her 1897 memoir, wrote: 'At our holiday frolics', her father 'used sometimes to conjure for us, the equally "noble art" of the prestidigitateur being amongst his accomplishments.'

Charley Dickens, the eldest son, also recalled the holiday shows: 'There seem to me to have been continual excursions and picnics during the day; constant impromptu dances, and games, and forfeits, and such like diversions; performances of conjuring tricks, with my father as the magician and John Leech as his attendant, in the evenings.' Here was another assistant, following in the footsteps of Clarkson Stanfield and John Forster, to Dickens's conjurer. John Leech did the illustrations for *A Christmas Carol* and later became a major cartoonist for *Punch* magazine.

Here is Mamie, writing again, this time about the Twelfth Night performances.

Then, again, at the juvenile parties he was always the ruling spirit. He had acquired, by degrees, an excellent collection of conjuring-tricks; and on Twelfth Nights, – the eldest son's birthday, – he would very often, dressed as a magician, give a conjuring entertainment, when a little figure, which appeared from a wonderful and mysterious bag, and which was supposed to be a personal friend of the conjurer, would greatly delight the audience by his funny stories, his eccentric voice and way of speaking, and by his miraculous appearance and disappearances.

Of course, a plum-pudding was made in a hat, and was always one of the great successes of the evening. It would be almost impossible, even to guess *how* many such puddings have been made since. But surely, those made by Charles Dickens must have possessed some special fairy-power, no other conjurer being able to put into *his* pudding all the love, sympathy, fun, and thorough enjoyment which seemed to come from the very hands of this great magician!

Then, when supper-time came, he would be everywhere at once, – carving, cutting the great Twelfth Cake, dispensing the *bonbons*, proposing toasts, and calling upon first one child, and then upon another, for a song or recitation. How eager the little faces looked for each turn to come round, and how they would blush and brighten up when the magician's eyes looked their way!

Mamie Dickens stressed that Dickens would always make an effort with his costume – she wrote that he 'dressed as a magician'. And it was seen in an earlier letter to his younger brother how he was planning on dressing up, complete with black beard. At one Twelfth Night performance Dickens tried a different style of dress. On 11th January, 1849, he wrote to Angela Burdett Coutts: 'Charley had a very merry birthday – I had the honor of conjuring for the party, in a chinese dress and a very large mask – and his noble cake was the admiration and wonder of all beholders.'

This was at least the third costume Dickens had worn. And for his next performance yet more attire was required. It was in this show that Dickens created the name, image and selection of tricks for which he is best remembered as a conjurer.

# Chapter Two Supplement

## Note on Sources

By far the most information about Dickens's exploits as a conjurer come from letters that he wrote. He was an inveterate letter writer, with up to a dozen a day. Some twelve thousand of these have been collected in twelve volumes, which are collectively known as *The Pilgrim Edition of the Letters of Charles Dickens*. The first volume was published in 1965 and the final one in 2002. Alongside the letters themselves are invaluable notes by the editors. Even with such an esoteric subject as conjuring, their commentary is perceptive and invariably correct.

The quotations from Dickens's letters in this chapter are referenced as follows in the Pilgrim volumes:

CD turning down a dinner invitation to see the conjurer.
[Pilgrim, Vol. 3] p. 277          18-25/7/1842
CD to John Forster about some new wrinkles.
[Pilgrim, Vol. 3] p. 325          16/9/1842
CD to Frank Stone inviting him to party.
[Pilgrim, Vol. 3] pp. 406-7          8/12/1842
CD to Cornelius Felton coming out as a conjurer.
[Pilgrim, Vol. 3] p. 416          31/12/1842
CD to Frank Stone follow up party invitation.
[Pilgrim, Vol. 3] p. 419          2/1/1843
Catherine Dickens inviting friends to party.
[Pilgrim, Vol. 3] p. 419 n. 3          3/1/1843
CD to Leigh Hunt inviting him to party.
[Pilgrim, Vol. 3] pp. 419-20          3/1/1843
CD to Frederick Marryat inviting him to party.
[Pilgrim, Vol. 3] p. 420          3/1/1843

CD to Clarkson Stanfield about rehearsing for show.
[Pilgrim, Vol. 3] pp. 437-8        3/2/1843
Suggesting Ivory was the name of a conjurer's assistant.
[Pilgrim, Vol. 3] p. 438 n 1
CD to Thomas Mitton comparing Döbler & Anderson.
[Pilgrim, Vol. 3] p. 439        6/2/1843
CD to Angela Coutts about including Döbler's best tricks.
[Pilgrim, Vol. 3] pp. 613-4        27/12/1843
CD to Cornelius Felton writing about 'such conjurings'.
[Pilgrim, Vol. 4] pp. 2-3        2/1/1844
CD to William Macready about success of his wife's party.
[Pilgrim, Vol. 4] p 10        3/1/1844
CD to brother Fred about buying new costume.
[Pilgrim, Vol. 4] p. 14        4/1/1844
CD apologising for not going to see Döbler.
[Pilgrim, Vol. 4] pp. 113-4        26/4/1844[1]
CD to Angela Coutts about performing in a chinese dress.
[Pilgrim, Vol. 5] p. 473        11/1/1849[2]

Third party letters and diaries also played their part and three are cited in this chapter.

Jane Carlyle to Jeannie Welsh about CD playing the conjurer.
[Carlyle] Vol. 17, 28/12/1843, cited in [Pilgrim, Vol. 3] p. 613 n 4
Jane Carlyle[3] to Thomas Carlyle about CD performing as Bobadil.

---

[1] Note 1 of the Pilgrim footnote on page 114 states 'In 1843', but it should be 1842. 'I walk about brimful of letters, facetious descriptions, touching morsels, and pathetic friendships, but can't for the soul of me uncork myself. The Post-Office is my rock ahead. My average number of letters that *must* be written every day, is, at least, a dozen.' Letter to Cornelius Felton, 1 Sept, 1843 [Pilgrim, Vol. 3] p. 548.

[2] A reference to this letter was found in [Tomalin] p. 216; the citation was obtained personally from her. CD spelt Chinese with a lowercase 'c'.

[3] This is wrongly attributed as having been written by Thomas Carlyle in a rare

[Carlyle] Vol. 19, 23/9/1845
Mrs Watson recording having meal with CD in Lausanne.
'Sidelight on a Great Friendship', [Dickensian] No. 47, 1 Jan, 1951, p. 17

A further source of Dickens's conjuring came from his children. The references are:

'At our holiday frolics...' [Mamie Dickens, My Father] Chapter 2, p. 33
'There seem to me...' [Dickens, Charley] p. 15
'Then, again, at the juvenile...'
[Mamie Dickens, Dickens with his Children] pp. 33-4

## Magic Sets and Magic Books

Almost without exception, in pre-television and internet days, people were inspired to take up magic arising out of one of three circumstances, or a combination of them. They were given, or purchased, a magic set; they read a book on magic; or they saw somebody, whether an amateur or professional, perform magic. It is argued in this chapter that it was seeing Ludwig Döbler that galvanised Dickens into conjuring. Why, though, could he not have been motivated by a magic set or a book?

It is difficult to know whether magic sets were on sale in London in 1842. The earliest surviving magic set would appear to be in the Goethe Museum in Dusseldorf and it dates from 1830; so it is quite possible that some had been imported, or indeed produced, in England a decade later. Another German company that made magic sets, Baudenbacher of Nuremberg, claimed to have exhibited at the world exhibition in London in 1862; and again it is feasible that they were selling sets prior to this.[4]

lapse in [Tomalin] p. 170.
[4] This information came from [Witt]: a German book devoted to the history of magic sets.

What counted against Dickens buying one was primarily the types of trick that were contained in them – which do not match up with the tricks Dickens actually performed. Magic sets comprised scaled down props, aimed at children, and designed for performing to small groups. Dickens was using apparatus suitable for adults and for reasonably large audiences. Also initially Dickens wrote about buying the 'stock in trade of a conjurer', which does not suggest the purchase of a magic set.[5]

The possibility that Dickens was first inspired by reading a book on conjuring would, on first reflection, appear very likely. He was a voracious reader in his youth and by the end of his life had an impressive library. The problem is the lack of magic books which were published up to the middle of the nineteenth century that could genuinely teach someone how to be a conjurer. In some ways the extent of magic knowledge written down had not really progressed a great deal from the chapters on conjuring in Reginald Scot's 1584 *The Discoverie of Witchcraft*.[6]

After Scot's *Discoverie* the most important milestone in magic literature was *Hocus Pocus Junior* in 1634. There were some new tricks, amidst some that had been copied from Scot, including one in Dickens's own repertoire. Later important contributions were Henry Dean's *The Whole Art of Legerdemain* (1722), *Breslaw's Last Legacy* (1784), Henri Decremps, *The Conjurer Unmasked* (1785)

---

[5] The approximate size of Dickens's audiences for one show is known about through asking his brother to try and buy him a magician's attire. He wrote: 'If you can effect this wonderful work, fifty people are expected to fall into fits.' [Pilgrim, Vol. 4] p. 14.

[6] [Scot] pp. 182-203. [Dawson] p. 136 wrote: 'Dickens appears to have read Reginald Scot's *Discoverie of Witchcraft*. This was predicated on the incorrect attribution to CD of an article 'Mediums Under Other Names', Eliza Lynn Linton [AYR] Vol. VII, No. 156, 19 April, 1862, pp. 130-37.

and *Gale's Cabinet of Knowledge* (1796); but none were especially revolutionary in their content – and the instructions remained fairly cursory with little in the way of useful illustration.[7]

The production of new magic books in the first forty years of the nineteenth century meant it was even more poorly served than in previous decades. There were plenty of general fun books published, principally aimed at children, that had conjuring sections in them (for instance *Endless Amusements*, 1818, John Babcock's *Philosophical Recreations or Winter Amusements*, 1820 and *Parlour Magic*, 1838); most of these regurgitated earlier material and none of them revealed the methods of the apparatus magic performed by contemporary theatre conjurers.

Some thirty five years later doubtless Dickens would have had a copy of Professor Hoffmann's *Modern Magic* in his library. This was the game-changing book, published in 1876, in which the author, real name Angelo Lewis, revealed most of the secrets of the professional repertoire of conjurers at the time; which many incorrectly anticipated would ruin their livelihood. Instead it heralded the start of the golden age of magic.[8]

However in 1842 there was no equivalent 'must-have' book for Dickens to own. Indeed, if the catalogue that was produced of his library at Gad's Hill after he died is anything to go by, it would seem

---

[7] The relative importance of some of these books could certainly be argued about. This particularly might apply to Henri Decremps's *The Conjurer Unmasked* which was translated from the French *La Magie Blanche Dévoilée*. Decremps wrote other significant books on magic which were not translated. Although Dickens spoke French, and it is known that he bought some of his magic apparatus in France, there is no evidence that he had read any of these.

[8] [Hoffmann, Modern Magic]. It is often said that the best way to keep a secret is to publish it. The reason why exposing tricks in books does not necessarily result in audiences being much the wiser is addressed in the 'Introduction' [Steinmeyer] pp. xix-xxi.

that Dickens did not actually possess any books on conjuring. It was possible he had bought some and then got rid of them; alternatively, when his library was sold after his death, some magic books might have been bundled into general lots and therefore not separately listed. But the fact that, to quote one magic historian, 'not a single work in the category of "practical magic" was catalogued', certainly counts against Dickens consulting books for his magic knowledge.[9]

There are a couple of books that it is known Dickens did possess, with at best a passing interest in magic. One was Sir David Brewster's *Letters on Natural Magic*, the 1838 edition: this exposed Wolfgang von Kempelen's automaton chess player, in which a human was hidden inside a life-sized model of a mechanical Turk and proceeds to beat all-comers at chess. But most of the rest of the book was more scientific. He also owned Joseph Strutt's *The Sports and Pastimes of the People of England*, from the same year. Again there was no reference to any specific conjuring tricks in it; the nearest was a description of fire eating and animals dancing and other feats, including a horse that was able to 'tell the number of spots on a card and leap through a hoop'.[10]

There is a possibility that Dickens also owned a copy of Hans Jacob Wecker's *Eighteen Books of The Secret Art and Nature*, 1661. This copy is in a private collection and on the paste-down front endpaper it has the Dickens bookplate and, at the bottom, a sticker stating 'From the Library of Charles Dickens, Gadshill Place, June 1870'; so the provenance would seem to be good, even though it was not listed in the sale catalogue. The book does have a few tricks in it, such as cutting and restoring a piece of string, but again they are relatively basic – and it does not contain any tricks that Dickens

[9] 'Charles Dickens and his Library' [Magic Circular] Edwin A Dawes, Vol. 60, Feb, 1966, p. 90. See also [Dawson] Chapter XVII 'Dickens' Library', pp. 185-195.
[10] 'Descriptions of a Horse in Queen Anne Reign', [Strutt] p. 245.

performed.

This exposes the crux of the argument against Dickens having read any sort of text books in learning his magic – Dickens did not perform 'magic-book' conjuring. All of his tricks involved some sort of apparatus which, with one or two exceptions, were not even explained in any existing book. The conclusion is that Dickens must have bought his apparatus from a magic shop or dealer. The likely sources are looked at in the next chapter.

## John Henry Anderson

John Henry Anderson, or the Great Wizard of the North, has already been suggested as the conjurer Dickens was most likely to have seen prior to 1842. And if he did see him, could he not be a possible candidate, rather than Döbler, for inspiring Dickens to take up magic?

Apart from the sheer length of time that Anderson was in London, there is other supporting evidence that Dickens saw him. The most robust is contained in the letter of 6th February, 1843 that Dickens wrote to Thomas Mitton about an unnamed trick he was doing: 'It is better than the Northern Wizard and as good as Doebler.' Such a comparison, one feels, could only be made if Dickens had seen both conjurers. Another mention of Anderson to Mitton, a couple of years later, turned up in this letter written on 25th July, 1845: 'I suppose he ['he' is probably a reference to his father – as a cheque was paid to him on 25th August for £4] must have it. Am I right? – As the Wizard of the North used to say.' 'Am I right?' was clearly the catch-phrase of Anderson.[11]

---

[11] The two letters to Mitton are in [Pilgrim, Vol. 3] p. 439 and [Pilgrim, Vol. 4] p. 336. Whilst there is no other external confirmation that this was Anderson's catch-phrase, there is also no existing record of any of Anderson's scripts to contradict it (confirmed by Edwin Dawes, author of

A further name check for Anderson occurred in a speech Dickens made in London on 6th April, 1846 at the seventh anniversary festival of the General Theatrical Fund Association, which was founded for the purpose of granting pensions to retired actors. In it Dickens referred to the lack of theatres situated in Covent Garden and he said that the human voice is rarely heard within their walls anymore 'save in connexion with corn, or the ambidextrous prestidigitation of the Wizard of the North.'[12]

Finally, there is one last piece of circumstantial link between Dickens and Anderson. In July, 1843 Dickens chaired a fund-raising committee for the children of an actor, Edward Elton, who drowned returning home from an engagement. Various artists offered a night's receipts to the fund and these included Anderson, who was performing at the Adelphi Theatre. It was likely that Dickens would have been in contact with Anderson at some point about this charitable donation.[13]

If it is accepted that Dickens did see Anderson, he would almost certainly have seen him prior to Döbler.[14] This was because Dickens made his relative comparison between Döbler's and Anderson's same trick in February 1843. But after his appearance in London in 1841, Anderson did not return again to the capital until April 1843.

[Dawes, Anderson]).

[12] [Dickens, Speeches]

[13] [Pilgrim, Vol. 3] p. 534, n 3.

[14] That is not to say that CD could not have seen Anderson more than once of course. [Dawes, Anderson] researches have picked up on the intriguing scenario that both 'Anderson and CD appeared simultaneously under the same roof at the Rotundo in Dublin in mid-March 1867 (presumably in different but adjacent auditoria, as both performances commenced at 8pm). CD arrived in Dublin, from Belfast, on Thu 14 and gave his readings there on Fri 15, Mon 18 & Fri 22 March, leaving him an opportunity on Sat 16 Mar to pop round to see Anderson's show, which had its last night of a run there on Mon 18 Mar.'

So Dickens must have seen Anderson either in 1840 or 1841, which of course preceded his taking a 'whole bevy of young people to see' Döbler.[15]

So if Dickens saw Anderson before Döbler, why is the latter a more likely motivator? Firstly, because there is no evidence of his getting actively involved in conjuring until over a year later – that is a long gestation period. Given Dickens's impulsiveness and eagerness to throw himself into something wholeheartedly once he had 'caught the bug', having seen Döbler in July 1842, and performing to an audience of friends and family less than six months later, is more consistent with his character.

Secondly, in comparing the two, Dickens rated Döbler higher – as the quotation, 'It is better than the Northern Wizard and as good as Doebler', suggests. This assessment was shared, not just by magic historians, (Clarke considered 'Döbler was the best of the decorative conjurers'), but by contemporary newspaper reports. 'Anderson,

---

[15] Döbler opened at the St James's Theatre early in April 1842 and performed on two, sometimes three evenings a week, until 25 July: [Clarke] p. 233 and playbill in Peter Lane Collection. Anderson's actual dates were as follows: Easter Mon 17 Apr - Sat 9 Sep, 1843: Adelphi Theatre, London (originally had been advertised to open Mon 10 Apr); Easter Mon 8 Apr - Mon 17 Jun, 1844: Adelphi Theatre, London. Data from [Dawes, Anderson]. Reinforcing the judgement that Dickens saw Anderson prior to Döbler is that he also used Anderson's catch phrase in a letter to John Forster, written from the Niagara Falls on his first trip to America on 26 April, 1842: 'One word on the precious letters before I close. You are right, my dear fellow, about the papers; and you are right (I grieve to say) about the people. *Am I right?* quoth the conjuror. *Yes!* from gallery, pit, and boxes.' [Pilgrim, Vol. 3] p. 211. CD here was referring to his controversial speeches in America about his concerns over international copyright which received a lot of criticism in the US press. He was essentially echoing Anderson's words that 'he is right' to raise the subject.

"the Great Wizard of the North", who figured at the Strand...was unequal to Herr Döbler', wrote *The Times* in April, 1842. Similarly, the *Morning Chronicle* had: 'Henceforth all minor magicians must hide their diminished heads, Wizards of the North and Wizards of the South are no more to paralleled with our Herr [Dobler]'. The conjurer that impressed Dickens the most was likely to be the one who motivated him to take up conjuring.[16]

Ironically Dickens undoubtedly did more from Anderson's repertoire than he ever did from Döbler's. Indeed it is hard to ascertain what it was specifically out of Döbler's repertoire that Dickens was referring to, when he wrote to Anglea Coutts claiming he had performed 'some of Doëbler's best tricks'. In contrast Anderson certainly cooked a pudding in a hat, found a handkerchief inside a wine bottle, produced a guinea pig, discovered a watch in a loaf of bread and questioned some dancing coins – all of which tricks Dickens would go on to do himself. Such tricks were much more practical for the front room of a private house than most of what Döbler did.[17]

There is one other possible inspiration for Dickens that has been suggested: this was the famous clown Joseph Grimaldi. Heathcote Williams, in his booklet *What Larks! Charles Dickens, Conjuror* wrote: 'Of those who might have been responsible for awakening

---

[16] [Clarke] p. 232; it was also Clarke who wrote that Döbler had a 'real genius for artistic presentation'. Quotations in the main chapter about Döbler being young and appealing to the middle-classes came from [Frost] p. 266 and [During] p. 113. Quotations in this paragraph were from *The Times*, 16 April, 1842 and the *Morning Chronicle*, 13 April, 1842.

[17] Döbler's repertoire of tricks, as noted in the main chapter, came from *The Times*, 16 April, 1842, *The Morning Post*, 23 April,1842 and [Frost] p. 267. Anderson's early repertoire is listed in [Clarke] p. 213 and the playbill in [Houdini, Unmasking] p. 150. The quotation from CD letter to Angela Coutts is [Pilgrim, Vol. 3] p. 614.

Dickens's interest in magic the most likely was Grimaldi.' Whilst Tigner similarly put him forward as a possibility. The main reason for this supposition was that Dickens edited Grimaldi's memoirs in 1838. However, even though there is evidence that Grimaldi did incorporate some magic into his act it was, by all accounts, very peripheral. Indeed Dickens did not mention conjuring at all in his book: for that reason alone he is not really a credible contender with Döbler.[18]

## When was Dickens's First Conjuring Performance?

It has been long accepted that Dickens's first conjuring performance was announced when he wrote to Cornelius Felton on 31st December, 1842 stating that he had bought 'the entire stock in trade of a conjurer' and was planning a show on 6th January, 1843.[19] The

---

[18] [Williams] pp. 18-9. However Williams goes on to rule Grimaldi out himself, preferring instead to put forward the even more unlikely candidate of the thimble-rigger (Williams seems to confuse him with being a conjurer) that CD portrayed in his chapter on 'Greenwich Fair' in *Sketches by Boz*. [Tigner] p. 92: 'We do not need to credit Grimaldi for rousing Dickens' interest in conjuring tricks, however, if an article [Performing Animals] in Dickens' journal...may fairly be credited to him'. [Tigner] quoted this from *Clowns*, John H. Towsen, New York, Hawthorn Books, 1976, p. 157: 'Grimaldi was well versed in trickwork and was himself the designer of many effective "tricks of construction".' *Memoirs of Joseph Grimaldi*, edited by Boz, London 1838.

[19] [Tigner] p. 95: 'It was not long after his return from America that Dickens had first seen Dobler. And it was late in that same year that Dickens – judging from both the tone and the contents of his year's end letter to Felton – was first bit by the performer's bug.' The Pilgrim editors stated: 'This was clearly the first of a long series of Twelfth Night parties with conjuring'. [Pilgrim, Vol. 3] p. 437 n 3. [Dawes, Great Illusionists] p. 131 wrote that the letter was the 'earliest record we have of Dickens as a performer.'

only person who seriously disputed this was Trevor Dawson in *Charles Dickens: Conjurer, Mesmerist and Showman.* His supposed evidence to prove that Dickens performed magic prior to 1842 has already been dealt with. But having taken that stance, he needed to somehow show that the letter to Felton demonstrated an ongoing interest, rather than a starting point, in Dickens's conjuring.

He did this by the rather tortuous route of claiming that Dickens previously 'must have performed some conjuring tricks for Fenton [sic, should be Felton], who must have been suitably impressed, otherwise...he would not have written' the letter. The only occasion Dickens could have 'performed some conjuring tricks' on Felton was in America, which is when he first met him on his trip there earlier that year. Unfortunately Dawson failed to enlighten as to where, or indeed how – given that Dickens specialised in apparatus-based magic tricks – this conjuring performance took place.[20]

The only other contentious area over Dickens's first conjuring performance arose as a result of some confusion over dates. Heathcote Williams in *What Larks! Charles Dickens, Conjuror* stated that Dickens's letter to Cornelius Felton about first taking up conjuring, was written a year later than it was – 1843, instead of 1842. Simon Callow, in his 2012 book, *Charles Dickens and the Great Theatre of the World,* used Heathcote Willams exclusively as his source for his own research into Dickens and conjuring.

Callow therefore erroneously proclaimed that Dickens 'bought up the entire stock-in-trade of a retired conjuror' *after* he had done his first show (which he dated as 6th January, 1842, rather than 1843); and, as a result of this purchase, 'the tricks became

---

[20]See Chapter One Supplement: 'Interest in Conjuring prior to 1842' with regard to CD performing conjuring prior to 1842. [Dawson] p. 82: Dawson's logic is surely at fault here: why would you have had to perform some tricks for someone before telling them you were doing a conjuring show?

spectacular...magic had become a full-scale obsession: he acquired ever more elaborate devices' and he 'performed large-scale illusions'. There is no evidence of any such change in the complexity or size of Dickens's repertoire over time. [21]

---

[21] [Williams] p. 5. Just to confuse matters even more, Williams later quoted another extract from Felton's letter, but this time gave the correct year, p. 20. He also quoted from the letter – this time with the correct date – but stated that it was a diary entry, writing incorrectly that 'Dickens's diaries also contain several mentions of his conjuring practices', p. 5. It is unsurprising that [Callow] p. 132 got rather muddled with his own narrative.

# CHAPTER THREE

# The Showman

## The Bonchurch Playbill

Indirectly it is Alfred de Caston, the French conjurer, who has to be thanked for information about Dickens's show on Bonchurch on the Isle of Wight. It was because Dickens was clearly so enamoured by his performance (which he saw in June, 1854) and wrote to Forster to say just that, that his biographer was reminded about an earlier performance Dickens himself had done five years previously.

Forster wrote about Dickens's credentials for giving an opinion on de Caston's abilities: 'Nor was he a mean authority as to this, being himself, with his tools at hand, a capital conjuror*...' The asterisk referred to a footnote – clearly Forster did not think it was important enough to put in the main text. But it is arguably the most significant footnote in the history of magic. This is it in full:

I permit myself to quote from the bill of one of his [Dickens] entertainments in the old merry days at Bonchurch, (ii, 425-434), of course drawn up by himself, whom it describes as:

The Unparalleled Necromancer RHIA RHAMA RHOOS educated cabalistically in the Orange Groves of Salamanca and the Ocean Caves of Alum Bay, [some of whose proposed wonders it thus prefigures:]
### THE LEAPING CARD WONDER.
Two Cards being drawn from the Pack by two of the company, and placed, with the Pack, in the Necromancer's box, will leap forth at the command of any lady of not less than eight, or more than eighty, years of age.

# CHARLES DICKENS MAGICIAN

*This wonder is the result of nine years' seclusion in the mines of Russia.*

### THE PYRAMID WONDER.

A shilling being lent to the Necromancer by any gentleman of not less than twelve months, or more than one hundred years, of age, and carefully marked by the said gentleman, will disappear from within a brazen box at the word of command, and pass through the hearts of an infinity of boxes, which will afterwards build themselves into pyramids and sink into a small mahogany box, at the Necromancer's bidding.

*Five thousand guineas were paid for the acquisition of this wonder, to a Chinese Mandarin, who died of grief immediately after parting with the secret.*

### THE CONFLAGRATION WONDER.

A Card being drawn from the Pack by any lady, not under a direct and positive promise of marriage, will be immediately named by the Necromancer, destroyed by fire, and reproduced from its own ashes.

*An annuity of one thousand pounds has been offered to the Necromancer by the Directors of the Sun Fire Office for the secret of this wonder — and refused!!!*

### THE LOAF OF BREAD WONDER.

The watch of any truly prepossessing lady, of any age, single or married, being locked by the Necromancer in a strong box, will fly at the word of command from within that box into the heart of an ordinary half-quartern loaf, whence it shall be cut out in the presence of the whole company, whose cries of astonishment will be audible at a distance of some miles.

*Ten years in the Plains of Tartary were devoted to the study of this wonder.*

### THE TRAVELLING DOLL WONDER.

The travelling doll is composed of solid wood throughout, but, by putting on a travelling dress of the simplest construction, becomes invisible, performs enormous journeys in half a minute, and passes from visibility to invisibility with an expedition so astonishing that no eye can follow its transformations.

*The Necromancer's attendant usually faints on beholding this wonder, and is only to be revived by the administration of brandy and water.*

## THE PUDDING WONDER.

The company having agreed among themselves to offer to the Necromancer, by way of loan, the hat of any gentleman whose head has arrived at maturity of size, the Necromancer, without removing that hat for an instant from before the eyes of the delighted company, will light a fire in it, make a plum pudding in his magic sauce pan, boil it over the said fire, produce it in two minutes, thoroughly done, cut it, and dispense it in portions to the whole company, for their consumption then and there; returning the hat at last, wholly uninjured by fire, to its lawful owner.

*The extreme liberality of this wonder awakening the jealousy of the beneficent Austrian Government, when exhibited in Milan, the Necromancer had the honour to be seized, and confined for five years in the fortress of that city.*

Forster had reproduced Dickens's playbill, which he had stated was written by the novelist, which not only gave his performing persona for this occasion, but also displayed his characteristic humour of exaggeration for comic effect in listing and describing the actual tricks he did. Tantalisingly Forster wrote 'some of whose proposed wonders...' suggesting that he did not even copy out the entire playbill.

Dickens came to Bonchurch in July 1849 (see Plate 14). He was thirty seven years old. After *Martin Chuzzlewit*, which he had just begun when he took up conjuring six and a half years earlier, he had written one other novel, *Dombey and Son*. However he was now embarked on his own particular favourite work, and which is considered to be his most autobiographical in content, *David Copperfield*. By the time he completed it, his own conjuring career was almost certainly over.

Bonchurch was an exclusive village; most of the properties were owned by the Reverend James White – an author of history books and a regular contributor to both *Punch* and *Blackwood's Magazine* – and his wife Rosa Hill. They were also great friends to many literary celebrities of the day including Carlyle and Thackeray. They had a house called Winterborne which they leased to Dickens and his family for the summer. Dickens's schedule was to work until two in the afternoon and then enjoy himself for the remainder of the day.

The Bonchurch show took place sometime in August or September. It is possible to date it to this period because, in an earlier extract from his biography, Forster alluded to the same performance, quoting from a letter he had received from Dickens.

"Last night we had some very good merriment at White's, where pleasant Julian Young and his wife (who are staying about five miles off) showed some droll new games" – and roused the ambition in my friend to give a "mighty conjuring performance for all the children in Bonchurch", for which I sent him the materials and which went off in a tumult of wild delight.

As well as 'some droll new games' there was some warm-up conjuring from Dickens, as Julian Young wrote the following in his diary.

Spent a delightful evening at Bonchurch with James White, Mr Danby, Mr and Mrs John Leech, Charles Dickens, Mrs Dickens, and Miss Hogarth. Dickens showed us one or two capital conjuring tricks which he had just brought from Paris.

It has been argued that in this letter to Forster Dickens was referring to a different show, as the one with the playbill was put together primarily for adults. Dickens though usually performed for all ages – 'family shows' as they are now termed. All the tricks which were featured on the playbill would be equally understood and enjoyed by children; and if the youngsters had not latched on to some of the jokes and allusions in the written programme, this would not have lessened their enjoyment of the magic.

Unfortunately there is no other known factual account or newspaper report of the show, but the playbill itself provides plenty of scope for analysis. It starts with the long introduction to who is performing, with Dickens hiding behind a fleshed out *nom de théâtre*. The opening expression 'The Unparalleled Necromancer' is typical Dickens as it is well-known that he liked to refer himself as the 'Inimitable'.

A necromancer is defined as someone who communicates with the deceased in order to predict the future; in the context of a magic show, the suggestion is that it is some extraneous power, under the control of the conjurer, that is causing the magic to happen – a throwback to an era when people believed in the supernatural, witches and ghosts. However it was an epithet that showmen often applied to themselves in the early years of the nineteenth century; so it is likely that Dickens copied the word from an existing playbill.

Next comes the wonderfully evocative Rhia Rhama Rhoos. In creating this name, Dickens parodied an Indian conjurer called Khia Khan Khruse. Khruse arrived from India in 1815, along with Ramo Samee – who made an appearance in Dickens's 'An Unsettled Neighbourhood' article about his memories of growing up in London. They were part of a troupe known as 'The Four Surprising Indian Jugglers', before splitting up and going their separate ways.

Ramo Samee became the better known of the two; but that might partly be due to the longevity of his career in England, rather than their relative performing skills. According to one source Khruse only remained in the country for ten years – which meant, if Dickens had seen him perform, it would have been before he was twenty. Little is known about Khruse apart from what is stated on his playbills: there is only one existing image of him; a caricature that is in a children's illustrated book (see Plate 13).

Any doubt that it might be Khruse that Dickens was citing is dispelled by the words which immediately follow the name Rhia Rhama Rhoos: 'educated cabalistically in the Orange Groves of *Salamanca* and the Ocean *Caves* of Alum Bay' [my italics]. A playbill of Khruse noted that he was 'Instructed in the *Caves* of *Salamanca*' [my italics]. Given Dickens's fascination for names, it is understandable how the alliteration of Khia Khan Khruse was locked in his memory bank; but to recall the reference to Salamanca, that appeared on a twenty-five year old playbill, demonstrates Dickens's phenomenal visual memory – either that or he had kept a copy!

Dickens was only interested in the name of Khia Khan Khruse, not in his repertoire of tricks – which were very different from his own. Khruse performed such feats as catching a bullet in his hand, dancing on a sheet of red-hot iron, swallowing pins and extracting them from his eyes (a similar stunt to the one that Sweet William did in *The Old Curiosity Shop* of putting 'small leaden lozenges into his eyes' and bringing 'them out at his mouth'), walking on his hands with one foot in his mouth and changing a small toad into a large one.

It is clear from the pastiche of the name, and indeed the rest of the playbill, that Dickens was sending himself up. In this respect he was ahead of his time, as most conjurers of this period tended to take themselves, and their tricks, very seriously. There is no deliberate irony, for instance, in a genuine playbill of Khia Khan Khruse where he claimed 'He will Swallow a Small Bell, Which will be heard to Ring in various parts of his Body' or 'He will also Fry Bacon & Eggs upon a Sheet of common Writing Paper'.

Indeed when you compare Khia Khan Khruse's billing as 'Chief of the Indian Jugglers', with Dickens's Rhia Rhama Rhoos as 'The Unparallelled Necromancer', the latter does not necessarily seem comic by comparison. Like all good jokes, however, the punch line came at the end. Dickens stated that Rhia Rhama Rhoos was 'educated calabistically in the Orange Groves of Salamanca and the Ocean Caves of Alum Bay'. Alum Bay is located on the Isle of Wight and it was at this point his audience would have enjoyed the witticism (see Plate 15).

Whether they also would have appreciated that practically all the other words leading up to it came from the playbills of actual conjurers, is less certain. But it is a wonderful illustration of the inordinate lengths to which Dickens was prepared to go in his creativity. It is hard to think of anything more ephemeral than a playbill and yet it was still lovingly and amusingly composed.

After the name and credentials of the conjurer, Dickens listed his six intended tricks, detailing what it was the audience were going to see. He also penned a little addendum after each, essentially explaining how the trick was supposedly obtained. It was a humorous touch and appears to be original with Dickens, rather than copying the style of an existing playbill. It is possible that all of the references had some added meaning which is now lost, although the allusion to 'Russian mines' (*This wonder is the result of nine years' seclusion in the mines of Russia.*'), the Plains of Tartary (*Ten years in the Plains of Tartary were devoted to the study of this wonder.*') and a 'Chinese Mandarin' (*Five thousand guineas were paid for the acquisition of this wonder, to a Chinese Mandarin...*'), seem relatively generic.

There was one that was seemingly a topical gag. The Austrian empire, which back then ruled the states of Northern Italy, was threatened by revolution and a provisional government in Milan had indicated they wanted to be part of a united Italy. So it was transparent how anything exhibited in Milan might awaken 'the jealousy of the beneficent Austrian Government', where presumably Dickens's use of the word 'beneficent' was ironic. (*The extreme liberality of this wonder awakening the jealousy of the beneficent Austrian Government, when exhibited in Milan...*')

One of the appendages (*An annuity of one thousand pounds has been offered to the Necromancer by the Directors of the Sun Fire Office...*') related to an existing insurance company called the Sun Fire Office. Indeed Dickens used it himself. In a diary entry for

Tuesday 9th January, 1838 he wrote: 'Went to the Sun office to insure my life, where the "Board" seem disposed to think I work too much.'

It is perhaps unsurprising that the funniest to modern ears is the one that does not require any knowledge of Dickens's thought processes, but just paints a comical image: *'The Necromancer's attendant usually faints on beholding this wonder, and is only to be revived by the administration of brandy and water.'*

## Dickens's Tricks

The titles alone of each of the six tricks are not that informative. Dickens was lampooning the typical conjurer's playbill which listed headings with enticing and enchanting names but which were relatively meaningless when it came to determining what the trick actually was. He did this by calling all of them a 'Wonder' of some sort. However the combination of the heading, with the plot précis, enables the trick to be recognised.

The amount of descriptive detail Dickens gave is unusual because most magicians are wary of telling their audience too much in advance about what is going to take place. It decreases the element of surprise and increases the chance of the spectators working out how the trick is done. It suggests that by now Dickens had accumulated enough experience to be confident in his abilities to fool his audience despite this self-imposed handicap.

Dickens's tricks, converted into modern parlance, are as follows. 'The Leaping Card Wonder is the 'Jumping Cards'. Two cards are selected and returned to the pack. The pack is placed inside a wooden *houlette* and one at a time they shoot out from the top. 'The Pyramid Wonder' is 'Coin in Nest of Boxes'. A marked coin is placed inside a small box and vanishes. It reappears in the bottom-most box of probably seven boxes, all inside one another.

'The Conflagration Wonder' is 'Burnt and Restored Playing Card'. A selected card is placed inside a box and burnt. When the box is opened, the card is found restored. 'The Loaf of Bread Wonder' is 'Watch in Loaf of Bread'. A borrowed watch vanishes from a box and ends up inside a loaf of bread. 'The Travelling Doll Wonder' is 'Bonus Genius'. A small wooden doll disappears when it is placed inside a little cloak (see Plate 10).

Finally, 'The Pudding Wonder' is 'Baking a Cake in a Hat'. In a tin are mixed various ingredients – flour, eggs, sugar, milk etc. – that are required to bake a cake; the contents are poured into a borrowed hat. The hat is heated over a flame and a cake is removed; the hat is returned unsullied to its owner.

Leaving aside those on the Bonchurch playbill, there were other tricks that it is known Dickens performed. He wrote to Felton about 'conjuring the company's watches into impossible tea caddies, and causing pieces of money to fly, and burning pocket handkerchiefs without hurting 'em'. At Nina Macready's birthday party, he produced 'a pocket handkerchief from a wine bottle'; changed 'ladies' pocket handkerchiefs into comfits'; 'a box of bran was changed into a live Guinea Pig'; and 'three half crowns...put into a tumbler-glass' gave 'jingling answers unto questions asked of them by me.'

All of these tricks relied on some sort of specialist apparatus for their successful execution and were obtained from a magic shop or dealer. Dickens bought at least some of his props from the toy shop Hamleys. Hamleys was founded in 1760 and in the 1840s was based at 231 High Holborn under the name of Noah's Ark. It is known that Dickens spent two pounds and eight shillings there on 2nd January, 1843 and a further two pounds, nine shillings and six pence on 15th January, 1844. According to his daughter, he was a frequent visitor.

The instructions on how to perform these tricks would have come with the apparatus and, in addition, Dickens might well have had a lesson from the man serving him. Dickens would have also picked up tips by watching other conjurers, in particular Döbler and John Henry Anderson. This is shown by the letter Dickens wrote to his solicitor Thomas Mitton, that a trick he was doing 'is better than the Northern Wizard and as good as Doebler'. It is likely he was referring here to the production of a handkerchief from a wine bottle.

Dickens's extensive use of props, together with the presence of a confederate, or assistant, to help with the 'dirty work', meant he was not reliant on sleight of hand (the one exception perhaps was the Travelling Doll Wonder which required some palming ability). In this respect Dickens's show was very much in keeping with how the majority of popular conjurers performed their magic at this time. Dickens was not out of step; rather he was at the vanguard of the prevailing style of conjuring.

Nevertheless, Dickens must have brought more to his conjuring than a mere exhibition of a number of boxes that automatically did the magic for him. Watching any conjurer display self-working apparatus can be a tedious experience; and one suspects that would have been as true in Victorian times as it is now. So what was it about Dickens's performances that prompted Jane Carlyle to say he was 'the *best* conjuror I ever saw'?

## Presentation of the Tricks

A clue to Dickens's success perhaps lies with his performance of The Travelling Doll Wonder. This was the oldest recorded trick that Dickens did – its origins can be traced back to the 1634 first edition of *Hocus Pocus Junior* where it was called 'Bonus Genius or Nuntius Invisiblis'. Whilst it was one of the few tricks in Dickens's repertoire that was explained in a book, it is unlikely that Dickens would have come across it in his readings. Along with his other tricks, he would have bought the apparatus – a specially made wooden doll and cloth cloak – from a magic shop.

It was a trick Dickens would have seen as it was popular amongst street entertainers. One such, when interviewed by Henry Mayhew, talked about getting out his 'cards and card-boxes and the bonus genius or the wooden doll' prior to his show. There is possibly a reference to it in *Nicholas Nickleby*, written before Dickens took up conjuring. In Chapter 50 he wrote that part of the side-show entertainment taking place at a racing track were 'ventriloquists holding dialogues with wooden dolls'. This has more resonance when it is realised how Dickens presented the trick.

In its basic format, Bonus Genius involves putting a small wooden doll inside a bespoke cloak. After a little by-play, the doll vanishes and the cloak is shown empty; the doll can then be shown to have returned to the cloak. Mamie Dickens, his daughter, explained a little more how her father made it much more than a simple vanishing and reappearing trick.

> One of these conjuring tricks comprised the disappearance and reappearance of a tiny doll, which would announce most unexpected pieces of news and messages to the different children in the audience; this doll was a particular favourite, and its arrival eagerly awaited and welcomed.

She referred to the same trick here.

> A little figure, which appeared from a wonderful and mysterious bag, and which was supposed to be a personal friend of the conjurer, would greatly delight the audience by his funny stories, his eccentric voice and way of speaking, and by his miraculous appearance and disappearances.

The trick played to one of Dickens's strengths – his amazing ability as a mimic; no better illustrated than in his public readings where he recreated the voices of his own characters. It also would have given him an opportunity to display his acting skills. There is a quotation by the French conjurer, Robert-Houdin, which essentially says that a magician is an actor playing the part of a magician. In reality most successful magicians play an extension of their own character, rather than acting a part; although there have been some notable exceptions. One suspects, though, with Dickens that he really did act out being a conjurer and, given there are plenty of testaments to his abilities as a thespian, it was likely he pulled off this role with great success – whatever his actual ability at the mechanics of conjuring might have been

This hypothesis is further supported by the different persona, and various costumes he wore – whether it was the Chinese dress and mask, the black cloak with hieroglyphics and black beard, or whatever he put on in the guise of Rhia Rhama Rhoos. The downside to this is that the continual change suggests that Dickens had not really found the 'character' that worked best for him. The most successful conjurers often have a readily identifiable costume which they stick to; Döbler, for instance, was instantly recognisable in the dress of a fifteenth century German student.

Besides his acting skills, another area Dickens would surely have excelled in is in the script of his tricks – or 'patter' as magicians normally term it. Some might question this on the basis of his playwriting, which is closer to the technique required in coming up with conjurer's patter than writing dialogue in novels; and it is claimed by one biographer that Dickens could not 'write plays at all.' What Dickens had an instinct for, though, was what worked in public performance. With patter for tricks you can amend and add and cut back over a number of performances as you judge the reaction of your audience; and it is known that Dickens did precisely that for the readings from his books.

The difference is that with Dickens's readings, he had a pretty good starting script, to put it mildly, to work from; and, of course, numerous opportunities to fine-tune it. Whereas in his conjuring he was starting from a blank canvas, and his total shows were unlikely to have exceeded much more than a couple of dozen or so. Nevertheless it is reasonable to assume that a combination of Dickens's genius as a wordsmith (even though he was not working in his natural genre) and his obvious ability to learn and adapt extremely quickly, would have resulted in some entertaining patter to go alongside his tricks.

Is there any indication of what that patter might have been? The only guide available is the wording he used on his playbill, where he mixed deliberately over-the-top, outlandish claims, with comic phraseology that demonstrated that what he had written should not be taken too seriously. Maybe this was how he played it in performance: sending up the exaggerated delivery of contemporary conjurers.

As a generalisation 'wordy humour', which can be mulled over and studied at your own pace when written down, does not transcribe too well into spoken patter. There is evidence though that Victorian conjurers were rather verbose in their delivery – maybe it was a style that audiences enjoyed and were comfortable with.

If Dickens's development of entertaining patter is something that has to be taken on trust, there is another element to being a successful conjurer that Dickens demonstrably possessed: his choice of tricks. There were plenty of examples, apart from the Bonus Genius doll, to show that Dickens's selection of material was exemplary. Any trick involving livestock is bound to get a great reaction: and the transformation of 'a box full of bran into a box full of – a live-guinea-pig!' certainly made a memorable impression on Jane Carlyle. The apparatus does most of the work: it would be the sheer surprise and unexpected nature of the production of a living creature that would provoke the wonder. That Dickens used his own guinea-pig is made clear in a letter he wrote to a friend in January, 1844, where he announced: 'The Guinea Pig Is Dead. He left it in his Will, that he thought Conjuring had been the Death of him.'

One way to entertain an audience with the minimum of skill is to borrow an object from someone – especially if somehow you contrive to lose or destroy it accidentally in some way – and then for it to turn up in a totally bizarre and unexpected location. The plot of Dickens's The Loaf of Bread Wonder encapsulates this perfectly. A borrowed watch, despite been locked in a 'strong box', somehow vanished; and was found in a loaf of bread. It is a timeless scenario that plays as well today as it would have doubtless done back then. In a letter Dickens wrote about the sheer entertainment emanating from just borrowing a watch, even before the trick had started: 'to see a blushing sleek-headed footman produce, for the watch-trick, a silver watch of the most portentous dimensions, amidst the rapturous delight of his brethren and sisterhood'.

Some of his other tricks had a visceral appeal about them: anything involving fire – as in his burnt and restored playing card (The Conflagration Wonder) – would retain the rapt attention of an audience. Selected cards jumping out of a pack (The Leaping Card Wonder), in its defiance of the basic law of gravity, has always appealed to spectators. Whilst even the relatively unsensational impact of a coin appearing in a nest of boxes (The Pyramid Box Wonder ) would have been enhanced by the fact that the coin was borrowed and marked.

The trick that undoubtedly appealed most, though, was the production of a steaming hot pudding: The Pudding Wonder. Mamie Dickens said its appearance was 'always one of the great successes of the evening' whilst Jane Carlyle noticed 'the eyes of the astonished children, and astonished grown people!' On the occasion when Jane saw it, there was an amusing follow up in the aftermath of the show.

She observed one of Dickens's small children, 'about the size of a quartern loaf sitting on a low chair gazing in awestruck delight at the reeking plum-pudding which its Father had just produced out of a gentleman's hat.' A certain Mrs Reid, determined to apply some socialist teaching, stage whispered to the child:

"Would not you like that there was such a nice pudding as that in every house in London to-night? I am sure *I* would". The shrinking uncomprehending look which the little blouzy face cast up to her was inimitable – a whole page of protest against *twaddle*! if she could but have read it!

The trick is still performed today, although now it tends to be a cake, rather than a pudding, that is produced. And it does not play so well because the magician has to use his own hat. The strength of the trick in Victorian times was that there would be plenty of appropriate hats to borrow from members of the audience. In its simplest form, producing a cake from a hat is relatively easy.

Dickens's presentation raised the bar, in that his pudding came out hot. This is known not just from his own description – in his letter to Macready, quoted in the last chapter, he wrote about a 'hot plum pudding [that] was produced'; but also Jane Carlyle recorded the appearance of a 'reeking plum-pudding': 'reeking', in this context, meaning smoking or steaming.

This gave an added dimension to the trick and made it even more incomprehensible. It also demonstrated Dickens's flair for showmanship and explained why, despite perhaps lacking in other areas of expertise of the magician's craft, he was ultimately a good conjurer.

## His Final Show?

After Bonchurch, there is only one more reference to a magic show performed by Dickens. This was when he visited Rockingham Castle in Leicester, the home of Mr and Mrs Watson, in November 1849; they were a wealthy couple he had first met in Lausanne. This is the same Mrs Watson who had noted in her diary 'Tricks', when dining with Dickens and his wife three years before.

Dickens wrote to Forster on 30th November, 1849 imitating the style of the character of an American visitor to an English castle.

Picture to yourself, my dear F, a large old castle, approached by an ancient keep, portcullis, &c, &c, filled with company, waited on by six-and-twenty servants; the slops (and wine-glasses) continually being emptied; and my clothes (with myself in them) always being carried off to all sorts of places; and you will have a faint idea of the mansion in which I am at present staying. I should have written to you yesterday, but for having had a very busy day. Among the guests is a Miss B, sister of the Honourable Miss B (of Salem, Mass.), whom we once met at the house of our distinguished literary countryman Colonel Landor. This lady is renowned as an amateur actress, so last night we got up in the great hall some scenes from the *School for Scandal*; the scene with the lunatic on the wall, from the *Nicholas Nickleby* of Major-General the Hon. C. Dickens (Richmond, Va.); some conjuring; and then finished off with country-dances; of which we had two admirably good ones, quite new to me, though really old.

He concluded the letter as follows, part of which was quoted above.

To see all the household, headed by an enormously fat housekeeper, occupying the back benches last night, laughing and applauding without any restraint; and to see a blushing sleek-headed footman produce, for the watch-trick, a silver watch of the most portentous dimensions, amidst the rapturous delight of his brethren and sisterhood; was a very pleasant spectacle, even to a conscientious republican like yourself or me, who cannot but contemplate the parent country with feelings of pride in our own land, which (as was well observed by the Honorable Elias Deeze, of Hertford, Conn.) is truly the land of the free. Best remembrances from Columbia's daughters. Ever thine, my dear F,--C.H.

The same show was commented upon in a letter dated 29th December, 1849 to de Cerjat, another friend who lived in Lausanne and who knew Mr and Mrs Watson: 'The entertainments concluded with feats of legerdemain (for the performance of which I have a pretty good apparatus, collected at divers times and in divers places) and we then fell to country dances of a most frantic description and danced all night.'

Dickens was now talking the language of a seasoned performer. He referred to the Watch in Loaf of Bread trick merely as 'the watch-trick'; he did not need to explain the effect to Forster, highlighting instead the unusual watch that was lent to him. He was taking it for granted that the magic would work – he was concentrating instead on the audience reaction. And, in the final letter, he casually remarked that he had now been doing magic for some time and had a pretty good collection of props. If this was indeed his last performance, he seems to have bowed out at the top of his game.

Suggestions for exactly when Dickens stopped conjuring, and his reasons for giving up, are pure conjecture. One possibility is that, like many an amateur conjurer, he ran out of audiences. Most of his friends would have seen his repertoire of tricks, perhaps on more than one occasion. However good a performer might be, you do not want to keep seeing the same show.

Another barrier against Dickens continuing to perform – and it is a perennial problem when you are so dependent on apparatus – was that he does not appear to have been well-versed in sleight of hand. Unlike the street entertainer, he could not just borrow a pack of cards, a few coins and a piece of string and launch into an impromptu show. He could only do his Bonchurch show after Forster had organised the despatch of his props – Forster wrote that he 'sent him the materials'. Forster also qualified his assessment of Dickens as 'a capital conjurer' by noting that he required 'his tools at hand'.

When Julian Young made his journal entry that Dickens showed 'one or two capital conjuring tricks', he highlighted that they had been 'brought from Paris'. It was almost as if their provenance was more important to Dickens than the tricks themselves. Similarly, rather than showing off about his conjuring prowess in his letter to de Cerjat, Dickens chose to draw attention to his 'apparatus, collected at divers times and in divers places'. If Dickens had wanted to carry on conjuring, he would have needed to purchase more props.

Of perhaps more significance, though, was that Dickens found other outlets for his love of performing. Although he had done a fair amount of amateur dramatics previously, in 1844 he took on his first major acting role: in Ben Jonson's comedy *Every Man in His*

*Humour*. He continued with various theatrical projects over the next decade, through to 1857. It was in that year, in a production of Wilkie Collins's *Frozen Deep*, that he was first to meet the eighteen year old actress Ellen Ternan, who then became either his mistress or his muse, depending on which biographer you believe. He was particularly involved in acting in the years 1850-52 and this would fit in with the cessation of conjuring in the years immediately after 1849.

As he cut down on his acting, so public readings of his own works came to the fore. His first reading, for charity, was in 1853. However from 1858 onwards it became a commercial enterprise, from which he earned considerable sums of money. His readings were completely different, in terms of the sheer size of his audiences and the doting reception he received, from anything he had done before. They were also something, along with his writing, that he was clearly brilliant at – a questionable label when applied to either his acting or his conjuring.

One senses that Dickens would have known this instinctively; and, leaving aside the spare time he could have devoted to his other interests, he surely received all the necessary adrenalin feedback and sating his love of performing from these public readings. After hearing the applause from a packed hall of up to three thousand adoring fans, the response for his conjuring from a household of people, however warmly given, would have rather paled by comparison.

From this perspective, it makes complete sense that Dickens did not refer to his own conjuring again after 1849; and the absence of references from any other sources reinforces the belief that he stopped doing shows from 1850 onwards. However, even if Dickens was not performing himself, he had not entirely lost his interest in conjuring. He saw at least two conjurers after 1849; and his reports on these turn out to be as momentous to conjuring history as is Dickens's own show on the Isle of Wight.

# Chapter Three Supplement

## Note on Sources

Once again a number of quotations have been taken from Dickens's letters in this chapter. They are referenced as follows.

CD diary entry insuring his life with the Sun Office.
[Pilgrim, Vol. 1] p. 630                    9/1/1838
CD to Thomas Mitton comparing Döbler & Anderson.
[Pilgrim, Vol. 3] p. 439                    6/2/1843
CD to William Macready describing some of his tricks.
[Pilgrim, Vol. 4] p 10                      3/1/1844
CD to Forster about conjuring show at Rochester Castle.
[Pilgrim, Vol. 5] pp. 661-3                 30/11/1849
CD to de Cerjat about Rochester Castle show.
[Pilgrim, Vol. 5] p. 683                    29/12/1849
CD to Marion Ely on death of his conjuring guinea pig
[Dickensian] 'The Letters of Charles Dickens: Supplement V', Summer 2005, Vol. 101, No. 466, p. 141            22/1/1844

The recollections of his children are noted here:

'a little figure, which...'
[Mamie Dickens, Dickens with his Children] pp. 33-4.
'One of these conjuring...' [Mamie Dickens, My Father] Chapter 2, p. 34.

And this letter by Jane Carlyle.

Jane Carlyle to Jeannie Walsh on the production of a hot pudding [Carlyle] Vol. 17, 28/12/1843, cited in [Pilgrim, Vol. 3] pp. 613-4 n 4.

## Necromancer

Dickens's use of the term 'necromancer'in his Bonchurch playbill billing[1] predominantly refers back to an earlier time in conjuring history. But it had been alluded to occasionally by conjurers that Dickens might well have seen. George Sutton, in his 1838 show at the New Strand Theatre included '90 Minutes of Witchcraft', which embraced not only 'Legerdemain' and 'Magic Illusions' but also 'Physical Necromancy'. When starting out, John Henry Anderson in 1836 called himself the 'Caledonian Necromancer' and from 1837-8 the 'Great Magician, Scottish Necromancer'. It was in his Edinburgh Christmas/New Year season of 1838-39 that he dropped 'Necromancer' and adopted the sobriquet for which he is best known: 'The Great Wizard of the North'.[2]

---

[1] The playbill is found in [Forster, Vol. 3] Chapter IV, 'Three Summers at Boulogne'. The letter which dates the show as taking place in August or September 1849 can be located here [Forster, Vol. 2] Chapter XVIII, 'Seaside Holidays'. The fact that Alum Bay, mentioned in the billing, is located on the Isle of Wight was first pointed out by [Findlay] p. 9. As Findlay lived on the island, this was not altogether surprising! It was a place CD knew well as he stayed there in September 1838. He composed a poem to the owner of the hotel, John Groves. The first verse was as follows: 'Oh Mr. Groves/If so be you approves/Of writings in rhyme/Knocked off in quick time/And set down at once/By an indolent dunce/Who to Alum bay runs – /Read these lines Mr. Groves'. [Pilgrim, Vol. 1] p. 432. Information on CD and his time on the Isle of Wight can be found in [Hutchings].

[2] Sutton playbill is in [Price] p. 51. Information about Anderson dropping 'Necromancer' comes from [Dawes, Anderson]. The playbill of The Great Caledonian Magician, which featured several tricks which Dickens himself performed, can be found in [Houdini, Unmasking] p. 150. By contrast the only Döbler trick which it is known CD performed – producing a pocket handkerchief from a wine bottle – appeared in [Frost] pp. 267-8. An example of CD calling himself the inimitable is in a letter to John Forster from the Isle

Anderson still seemed keen to use the word in some capacity. When he first performed at St James's Bazaar in London in June 1840 the venue was described on his playbill as the 'Grand Fashionable Palace of Necromancy'. And in his show at The Strand Theatre on Boxing Day 1848, his playbill informed the public that 'He will Make his Appearance, and give his Royal Entertainment, Illustrative of the Fallacy of Magic, Necromancy, Witchcraft and Demonology', which certainly ticked all the boxes.[3]

Whilst its popularity as a term gradually faded out from the playbills of conjurers, using 'necromancer' as a substitute word for 'conjurer', without any particular nod to the dark side of magic, continued to be relatively commonplace. In an extract from an 1852 article entitled 'Wonderful Toys', WH Wills – Dickens's assistant on *Household Words* – wrote about 'a jeweller, who has devoted eight years of his life to the perfection of a clock-work conjuror' and went on to say that 'Dressed in an Eastern costume, this necromancer stands behind a table'.[4]

Having called himself a 'necromancer' made it logical that Dickens should claim that he had been 'educated cabalistically', as this suggested he had been taught some sort of occult secret. Again this was a term often used by conjurers of that period. One of the celebrated tricks performed by the French magician, Robert-Houdin, was called The Cabalistic Clock – which comprised a clock where the hands appeared to revolve by their own volition. A lesser known conjurer called Buck, who copied the repertoire of the likes of Anderson, appeared in various towns in England between 1840

of Wight, which also recorded his working schedule: 'I have made it a rule that the inimitable is invisible, until two every day.' [Pilgrim, Vol. 5] p. 590.

[3] Anderson's two playbills: 'Edwin Booth Collection, New York' (now in the David Copperfield collection), cited in [Bayer] p. 29; and [Houdini, Unmasking] p. 309.

[4] [HW] Vol. IV, No. 99, 14 Feb, 1852, p. 504.

and 1844; he claimed on an 1844 playbill that he would 'open his cabinet of cabalistic phenomena'.[5]

## Rhia Rhama Rhoos and Ramo Samee

There have already been references to Ramo Samee and the question of whether Dickens saw him in either 1822 (because he was mentioned in an article that Dickens wrote) or in 1838 (when he was on the same bill as a production of *Nicholas Nickleby* in Hull). And here he crops up again – this time in respect of Dickens's *nom de théâtre* for his show on the Isle of Wight. It was Grove, in his 1921 article in *The Dickensian*, who first postulated that Dickens had seen him in 1838; and he also suggested that the name Rhia Rhama Rhoos was 'apparently imitative of Ramo Samee'.[6]

This was supported by Peter Warlock who wrote 'and obviously the pseudonym chosen, Rhia Rhama Rhoos was inspired by his seeing Rama [sic] Samee at Hull.' This supposition continued to be made as late as 1995 when David Goodsell wrote in an American magic journal, 'while vacationing with his family on the Isle of Wight, Dickens prepared a magical performance based, loosely, on that of "The Celebrated East Indian Ramo Samee".'[7]

---

[5] Cabalistic Clock: [Sharpe] p. 21 and [Houdini, Unmasking] pp. 156-66. Buck ref: [Clarke] p. 225. Playbill: [Houdini, Unmasking] p. 261. An earlier playbill of Mons. Felix Testot featuring Cabalistic Art can be seen on p. 254.

[6] The correct spelling is Rhia Rhama Rhoos; both [Dawes, Great Illusionists] p. 134 and [Dawson] pp. 109 & 112 misspell the last name as Roos. The repetition of the rH, as in kH, reinforces the likelihood of Khia Khan Khruse having been the sole name inspiration. Perversely [Williams] had the correct spelling whilst [Callow] p. 133, who copied all his conjuring information from that source, did not.

[7] 'Ramo Samee and the Three Potatoes', JSP Grove [Dickensian] Vol. 17, No. 4, Oct, 1921, p. 214; 'Magic and Charles Dickens', Peter Warlock [Magic Circular] Vol. 79, December 1985, pp. 478-9; : 'Up My Sleeve, Editorial',

No excuses really for either Warlock or Goodsell in respect of this error. It was made clear in *The Great Illusionists* by Edwin Dawes that it was Khia Khan Khruse who was the principal influence on Dickens's choice of name. This book was published in 1979. Heathcote Williams in *What Larks! Charles Dickens, Conjuror*, by pointing out Khia Khan Khruse's by-line of 'Instructed in the Caves of Salamanca' (similar to the 'Orange Groves of *Salamanca* and the Ocean *Caves* of Alum Bay' in Dickens's playbill) confirmed who Dickens had in mind in his parody.[8]

The suggestion that Ramo Samee might also have had an influence on the choice of Dickens's stage name – presumably because Ramo begins with the letter 'R', as does Rhia Rhama Rhoos – is rather tenuous: and one suspects would not even have been conjectured if Khia Khan Khruse had been recognised earlier as the likely source. Nevertheless Trevor Dawson, in *Charles Dickens: Conjurer, Mesmerist and Showman*, was still keeping his options open. He conceded that Khia Khan Khruse was the 'more logical'

---

*MUM*, David R Goodsell, Nov, 1995 p. 13. For consideration of whether CD saw Ramo Samee in 1822 or 1838, see 'Ramo Samo' in Chapter One Supplement.

[8] [Dawes, Great Illusionists] p. 134 wrote, in respect of an image of a playbill of Khia Khan Khruse, that his 'conjuring performances probably influenced Charles Dickens in his choice of Rhia Rhama Roos [sic] as a *nom de théâtre* for his drawing-room entertainment in 1849'. Information from his playbills have been extracted for stating the repertoire of Khia Khan Khruse in the main chapter. One such playbill was featured in [Dawes, Rich], No. 27: 'Kia Khan Khruse and the Bullet Catch', Vol. 69, Feb, 1975, p. 31: another is in [Houdini, Conjurers' Monthly] Vol. 1, Nov, 1906, p. 74, dated 9 Sept, 1818. Both have 'Instructed in the Caves of Salamanca' on them, a link first noted by [Williams] p. 5. Another playbill of Khia Khan Khruse is clearly in the collection of Ricky Jay, as he quoted from it in [Jay, Learned Pigs] p. vii: performance at the Green Man Assembly Rooms, Blackheath, 18 March, 1822.

name inspiration; but that did not stop him speculating that 'the probability is that having known Ramo Samee from 1822, [Dickens] derived this name Rhia Rhama Roos [sic], years before 1838 for his performances. However, at this Bonchurch holiday we have the first written record of the name'.[9]

Whether or not Dickens saw Ramo Samee back in 1822 has already been addressed. As to Dickens having come up with the name, Rhia Rhama Rhoos, 'years before', this would be predicated more on Khia Khan Khruse, who stopped performing in England in the late 1820s. Ramo Samee died in the same year as the Bonchurch show, so, if he did have any influence on Dickens's choice of name, you could imagine he might have been on Dickens's 'radar' at this time rather than earlier.[10]

## Blacking Up?

Of all the quotations that have been attributed to Dickens as a conjurer, this is perhaps the most potentially inflammatory to modern sentiments. It was stated in Ricky Jay's *Celebrations of Curious Characters*:

On one auspicious occasion in 1849 on the Isle of Wight, according to one writer, he [Charles Dickens] "studiously blackened up his face and hands, dressed himself in exotic robes that concealed a morass of 'fekes,' 'steals,' clips, pulls, and loads, tied in a gibecière, or magician's pouch, around his midriff, and appeared before an assembled company of neighbors and friends as the Unparalleled Necromancer

---

[9] [Dawson] p. 109.

[10] [Clarke] p. 395 references KKK arriving in 1815 with Ramo Samee; [Whaley, Who's Who] p. 185 has him performing in England up to c1828; [Clarke] p. 396 stated he only remained in the country for ten years (therefore to 1825). [Jay, Celebrations] p. 72 stated that there is only one existing image of KKK (reproduced in Plate 13).

Rhia Rhama Rhoos, educated cabalistically in the Orange Groves of
Salamanca and the Ocean Caves of Alum Bay".[11]

The second part of this sentence is clearly true; but what is the
provenance for all the paraphernalia that Dickens apparently
attached to himself? And, more controversially, who recalled that he
'blackened up his face and hands'?

Ricky Jay is a well-respected magic historian, so it is unsurprising
that others should repeat what he had written. Dawson correctly
asserted that the quotation came from Ricky Jay, adding that it was
'an unidentified source'. It is clear that Simon Callow, in his 2012
book *Charles Dickens and the Great Theatre of the World*, had
found the same reference. He wrote that Dickens 'invented a
character for himself: blacked up, in flowing magical robes with a
turban, as if he had stepped straight out of the *Arabian Nights*, he
now appeared as the Unparalleled Necromancer, Rhia Rhama Roos
[sic].'[12]

The provenance turned out to be Heathcote Williams's 1995
*What Larks! Charles Dickens, Conjuror.* This was the opening line.

On a summer evening in 1848 [sic, should be 1849], at a house called
Winterbourne, which he had rented in Bonchurch on the Isle of
Wight, Charles Dickens studiously blacked up his face and hands,
dressed himself up in exotic robes that concealed a morass of 'fekes,'
'steals,' clips, 'pulls', and 'loads', tied a gibecière, or conjuror's pouch,
around his midriff, and appeared before an assembled company of
neighbours and friends, as the Unparalleled Necromancer RHIA
RHAMA RHOOS.[13]

[11] [Jay, Celebrations] p. 73.
[12] [Dawson] p. 109. [Callow] p. 133: in his description Callow implied that
Dickens played the part of Rhia Rhama Rhoos from his very first conjuring
show.
[13] [Williams] p. 1.

Of course it was conceivable that Heathcote Williams had tracked down his own independent source. Following a courteous exchange of emails, the conclusion reached was that it was in fact his interpretation of how Dickens would have appeared in performance as an Indian conjurer. The booklet arose out of a television film he wrote called *What the Dickens!* It was about a Christmas magic show that Dickens did for orphaned children at the Foundling hospital[14] in London and aired at Christmas in 1983 on Channel 4. Ben Cross, later to star in the film *Chariots of Fire*, played Charles Dickens and Victoria Plucknett his wife Catherine. This was how Dickens's first appearance was described in the script.

A GOOD LOOKING, SLIGHTLY SATURNINE YOUNG MAN, AGED AROUND TWENTY-NINE, STARES AT HIMELF IN A MIRROR. HE RAISES A STURDY LUMP OF BLACKING THOUGHTFULLY TO HIS FACE. HE STREAKS HIS CHEEKS AND FOREHEAD WITH IT – MOMENTARILY MAKING HIMSELF LOOK LIKE A TIGER.

DICKENS:

(WHISPERING, CONINUING HIS MAKE-UP, RUBBING IN BLACKING WITH INCREASING VIGOUR.)

Christmas...! When ordinary things become extraordinary? All common things become uncommon and enchanted...

Later on in the script it has Dickens looking at his table of props and concealing about his person 'Steals', 'Loads', 'Fekes' and 'Conjurors' Gimmicks'.[15]

---

[14] There is no evidence that such a show took place.

[15] Copy of the film script, *What the Dickens!* by Heathcote Williams, undated, pp. 20 & 22: from the author's collection.

In trying, understandably, to create a visual image for Dickens playing the part of Rhia Rhama Rhoos, Williams opted for the theatrical device that Dickens blacked himself up and attached sundry gimmicks to his person. He took that conceit forward into his book and from there it was picked up, without any citation, by Callow and Jay. There is evidence that Dickens, like many a Victorian writer, did show racist tendencies; it will be interesting to see whether that misquote will ever be used against him in supporting that argument.

Just to add one final possible twist into this controversy, a reminder of a quotation from Chapter Two. When Dickens played the part of the braggart, Captain Bobadil, in a performance of the play *Every Man in His Humour* by Ben Jonson on 20th September, 1844, Jane Carlyle wrote 'poor little Dickens, all painted in black and red'. This might suggest that Dickens was happy to 'black up'. However a letter from Dickens four days later about his make-up throws a different light on it. He wrote: 'I drank to you in a great black wig, and with a peaked beard and black moustache, all stuck on singly, by the individual hair! I had a dresser from one of the large Theatres to do it.[16]

## Purchase of Magic Tricks

Dickens probably bought some of his magic tricks from Hamleys. Hamleys was founded in 1760 by William Hamley and in the 1840s was based at 231 High Holborn under the name of Noah's Ark. In 1881 it opened a new branch in Regent Street, which is where it is based today. However it is likely that the 'Noah's Ark' Magic Depot, as it was known, remained at High Holborn for some years after

---

[16] Letter from Jane to Thomas Carlyle, [Carlyle] Vol. 19, 23/9/1845. Letter from CD to Mme. De la Rue, dated 27 Sept, 1845, cited in [Johnson].

that.[17]

The evidence for Dickens visiting Hamleys is twofold. Firstly, there is his daughter Mamie's recollection.

> In our childish days my father used to take us, every twenty-fourth day of December, to a toy shop in Holborn, where we were allowed to select our Christmas presents, and also any that we wished to give to our little companions. Although I believe we were often an hour or more in the shop before our several tastes were satisfied, he never showed the least impatience, was always interested, and as desirous as we, that we should choose exactly what we liked best.[18]

Secondly, there is a letter dated 6th February, 1843 which Dickens wrote to his solicitor, Thomas Mitton: 'I have made a most splendid trick of that apparatus which Hamley* couldn't manage: by the addition of one or two simple contrivances. It is better than the Northern Wizard and as good as Doebler.' The asterisk refers to a Pilgrim footnote as follows: *W. Hamley, Noah's Ark . Toy Warehouse, 231 High Holborn; CD had paid him £2. 8. 0 on 2 Jan (Account-book, MS Messrs Coutts).[19]

This cheque of two pounds and eight shillings (around £200 in today's earnings) to Noah's Ark, did not necessarily represent the purchase of conjuring apparatus – it could well have been for toys. But the inference of the statement 'apparatus which Hamley couldn't manage' is that at least some of Dickens's conjuring props must have been bought from this shop – even if this particular trick was not. Certainly the Pilgrim editors believe that Dickens's initial

---

[17] An undated, but possibly the oldest known existing catalogue, is in the private collection of Peter Lane: this has 229, 230 & 231 High Holborn as the address of The 'Noah's Ark' Magical Depot.

[18] [Dickens, Mamie, My Father] p. 26.

[19] [Pilgrim, Vol. 3] p. 439 and n 3. The archivist at Coutts has stated that strictly the 'Account-book' should be called a 'Ledger'.

purchases of the 'stock in trade of a conjurer', which he referred to in his letter of 31$^{st}$ December, 1842 to Cornelius Felton, came from Hamleys.[20]

Confirmation of this is impossible as unfortunately no Hamleys catalogues of this era, if indeed they ever existed, have survived. Furthermore, all their records were lost during the Second World War, so there is no means of tracing what magic apparatus they might have had in stock in the 1840s and attempting to tie it up with Dickens's known props.[21]

Was there an alternative source? The most likely was a specialist magic dealer called WHM Crambrook, who conducted their business from the Necromantic Tent in the Royal Adelaide Gallery, West Strand in London. The date of the establishment of the business is unknown, but in 1843 they produced the second edition of their catalogue; there is no known existing copy of the first. So, working backwards, it is conceivable that Dickens did have access to an earlier catalogue in 1842; or indeed that he just walked into the Necromantic Tent and bought the items there.[22]

---

[20] The footnote states 'Clearly from Hamley's' [Pilgrim, Vol. 3] p. 416, n 1. The archivist at Coutts, where CD used to bank, has confirmed the following payments to 'Mr Hamley': 12 March 1838, £11 17s; 2 January 1843, £2 8s; 15 January 1844, £2 9s 6d and 17 April 1851, £3 4s. It is highly unlikely that either the 1838 or the 1851 payments related to magic apparatus, so it makes it hard to extrapolate that the sums paid in 1843 or 1844 therefore were. The archivist clarified that: 'The date in the ledger relates to the date of the cheque written by Dickens. Whether it was written on the date of purchase, or whether the items were sent to Dickens and he paid for them once he'd received them I don't think it's possible to say from this source.'

[21] [Sperber] Item No. 1580 gives 1898 as the earliest Hamleys catalogue; but the one in Peter Lane's collection almost certainly predates that. Peter Lane confirmed with Hamleys that existing records no longer survive.

[22] The archivist at Coutts has found no references to any payments by CD made to Crambrook.

There were apparently a couple of other magic dealers around in 1842: if, that is, their own hype is believed. Frank Hiam, of the London Conjuring Trick Works, claimed his firm had been established in 1818 and therefore 'is the oldest in London for the Manufacture of Conjuring Tricks'. Also J Theobald & Company stated they had been established around 1840. However, the earliest known catalogues for these two are dated 1882 and 1889 respectively. There is no corroborating evidence suggesting that they were in business when Dickens would have been purchasing his apparatus.[23]

Using the 1843 Crambrook catalogue there were a number of items listed for sale which could well have been in Dickens's armoury. Below are the names of Dickens's tricks, which he performed as Rhia Rhama Rhoos, followed by how the items were described in the catalogue and its price.

The Leaping Card Wonder: 'Card Machine, by which any chosen card is made to jump from the pack 5s'.
The Pudding Wonder: 'To make a Pudding or Cake in a Hat 5s'.[24]
The Loaf of Bread Wonder: 'The Watch Trick – The method of shooting a watch into a loaf 5s'.
The Travelling Doll Wonder: 'The Invisible Traveller, a figure which

[23] [Albo] pp. 339, 346 & 355. [Sperber] Item No. 3511, Theobald & Co. J, Catalogue of Conjuring Apparatus, 1889, 20 Church Street Kensington; and Item No. 1715, Frank Hiam (London, Conjuring Trick Works), 1882, 15 Nile Street, City Road, London.

[24] It was stated in the main chapter that part of the evidence that CD produced a hot pudding was Jane Carlyle noting that it was a 'reeking plum-pudding'. 'Reeking' today normally means an unpleasant smell; but a common usage in Victorian times was that of emitting smoke. R. Nicoll *Poems* (1842) 'Where the shepherd's reeking cot Peeps from the broomy glen', cited in *The Oxford English Edition*, Second Edition, Clarendon Press, Oxford, JA Simpson and ESC Weiner, Vol. XIII, 1989.

passes on any journey out of his Cloak of Darkness, and returns invisibly at the will of the performer 5s to 7s 6'.

After Crambrook, the next surviving magic catalogue is Henry Novra's Magical Repository Catalogue of around 1860; and there were a couple of items in it which would make up the remainder of Dickens's six tricks:

> The Pyramid Wonder: 'The Rattle Box, to send a marked coin to the other hand; may be examined. 2s 6d (this would be used in conjunction with The Nest of Seven Boxes).'
> 'The Nest of Seven Boxes, a marked coin passes into the last box from any other apparatus. 7s 6d.'
> The Conflagration Wonder: 'Burning Box, to burn or change a card. 1s 6d'.

Also contained in this catalogue is 'The Bonus Genius, a wooden doll that vanishes from a cloak and re-appears. 3s 6d'. This would be the same as the 'Invisible Traveller' from the Crambrook catalogue.

The total cost of these six tricks came to around £1 11s 6d: so one can see that with the Hamleys cheque of £2 8s you could indeed buy yourself a complete magic act.[25]

A couple of other tricks, which it is known Dickens performed on other occasions, were mentioned in these two catalogues. In the Crambrook catalogue, there was a 'Bran Tube, which is shewn first to contain bran, and afterwards change it into a guinea pig, 10s 6'; whilst in the Novra there was a 'Pedestal for Dancing Money' – that would have set Dickens back at least 21s: this would have been used for the three half crowns jingling answers in a tumbler-glass to questions put to them.

It is known that Dickens added to his magic collection over time.

---

[25] The names of the tricks, and their prices, were taken from [Crambrook] and [Novra].

This was noted both by his daughter Mamie who wrote: 'He had acquired, by degrees, an excellent collection of conjuring-tricks'; and also by Dickens himself when he wrote his final letter that mentioned conjuring: 'I have a pretty good apparatus, collected at divers times and in divers places.'[26]

One of those 'divers places' was France. As noted above, in the summer of 1849 Julian Young, who was part of Dickens's social group in Bonchurch on the Isle of Wight, wrote in his journal that whilst there Dickens 'showed us one or two capital conjuring tricks which he had just brought from Paris.' As far as is known, the last time Dickens had been to the continent was over two years before, in February 1847; so it is a matter of speculation as to whether he had purchased the apparatus back then, or more recently by mail order.[27]

Available to Dickens were both French catalogues to peruse and magic dealers to visit. The former predated the English equivalents with *Catalogue des Principaux Instruments de Physique Récréative Amusante* published by Père Roujol sometime in the 1820s. Père Roujol owned a shop in Paris, as did Charles-François Aubert who first started trading in 1830. In 1834 the brilliant mechanic André Voisin began supplying many of the great magicians of the time: he specialised in apparatus made of wood which included inlays in copper, mother-of-pearl and ivory.

Unfortunately there is insufficient information about what was on offer in Paris to tie up any of it with Dickens's known repertoire. Voisin, for instance, primarily sold tricks devised by Robert-Houdin, not the type of magic that Dickens did. However it seems reasonable to assume that French magic dealers would have carried

---

[26] [Dickens, Mamie, Dickens with his Children] p. 33. Letter to de Cerjat: [Pilgrim, Vol. 5] p. 683.

[27] [Young] p. 320. The journal entry is dated 4 July but that cannot be right as CD did not arrive in Bonchurch until 16 July.

similar stock to those held by their English counterparts; so it is not possible to retrospectively categorise Dickens's tricks by place of origin.[28]

Most magic historians have agreed that Dickens bought his tricks from a magic shop or dealer. One exception was JB Findlay in *Charles Dickens and his Magic*: 'We contend from the type of trick he actually performed himself that the apparatus he bought was of little account, and indeed may well have come from a street conjurer.' This is improbable: most of Dickens's tricks were not in the repertoire of street conjurers. Furthermore it is hard to envisage Dickens negotiating to buy the well-used and soiled props of an itinerant entertainer and then display them in the front parlour of middle-class Victorian houses.[29]

## Bonus Genius Patter

There is no knowledge of the script which Dickens would have used to accompany any of his tricks. Indeed the patter of any Victorian conjurer is hard to come by: for instance there is no record of what Anderson or Döbler said. The closest it is possible to know what might have been spoken to accompany a magic trick is by studying the patter which turns up in magic books.[30]

---

[28] Information relating to French conjuring dealers came from [Albo] pp. 125-151.

[29] [Dawes, Great Illusionists] p. 138 first postulated WHM Crambrook as a possible source of CD's tricks. [Dawson] pp. 85-88 endorsed both Crambrook and Hamleys. [Findlay] p. 7 suggested that CD bought his magic props from a street conjurer who would have had to then 'replenish his own personal stock, otherwise he himself would be out of business'. [During] p. 113, clearly picking up from, but misreading, Findlay, stated that CD 'purchased the entire stock of a magic supply shop that was going out of business': as good an example of Chinese whispers as one could want.

[30] Ackroyd's dismissal of CD's ability as a playwright is on p. 199; but his ability

Unfortunately, as previously noted, hardly any of Dickens's tricks were written up in books at the time. One exception[31] was the Bonus Genius - the Travelling Doll Wonder as Dickens called it. By chance it is also one of the few tricks for which the authors of books often did provide some patter to go alongside the explanation of how the trick worked. By looking at three different examples, it might be possible to get a feel for some of the wording Dickens may have used. In all of these the trick itself is the same: a wooden doll is displayed, it is covered with a cloak, some money is handed up to the doll and it vanishes – to prove this, the cloak is shown empty.

The first script comes from *The Whole Art of Legerdemain* by Henry Dean, published in 1722. Its succinctness and easy-to-follow plot suggests its authenticity and that it was actually used in performance, perhaps by a street conjurer:

> Gentlemen, this I call my Bonus Genius. This is his coat. Look now as steadfast as you can, nevertheless I will cover you. Now he is ready to go on any Message I have to send him to Spain or to Italy, or whether I will, but he must have something to bear his Charges. There is three Crowns for you, now be gone. But he will look about him before he

---

to work on his own readings is here pp. 1035 & 1041 (CD 'revised passages in the light of the audience reaction...he cut out anything which was not directly and immediately entertaining or pathetic. No social polemic. No apostrophes. Only sadness and humour and drama.') The lack of existence of Anderson's scripts was confirmed by Eddie Dawes, author of [Dawes, Anderson] whilst Döbler did his act in German.

[31] Another was the 'Nest of Boxes' which appeared in *Nouvelles Recreations Physiques et Mathematiques*, Guyot, Vol. 3, 3rd Edition, 1786, pp. 231-2, 1st Edition is dated 1769. 'The Jumping Card' also featured in early books but not with the type of mechanical apparatus that Dickens would have used [Hoffmann, Modern Magic] p. 130. For instance 'How to make a Card jump out of the Pack and run on the Table' [Gale] p. 82, just required a piece of hair and some wax.

goes. Just as I thrust my Finger down so he shall vanish. See here he is gone.[32]

This next one comes in *The Boy's Holyday Book, for All Seasons*, not dated, but around 1843-44; so at a time when Dickens was probably coming up with his own script. The artificial set up of the trick – the author wrote that he is reciting the patter of a German quack doctor selling his medicine, and the trick is intended to entertain the potential buyers – makes one question how practical it would be. But it is interesting as the conjurer is allowing the doll to whisper in his ear and repeating back what it is supposedly saying, a presentation that Dickens used in his own version.

> Ladies and gentlemen this is my invisible courier, which I do send on all my most important errands. No one would suspect him to be a spy – he is welcome in all companies, and everybody considers that he is deaf and can't see.
>
> Ah Master Jean. I must send you to Durham to buy some mustard. And you must go by Windsor and kiss the Princess Royal, and tell me whether she sleep well last night. [Doll whispers in conjurer's ear] Ah! You are quite right to ask for your silk gown. [Doll again whispers in conjurer's ear] That is well said, I understand you. I know that a traveller without money is like a fire without coals. If you see nothing, ladies, you must not be surprised; my courier is invisible when he travels and I give Master Jean invisible money.[33]

The final extract comes from a conjurer whom Dickens saw, as will

---

[32] [Dean] pp. 28-9.

[33] *The Boy's Holyday Book, for All Seasons*, Second Edition, Greatly Enlarged, G. H. Davidson, London, c. 1844, pp. 164-5. I am indebted to James Smith for discovering this reference. He pointed out that the patter is a 'corrected' English translation from Henri Decremps's *Testement de Jermone Sharp* (1786). In the original French, Jean is sent to Dijon to buy some mustard, which certainly made more sense than going to Durham!

be discussed in the next chapter. His name was Colonel Stodare. It was written up in a book called *Stodare's Fly Notes or Conjuring Made Easy*. It is memorable as it seems to be an unusually dark take on what is traditionally a children's trick. But the sheer length (far too long, one suspects, to hold the attention of an audience), the reference to children being 'whipped' and the downbeat ending suggests this is not a routine Stodare performed himself.

In truth, as often happens with patter given in magic books, Stodare probably just made much of it up to fill some space. Nevertheless it almost certainly had elements which he heard others use – and you get an idea of the slightly convoluted phrasing, not to mention the bizarre insertion of a complete poem, that perhaps appealed to the Victorian middle-classes.

Allow me, ladies and gentlemen, to introduce my learned friend and assistant – indefatigable in travelling to the most distant parts on any message I may wish to send him. He used to be recognised by early conjurors as the Bonus Genius, their good familiar spirit. But, whatever his special title, he is gifted with the art of rendering himself visible or invisible, as he feels disposed, while he travels to distant countries.

I think he was brought up as a pupil of the learned Magician Dr. Faustus; of whom it is said in the rhyme of schoolboys –

Dr Faustus is a good man,
He whips his scholars now and then,
When he whips them he makes them dance,
Out of England into France,
Out of France into Spain,
And then they whip off back again.

Allow me to call your attention to the solid frame and unflinching nerves, at any rate to the well-seasoned constitution of my friend. [Rap him loudly, rap, rap, rap, on the table.] The raps he received during his education have doubtless accustomed him to bear much without flinching.

**1.** Ramo Samee, performing in 1822: the date at which 'An Unsettled Neighbourhood' article, that Dickens wrote, was set.

**2.** Detail from Plate 1. Ramo Samee was both a juggler and a conjurer.

**3.** A Thimble-Rigger at work at Derby Races, a familiar scene which Dickens described in *Sketches by Boz* and also mentioned in his letters. 'I even got some new wrinkles in the way of showmen, conjurors, pea-and-thimblers, and trampers generally.'

**4.** Portrait of Ludwig Döbler, the conjurer who inspired Dickens to take up magic when he saw the Austrian in 1842.

**5.** Playbill of Ludwig Döbler for the show Dickens attended in July 1842 at the St James's Theatre.

6. Portrait of The Great Wizard of the North, John Henry Anderson, as a young man. Dickens probably saw Anderson sometime in 1840 or 1841.

**7.** Playbill for John Henry Anderson, for his London debut at the New Strand Theatre in February 1840.

The Wizard of the North exposing the trick "Sauter La Coupe."

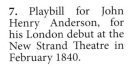

**9.** An engraving of Dickens in 1843, the year he first started performing as a conjurer.

**8.** Letter from Dickens to his solicitor, dated 1843, where he claimed a new trick he was doing was 'better than the Northern Wizard and as good as Doebler'.

**10.** The Bonus Genius trick, or Travelling Doll Wonder: a favourite trick of Dickens particularly enjoyed by children.

**11.** A portrait of Dickens in 1859, the same year as the 'Out-Conjuring Conjurors' article was published. This was long after he had stopped conjuring.

**12.** The 'Out-Conjuring Conjurors' article published in Dickens's *Household Words* reviewing the Memoirs of Robert-Houdin. This has been wrongly attributed as written by Dickens.

KIA KHAN KREUSE, the Conjurer, transmogrified them

**13.** Illustration of Khia Khan Khruse, from an 1824 children's book. The Indian conjurer inspired the name of Rhia Rhama Rhoos that Dickens used for his show in Bonchurch on the Isle of Wight in 1849.

**14.** Bonchurch village. Winterbourne house, where Dickens stayed, is the second house on the left in the foreground.

**15.** Alum Bay. According to Dickens's playbill, Rhia Rhama Rhoos was educated in 'the Ocean Caves of Alum Bay'.

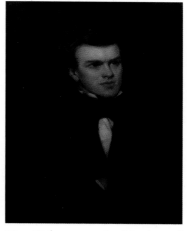

**17.** Dickens great friend and biographer, John Forster. It was in his *The Life of Charles Dickens* that Dickens's detailed description of de Caston's act first appeared.

**16.** Alfred de Caston, the French conjurer who Dickens saw in 1854 in Boulogne. Dickens described him as 'a perfectly original genius, and that puts any sort of knowledge of legerdemain, such as I supposed that I possessed, at utter defiance'.

**18.** Cartoon of Alfred de Caston. He completely fooled Dickens with a new type of magic that the novelist had never come across before: mind reading.

**19 & 20.** Frank Staff, or FS, and the article he wrote in the March 1931 copy of *The Magic Circular*, that announced the identity of the mystery conjurer as Alfred de Caston.

**21.** Cornelius Felton. Dickens first told him about taking up conjuring in December 1842; and he accompanied Dickens to see Robert-Houdin in 1853.

**22.** Portrait of Robert-Houdin, around the time he first performed in London in 1848.

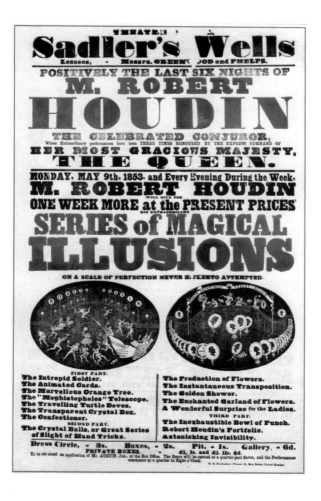

**23.**Playbill of Robert-Houdin of the show Dickens saw in May 1853 at Sadler's Wells. This would be the famous French conjurer's final appearance in London: he retired the following year.

**24.** Publicity shot of Colonel Stodare standing next to the Sphinx illusion, which Dickens saw in 1865, five years before his death.

**26.** John Leech's illustration from *A Christmas Carol,* which was written in 1843, of Scrooge vanishing the Ghost of Christmas Past. Dickens might have got the idea of the disappearance from the Extinguisher Trick.

**25.** Photograph also taken in 1865. Dickens attempted an explanation of the Sphinx in a letter to his daughter Mamie: she is on her father's left.

**27.** Detail from Plate 5 of a variation of the Extinguisher Trick as performed by Döbler in the show Dickens saw.

**28.** Henri Robin, the French conjurer who attended a séance with Dickens in 1862.

I perceive, however, by the glaring of his eye, that, after my too rough handling, he is desirous of starting on his travels. I suppose we must provide him with the needful for his expenses. Large sums are given nowadays to special correspondents in foreign countries; who will kindly give him sufficient? Oh, well, as there is a delay about it, I must myself supply him. I think I have a few disposable coins in my pocket: he shall have them.

There my good friend, you can now if you wish, proceed on your tour to Algiers, or Dahomey, or Timbuctoo, or wherever the English travellers fancy at the present to resort.

Ah, I see he is pleased and in good spirits again. He wishes apparently to bid you goodbye. You will excuse his looking also around about him, to judge whether the weather is fair to set out; after which I will lay my hand on his head to express my good wishes for his journey. I dare say he will not stay much longer after that than a schoolboy does after his master has bid him goodbye.

It is clear he has chosen to go to a hot climate, as he has left his cloak behind him. Alas! he is gone in earnest, like the sojourner of a day. When we have lost him, we feel our loneliness.[34]

Although the Bonus Genius trick has become perhaps the best known of Dickens's repertoire – partly because it played to his strengths as an actor[35] and mimic – it is unlikely that anybody

---

[34] [Stodare] pp. 112-116. This was published posthumously as Stodare died in October 1866. However it had originally been serialised in *Routledge's Magazine for Boys*, from January (with the exception of April) through to July 1866. [Dawes, Stodare] p. 151. A poem was also included in the Bonus Genius patter from Henri Decremps's *Testement de Jermone Sharp*, so it might have been common practice amongst 18th and 19th century conjurers.

[35] [Ackroyd] p. 499 quoted several well-known people praising CD's acting skills; although some did not agree. 'Lord Melbourne was heard to bellow in an interval, [of a play CD was in] "I knew this play would be dull, but that it would be so damnably dull as this I did not suppose"!' [Tomalin] p. 171. The quotation about a conjurer is an actor playing the part of a magician comes

outside his immediate friends and family would have been aware of his performance of it. Trevor Dawson assumed that Dickens was better known for his conjuring than he was. He quoted from a novel by Albert Smith who introduced his main character, Mr Ledbury, as living in a neighbourhood in London where 'the man who does the trick with the doll has been known to visit the thoroughfare'. Dawson wrote that this 'is almost certainly a reference to Dickens and his Bonus Genius doll effect, for which he was widely known among his family and friends'.[36]

The extract comes from a book that was first serialised in *Bentley's Miscellany* under the title of 'Mr Ledbury's Grand Tour' by Albert Smith; it only later came out in book form as *The Adventures of Mr Ledbury and His Friend Jack Johnson*. Dickens was friends with Albert Smith, and was later to employ his brother Arthur as his tour manager on his public reading shows. The problem with Dawson's suggested connection is that the article was published during 1842 and Dickens did not start conjuring until the end of that year.[37]

from [Robert-Houdin, Secrets] p. 43: 'A conjuror is not a juggler; he is an actor playing the part of a magician'. It is a controversial quotation that has been interpreted in many ways by magicians – some agreeing and some disagreeing with it. A modern day example of a successful magician who played a character is Geoffrey Durham aka The Great Soprendo. Although even he admits that eventually it outgrew him and he reverted back to 'being himself'. For more on this, check out his illuminating 'Prologue', pp. 1-27 in [Durham]. In the same book there is also an excellent chapter on the ability to select tricks, 'The Right Stuff' pp. 175-181, a skill that CD clearly had.

[36] [Dawson] p. 41.

[37] 'Mr Ledbury's Grand Tour', p. 217 first published in *Bentley's Miscellany*, Volume XII, London, Richard Bentley, 1842. A later edition is [Smith, Albert] 'Chapter 1, Which Introduces the Heroes to the Reader', p.2. It is clear from a reading of the book that the author is referring to a street entertainer who comes to the area. As well as the 'man who does the trick

Although only a tenuous connection with the Bonus Genius trick, the tendency to attribute too much contemporary interest in Dickens's conjuring is seen in another extract from Dawson. He correctly said that Dickens was good friends with many of the writers connected with *Punch* magazine, which was founded in 1841 under the editorship of Mark Lemon. However he went on to write: 'From their intimate knowledge of him and his writings, it is not surprising that many satirical cartoons in *Punch*, particularly of a political nature, feature [Dickens's] works and conjuring.'[38]

There are seven magic-related cartoons that appear in *Punch* between 1841 and 1849, the year Dickens probably stopped conjuring. These incorporate thimble-rigging, the Great Wizard of the North, the Bonus Genius trick, the von Kempelen automated Chess Player and Robert-Houdin's Inexhaustible Bottle trick. All of these conjuring references would have been familiar to the magazine's readership: that is the reason for their inclusion, not because the *Punch* staff happened to know Dickens was an amateur conjurer.[39]

## Dickens's Actual Shows

The total number of conjuring performances by Dickens is not known. Those he definitely did are as follows:

| | |
|---|---|
| 31st December, 1842 | John Forster's house, London. |
| 6th January, 1843 | Charley's Birthday & Twelfth Night, London. |
| 6th February, 1843 | Mrs Norton and her boys, London. |
| 26th December, 1843 | Nina Macready's birthday party, London. |
| 6th January, 1844 | Charley's Birthday & Twelfth Night, London. |
| 16th July, 1846 | Mr & Mrs Watson in Lausanne, Switzerland. |
| 7th January, 1849 | Charley's Birthday Party, London. |

with the doll', Smith also mentioned piano-organs and Punch & Judy.
[38] [Dawson] p. 31.
[39] *Punch* cartoons were extracted from [Claxton, Punch].

| August 1849 | Bonchurch House Party, Isle of Wight. |
| Aug/Sept, 1849 | Rhia Rhama Rhoos Show, Isle of Wight. |
| 30th November, 1849[40] | Rockingham Castle, Leicester. |

According to his children, Dickens did shows on holiday and on Twelfth Night; but they do not say how often – so it does not really help in trying to compute a total. Of the ten shows that are known about, Dickens used at least four different costumes: a Chinese dress and a very large mask; a black cloak with hieroglyphics on, a grave black beard and a high black sugar-loaf hat (assuming that his brother Fred was able to procure the costume wanted); the attire he used for Rhia Rhama Rhoos; and what he might have worn on other occasions. One suspects there were more as his daughter Mamie wrote that he 'dressed as a magician' for his performances.

Dickens also used at least three assistants: his biographer, John Forster; marine artist, Clarkson Stanfield; and the cartoonist, John Leech.

Given these known facts, one must be wary of generalisations about his conjuring. For example Dawson quoted, as if it was somehow a dependable source, from a 1988 biography of Dickens by Fred Kaplan.

No Twelfth Night party was complete without the slim novelist, an enthusiastic amateur magician, putting on a highly professional sleight-of-hand performance, with props and costumes, and the tall burley Forster playing straight man to the man of magic.[41]

---

[40] It has been argued in the main chapter that part of the reason CD might have ceased conjuring is that acting took over. [Tomalin] pp. 170-1 mentioned that his acting was particularly active from the years 1845 to 1857, especially in the years 1850-52, p. 171. After the 'acting years' Dickens concentrated on public readings, [Tomalin] p. 239. For full details about his meeting with Ellen Ternan in 1857, check out [Tomalin, Invisible].

[41] [Kaplan] pp. 155-6 cited in [Dawson] p. 84.

However there were only three definite 'Twelfth Night' parties in which it is known for certain that Dickens performed magic (and one of those was on the 7th January[42]); the tricks which he performed were largely devoid of 'sleight-of-hand'; John Forster did not always assist – Stanfield and Leech also fulfilled this role; and, if Dickens's comment in his 31st December, 1842 letter to Felton can be believed ('I am assisted...by Stanfield, who always does his part exactly the wrong way: to the unspeakable delight of all beholders'), it is unlikely that whoever helped him, played the 'straight man'.

Dawson inferred that Dickens was still actively conjuring in 1854, quoting from *The Making of Charles Dickens*, by Christopher Hibbert, to support this.

He was, however, in 1854, at a time in life when he was feeling restless and unbearably repressed by the frustrations of his own personal life. He had just finished *Hard Times* and was increasingly depressed by the tragic state of the world around him. On occasions he appeared cheerful and relaxed; and when he was at home rehearsing with the children, or showing them conjuring tricks at parties, so excited.[43]

---

[42] According to Forster, Charley's birthday was celebrated on the 7 January, 1849, as the 6 was a Sunday, [Pilgrim, Vol. 5] p. 473 n 1. In fact the 6 January, 1849 *was* a Saturday.

[43] [Hibbert] p. 143 cited in [Dawson] p. 129. The supposed reliability of Hibbert can be ascertained from this quotation from Peter Ackroyd: 'There are three separate accounts of Dickens's childhood. The first is Robert Langton's *The Childhood and Youth* of Charles Dickens which, published in 1912, has the benefit of some first-hand testimony. There are also Christopher Hibbert's *The Making of Charles Dickens* and Michael Allen's *Charles Dickens's Childhood*, the latter being noticeable for its meticulous scholarship.' [Ackroyd] p. 1147.

This is another example of a 'secondary source' writer aware that Dickens performed magic but not taking into account any relevant dates.

The most unlikely scenario when it comes to Dickens's tenure of conjuring was imagined by Heathcote Williams. He assumed that Dickens was performing right up to the year he died.

> There's little doubt that conjuring became an enduring preoccupation of his: up to his death at Gad's Hill Place in 1870 he devotedly organised convivial social occasions – particularly at Christmas and on Twelfth Night – in which his own magic was featured.[44]

---

[44] [Williams] p. 20. Any Dickensian historian relying on a combination of [Dawson] and [Williams] for their research would have CD conjuring for around forty years, compared to the seven known years. [Dawson] p. 26 suggested CD had been performing for 'years' before he was aged 23.

# CHAPTER FOUR

# The Fan

## Alfred de Caston

Five years after he had completed his final magic show, Dickens watched the 'most consummate master of legerdemain he had seen'. The year was 1854 and Dickens was holidaying in France in Boulogne. The conjurer was performing at a French army-camp, entertainment possibly laid on as a morale booster for those soldiers involved in the Crimean War.

The year before Dickens had completed what many modern-day critics believe to be his greatest work, *Bleak House*; a searing indictment in particular of the legal profession. He was now writing perhaps his least successful book, the only one of his novels that did not contain any scenes in London, *Hard Times*. 'Hard Times' was not something Dickens was going through. As well as the income from his books, he was also by now the editor of a weekly journal called *Household Words*; never again, even with a large family, and later on a mistress, to support, would he be short of money.

There are several reasons why this, on the surface, mundane occurrence of Dickens watching another conjurer is significant. Firstly, because it was only many years afterwards that this 'consummate master of legerdemain' was identified; secondly, because Dickens was so lavish in his praise of him – far exceeding any other conjurer he saw; and finally, because it would seem from the detailed description of his act that Dickens gave, that the conjurer deserves far greater recognition than he has hitherto received.

It was not until 1931 that the name of the conjurer was

established. He was called Alfred de Caston. The discovery was made by Frank Staff in 1931 and written up in *The Magic Circular*, the magazine of the prestigious Magic Circle (see Plates 19 and 20). Staff had found a book containing the memoires of Henry Chorley, who was a music and theatre critic and great friend of Dickens; in it he described a trick he had seen which was similar to what Dickens had recorded. More importantly he wrote that de Caston was 'the only Professor of his art who succeeded in puzzling Charles Dickens'.

Remarkably little is known about de Caston as a magician (see Plate 16). As one historian wrote: 'it is not that de Caston's name is forgotten, apparently it has never been remembered.' He was born on 9th March, 1822, so would have been thirty two when Dickens saw him. His real name was Léon François Antoine Aurifeuille and he taught high-school mathematics. He clearly had abilities in this field far exceeding his teaching post as he came up with a formula for determining the factors of extremely high numbers, a theorem known today as aurifeuillean factorization.

He only appears to have earned his living from conjuring over short periods, specialising in working fashionable French salons, seemingly more interested in writing (he authored at least nine books), exploring and travelling. He did a hundred performances at the Hotel d'Osmond in Paris; the final one was on 24th December, 1855. In 1857 through to 1858 he made long trips to Russia and Poland but there is no record of him doing any magic shows.

In April, 1859 he did a farewell show, when a newspaper report stated he was 'the successful rival of Robert-Houdin' (the pre-eminent French conjurer of that period) and in which he reprised his most famous feat of divulging the answers to questions while blindfolded. The reviewer commented that 'the only regret we were left with on the evening of Mr. Caston was that he did not conjure away the singers in the interlude'. That, as far as his conjuring biography is concerned, seems to be about it. He died in 1882 – although to add to his mystique there is a playbill with his name on it dated 1886; somebody doubtless trying to cash in on his name.

By far the most comprehensive record of the tricks that de Caston performed was from Dickens – in itself an extraordinary fact. That the famous novelist, in amongst all his other considerable achievements, also made a serious contribution to conjuring history has never been properly recognised. Perhaps magic historians have dismissed his narrative as the type of overblown exaggeration you might expect from a writer of fiction. Dickens's description was written up in John Forster's biography, extracted from his letters. Dickens recalled in great clarity not just what de Caston did but also much of his patter. Here is what he noted.

You are to observe that he [de Caston] was *with the company*, not in the least removed from them; and that we occupied the front row. He brought in some writing paper with him when he entered, and a black-lead pencil; and he wrote some words on half-sheets of paper. One of these half-sheets he folded into two, and gave to Catherine to hold.

"Madame", he says aloud, "will you think of any class of objects?" "I have done so."

"Of what class, Madame?" "Animals."

"Will you think of a particular animal, Madame?" "I have done so." "Of what animal?" "The Lion."

"Will you think of another class of objects, Madame?" "I have done so."

"Of what class?" "Flowers."

"The particular flower?" "The Rose."

"Will you open the paper you hold in your hand?"

She opened it, and there was neatly and plainly written in pencil – *The Lion. The Rose.* Nothing whatever had led up to these words, and they were the most distant conceivable from Catherine's thoughts when she entered the room.

Dickens continued, describing the next trick.

He had several common school-slates about a foot square. He took one of these to a field-officer from the camp, decoré [decorated] and what not, who sat about six from us, with a grave saturnine friend next to him.

"My General", says he, "will you write a name on this slate, after your friend has done so? Don't show it to me."

The friend wrote a name, and the General wrote a name. The conjuror took the slate rapidly from the officer, threw it violently down on the ground with its written side to the floor, and asked the officer to put his foot upon it, and keep it there: which he did.

The conjuror considered for about a minute, looking devilish hard at the General. "My General", says he, "your friend wrote Dagobert, upon the slate under your foot." The friend admits it.

"And you, my General, wrote Nicholas." General admits it, and everybody laughs and applauds.

"My General, will you excuse me, if I change that name into a name expressive of the power of a great nation, which, in happy alliance with the gallantry and spirit of France will shake that name to its centre?"

"Certainly I will excuse it."

"My General, take up the slate and read." General reads: DAGOBERT, VICTORIA. The first in his friend's writing; the second in a new hand.

I never saw anything in the least like this; or at all approaching to the absolute certainty, the familiarity, quickness, absence of all machinery, and actual face-to-face, hand-to-hand fairness between the conjuror and the audience, with which it was done. I have not the slightest idea of the secret.

Dickens came to the final trick.

One more. He was blinded with several table napkins, and then a great cloth was bodily thrown over them and his head too, so that his voice sounded as if he were under a bed. Perhaps half a dozen dates were written on a slate.

He takes the slate in his hand, and throws it violently down on the floor as before, remains silent a minute, seems to become agitated, and bursts out thus: "What is this I see? A great city, but of narrow streets and old-fashioned houses, many of which are of wood, resolving itself into ruins! How is it falling into ruins? Hark! I hear the crackling of a great conflagration, and, looking up, I behold a vast cloud of flame and smoke. The ground is covered with hot cinders too, and people are flying into the fields and endeavouring to save their goods. This great fire, this great wind, this roaring noise! This is the great fire of London, and the first date upon the slate must be one, six, six, six – the year in which it happened."

And so on with all the other dates. There!

Even by today's standards this was an astonishing performance. The first person, in 1911, who brought Dickens's summary of de Caston's show to the attention of other magicians wrote that 'one would find it difficult to accept these descriptions are absolutely unexaggerated and unembellished accounts of what this magician actually did, even from so great a writer as Charles Dickens'. With the benefit of hindsight it is possible to work out probable solutions of how de Caston did all of these tricks; and, if correct, far from exaggerating and embellishing, it can be concluded that Dickens's reporting was broadly accurate.

It is unsurprising that Dickens was flabbergasted by what he saw. He performed apparatus-type magic; he would also have been familiar with sleight of hand from watching street conjurers. But what de Caston was doing did not seem to involve either of these two branches of conjuring; he specialised in an entirely new category of magic. It is known today, although the expression was not used back then, as mind reading; a type of entertainment popularised by the modern-day exponent Derren Brown.

Robert-Houdin, in his seminal book *The Secrets of Conjuring and Magic*, called it Mental Conjuring and wrote that it comprised 'the kind of tricks performed by M. Alfred de Caston: a control acquired over the will of the spectator; secret thoughts read by an ingenious system of diagnosis, and sometimes compelled to take a particular direction by certain subtle artifices.' From this it is clear that de Caston was very much a pioneer and deserves perhaps to be called the first mind reader.

In performing his mind reading feats, de Caston was not just using available magic knowledge but also tapping into aspects of mesmerism (the precursor to hypnotism) and Spiritualism. One of the common claims of early mesmerists was the ability to see with your eyes covered. Dickens had been convinced by such a demonstration several years before. In 1841 he attended a demonstration of a young Frenchman called Alexis Didier, who was nicknamed the Magnetic Boy. Despite having his eyes tightly covered with cotton-wool and bandages, Didier was able to read from a book.

It was partly as a result of seeing Didier that Dickens embarked on his own enthusiastic foray into mesmerism; he treated a woman called Madame De La Rue, who suffered from a nervous disorder, by inducing hypnotic trances. Dickens never made the connection between the blindfolded Didier reading the words from a book and the similarly unsighted de Caston discerning the dates written on a slate. Despite the differences in how their feats were presented, both men would have used the same technique to bamboozle Dickens.

Compared to mesmerism, Spiritualism was a fairly new phenomenon and Dickens's attitude to it was considerably more sceptical. He condemned those who practised it, and mocked those who believed in it, both in articles and letters. Spiritualism had started six years before Dickens saw de Caston with the rather crude séances of the Fox sisters in America who conducted conversations with spirits through rappings or knockings. Its popularity swiftly spread over to England and Europe as the sophistication of the techniques of communicating with departed spirits increased.

One of the means of contact that quickly became popular was through so-called 'spirit writing'; writings miraculously appeared not just on paper but often scrawled on the wall, or even the ceiling, of a house. Over time the favourite way of revealing these communiqués from 'the other side' was on a slate, partly because it provided opportunities for the medium to use nefarious procedures to secretly compose their messages. The man who perfected spiritual slate-writing techniques was the medium Dr Henry Slade, who began his séances around 1860.

De Caston preceded by several years not just Slade, but possibly all other spiritualists, in producing a message on a slate. Furthermore his method would have been different, and rather more subtle, than that of Slade; the latter normally resorted to either crudely scrawling messages with some chalk attached to his finger, or switching one slate for another whilst it was hidden under a table, or with the help of an accomplice.

It would take even longer for conjurers to emulate de Caston. It was only with the introduction of a 'gimmicked' slate – known now as the flap slate – that they had the mechanical apparatus to duplicate de Caston's feat of making the word 'Victoria' appear. The date of the invention of the flap slate is unknown; but there are no reports of its use by conjurers until after 1880.

It is because of Dickens's reportage that due credit can now be given to how far ahead Alfred de Caston was of his contemporaries in both the way he presented his tricks and his technical abilities. Normally when hyperbolic terms are used to describe the feats of a conjurer, the words should be viewed through a highly sceptical prism. However when Dickens wrote to Forster that de Caston was 'so far as I know, a perfectly original genius, and that puts any sort of knowledge of legerdemain, such as I supposed that I possessed, at utter defiance', he was not exaggerating. You can easily understand why he wrote to Wilkie Collins enquiring if 'the great Conjurer' was 'the Devil'.

## Colonel Stodare and the Sphinx

In November 1865 Dickens described one of the most famous illusions of the nineteenth century – not in order to declare his admiration of the trick but rather to explain how it was done. The illusion was known as the Sphinx and was exclusively performed at this time by Colonel Stodare at the Egyptian Hall. Colonel Stodare had been born Joseph Stoddart in 1832 but it is not known exactly when he made the name change. He was once confronted by a genuine colonel at the end of a show demanding to know what regiment he was from; he got out of a potentially embarrassing situation by claiming he had been christened Colonel Stodare.

Colonel Stodare was performing a relatively pedestrian conjuring show at the Egyptian Hall in London when he purchased a new illusion, which was invented by Thomas William Tobin of the Polytechnic Institution. Tobin first offered it for sale to John Henry Anderson for £80 but as the Wizard of the North was going through one of his periodic bouts of impoverishment, he declined it. Anderson said later it was the one decision that he regretted most in his life.

With a combination of inspired publicity, a brilliant presentation and the application of an entirely new magic principle, Colonel Stodare caused a sensation with the Sphinx from the moment he debuted it on 16th October, 1865. He would continue to feature it at the Egyptian Hall right through to when tuberculosis forced him into retiring from the stage on 11th June, 1866.

At the start of the Sphinx illusion, there were two tables on stage; on the front one there sat a box large enough to contain a man's head. Stodare picked up the box and showed it empty. He placed it on the rear, oval-shaped, three-legged table with only a thin top, through the legs of which the audience could see to the back of the stage. He unlocked the box, letting the front drop down, revealing the disembodied head of a sphinx; a sphinx is a mythological Egyptian creature with the head of a human and a body of a lion – the most famous example being the Great Sphinx of Giza on the river Nile.

The sphinx had its eyes closed but after a time it opened one eye, opened another, winked and blinked and then started talking and answering questions, 'not only with perspicuity' as *The Times* newspaper wrote, 'but with something like eloquence'. It was apparent to the audience throughout that this was a human head talking, not some sort of ventriloquial dummy. At the finish, after the sphinx had recited some verses, Stodare closed the front of the box. When he opened it again, the sphinx had vanished, leaving just a pile of ashes.

It was less than a month after the Sphinx was first exhibited that Dickens went and saw it. He either went to the Egyptian Hall with his daughter Mamie or she attended separately (see Plate 25). She asked him how the illusion was done, presumably working on the assumption that because her father had studied conjuring, he must therefore be knowledgeable about all tricks, even if it was not one in his own sphere of expertise.

Dickens replied on 14th November, 1865. For ease of understanding some explanatory notes are inserted amidst Dickens's proposed solution.

My Dear Mamie,

As you want to know my views of the Sphinx, here they are. But I have only seen it once; and it is so extraordinarily well done, that it ought to be observed closely several times.

Anyone who attentively notices the flower trick will see that the two little high tables hung with drapery cover each a trap. Each of those tables, during that trick, hides a confederate, who changes the paper cone twice. When the cone has been changed as often as is required, the trap is closed and the table can be moved.

[*The 'flower trick' Dickens refers to, was the Instantaneous Growth of Flowers which Stodare had introduced into his show from his very first performance at the Egyptian Hall on 17th April, 1865. It was a stage version of the Mango Tree trick performed by Indian fakirs. It has been described as follows: 'A small plant pot filled with earth is covered with a previously-shown empty cone made of cardboard, and when the cone is lifted a small plant is seen. It is covered again and on this occasion a plant two to three feet high, in full bloom, is revealed when the cone is removed'.*]

When the curtain is removed for the performance of the Sphinx trick, there is a covered, that is, draped table on the stage, which is never seen before or afterwards. In front of the middle of it, and between it and the audience, stands one of those little draped tables covering a trap; this is a third trap in the centre of the stage. The box for the head is then upon IT, and the conjuror takes it off and shows it.

[*There are two tables on the stage at the start of the trick. The front, smaller table, contains the empty box in which the sphinx's head will later appear. Under that table, which is covered with a cloth, is a trapdoor – it is a 'third trap' because, according to Dickens, there need to be two other trapdoors to perform the Instantaneous Growth of Flowers. The empty box is picked up by the conjurer and displayed.*]

The man whose head is afterwards shown in that box is, I conceive, in the table; that is to say, is lying on his chest in the thickness of the table, in an extremely constrained attitude.

[*The man playing the part of the sphinx is concealed inside the larger, rear table, the top of which presumably would have to be hollowed out in order to accommodate him.*]

To get him into the table, and to enable him to use the trap in the table through which his head comes into the box, the two hands of a confederate are necessary. That confederate comes up a trap, and stands in the space afforded by the interval below the stage and the height of the little draped table! his back is towards the audience. The moment he has assisted the hidden man sufficiently, he closes the trap,

[*The man lying in the table is unable to manoeuvre his head up through the trap in the table on his own – so he needs some assistance. That assistance is provided by a confederate, who comes up the trapdoor which is hidden under the draped cloth of the front table. He stands, or squats, between the two so he cannot be seen – he is effectively hidden behind the front table. With his back towards the audience, he assists the concealed 'sphinx' to get himself into a position where he can poke his head up through the trap in the table top. He then drops down his own trapdoor back underneath the stage.*]

and the conjuror then immediately removes the little draped table, and also the drapery of the larger table; when he places the box on the last-named table *with the slide on* for the head to come into it, he stands with his back to the audience and his face to the box, and masks the box considerably to facilitate the insertion of the head. As soon as he knows the head to be in its place, he undraws the slide.

[*Once the confederate has dropped down the trap door, the conjurer can now remove the front table and also the cloth covering the back table. One presumes that the sphinx's head is hovering just underneath the table top trap, now that he has been somehow shoved into position by the assistant. The conjurer places the box on the back table, enabling the sphinx's head to be pushed up through the trap into the box. When Dickens writes about the 'slide', he probably means the front opening of the box which levers down to reveal the head of the sphinx.*]

When the verses have been spoken and the trick is done, he loses no time in replacing the slide.

[*The front of the box is closed.*]

The curtain is then immediately dropped, because the man cannot otherwise be got out of the table, and has no doubt had quite enough of it.

Dickens's solution to the trick has been rather ridiculed by magic historians. One has written that it was 'hopelessly inaccurate' whilst another preferred 'all we will say is, No comment!' However in a couple of crucial ways, Dickens was correct. There was a man concealed who pushed his head up through a trap in the table into the box. And the curtain did have to be dropped at the end of the trick in order for the man to be 'got out'. In some respects, the editors of Dickens's letters were therefore broadly correct when they wrote that Professor Hoffmann in *Modern Magic* 'describes how the trick is done, in terms very similar to CD's, except that he adds the use of a reflecting-mirror'.

It is quite possible that Dickens had come across the principle of using a mirror to create a stage illusion prior to the Sphinx. In 1862 John Henry Pepper took an idea devised by a civil engineer called Henry Dircks and came up with what was soon to be known as Pepper's Ghost: a means of producing ghostly apparitions on stage. On 24th December of that year it was first shown by Professor Pepper at the Polytechnic Institution in Regent Street in London to a group of literary and scientific colleagues and the press. As befitting the Institute, the plan was to inform the spectators of the method, but the audience was so impressed that Pepper decided it would be better to present it with no explanation.

A couple of days later it was part of the Polytechnic's Christmas programme. This comprised a variety of events around the building, most lasting around half an hour, although the pantomime was one hour in length. Pepper's Ghost was included as part of a 'Strange Lecture' and was illustrated by a scene from Dickens's fifth, and final, Christmas short story *The Haunted Man and the Ghost's Bargain*. Initially it was shown in one of the smaller lecture halls which meant the participants in the playlet had to be sitting or reclining throughout.

*The Morning Post*, on 27th December, 1862, reported it as follows:

Professor Pepper delivers "A Strange Lecture", illustrated by a series of curious illusions and other experiments, including the beautiful optical apparatus, invented and constructed by Mr. T. Rose, called the "Photodrone". A remarkable illustration of Mr. Chas. Dickens's idea of the "Haunted Man" is given in the course of the lecture, and must be seen to be appreciated.

Such was the popularity of the optical illusion that in the Easter season it was moved to the largest theatre; and remained part of the programme for the whole of 1863. Later in the year, audiences would have seen three scenes all involving ghosts in some capacity, the highlight perhaps being that of a ghost drinking water. The first scene comprised a reading from Dickens's *Haunted Man* in which Redlaw, the anti-hero of the story, was confronted by his phantom twin and the spectre of his sister. Pepper claimed that 'special written permission' had been obtained from Dickens to use his text.

Although there is no evidence that Dickens attended a performance, it is the type of show that surely would have intrigued him. If he had gone he would have seen a ghostly shape that materialised out of thin air, interacted with an actor on stage, walked through chairs and tables and who equally mysteriously faded away into nothingness at the end.

The chances were that Dickens would have been let in on the secret of how the appearing and vanishing ghost effect was created – as the Prince of Wales (the future Edward VII) was when he visited with his wife in May 1863 and was taken behind the scenes for a demonstration. It was achieved by placing a large sheet of glass, immaculately polished so the spectators were unaware of its existence, at an angle in front of the stage. Directly underneath the glass, but out of sight of the audience, stood the actor playing the ghost. When he was illuminated by a bright light, the image was reflected in the glass and he seemed to be onstage with Redlaw. As the light was dimmed, the ghost gradually disappeared.

The two actors could not see each other, so their timing had to be very exact to give the impression that they were communicating together. Furthermore, because of the obstruction of the glass, the person on stage could not speak. The performance was all done in mime, whilst there was a reading by Pepper from the relevant passage in *The Haunted Man*.

Pepper's Ghost proved a huge hit, with plenty of other impresarios appropriating it with varying degrees of success. It was not the most practical of stage setting for a theatre. It could only work in small venues because of the weight and therefore restricted size of the glass; this had to be secretly raised and lowered as and when the scene with the ghost was required. It was better presented in a lecture format, as happened at the Institute, or as a fairground attraction.

From a conjuring perspective, though, it ushered in plenty of other uses of transparent glass to create illusions; and Colonel Stodare with his Sphinx, some three years later, was almost certainly one of the principal beneficiaries of the creativity of Dircks and Pepper. Indeed Thomas Tobin, its inventor, was a colleague of Pepper at the Institute.

Even if Dickens had been privy to the methodology of Pepper's Ghost, it would hardly be fair to criticise him for not suspecting that a reflecting-mirror was also in play with the Sphinx; its application was very different and arguably more subtly applied. Dickens's alternative solution – involving a confederate coming up through a trap door to assist the man playing the part of the sphinx, who is concealed in the table top – might have been impractical. But given Dickens's level of knowledge and what he recalled of the illusion, it was not that bad a guess.

## The End of Conjuring References

His attempt to solve the secret of the Sphinx is the final mention of conjuring in any of Dickens's letters, papers or manuscripts. During the thirty years between Dickens first taking up conjuring, and his death in 1870, there had been many innovative changes in magic generally. Apart from Stodare and Alfred de Caston, both pioneers in their own speciality of illusions and mind reading respectively, other groundbreaking conjurers included Robert-Houdin, who revolutionised the presentation of old and new tricks and is known as the 'father of modern conjuring'; the Davenport Brothers who combined Spiritualism and conjuring with spooky manifestations that emanated from a large cabinet in which they were both tied up; and Alexander Herrmann, the ultimate all-round showman who anticipated the great touring shows in later years of Kellar and Thurston.

The days of the 'apparatus-type' conjurers, the magic that Dickens specialised in, were long gone. It was the likes of Robert-Houdin and Wiljalba Frikell who heralded the new era. So although Anderson, the Great Wizard of the North – some of whose initial tricks, Dickens had performed himself – continued touring right through to his death in 1874, after 1845 his repertoire and style were strongly influenced by Robert-Houdin. When Frikell appeared in London in 1857 he boasted on his playbill about doing magic 'Without the Aid of any Apparatus'. He wrote a book around the same year where part of the title was *Two Hours of Illusions without the Aid of Apparatus*, in which he referred disparagingly to modern conjurers becoming addicted to using 'complicated and cumbrous apparatus'.

Ludwig Döbler, the conjurer who had initially inspired Dickens, never returned to England after 1844 and retired from the stage in 1847. *Punch* magazine's satirical article titled 'Dobler Outdone', would seem, on this evidence, to be rather anachronistic when it was published in 1860. There were though numerous imitators who stole Döbler's name and copied his tricks – so the heading might have been referring to one of those, or maybe 'Döblers' in general; for the object of the article was to highlight that magic apparatus was 'sold at every counter, and feats of legerdemain are now in everybody's hands', so denigrating those who relied on such self-working devices for their conjuring.

If Dickens had still been conjuring at the end of his life, with the same apparatus that he began with, he would have looked rather dated by comparison with those working professionally. However only the props would seem outmoded. Dickens's choice of tricks remain as impressive as ever they did back in the 1840s; the difference was that, over the years, the way of doing the trick had altered, relying more on sleight of hand and subtlety, rather than the mechanics of the specially-made utensils, to do the magic.

It is unfortunate that the final reference by Dickens to conjuring related to a flawed attempt to explain how a trick worked; but the fact that he bowed out of performing when he did is a credit to his prescience. Whatever is thought about Dickens's magical abilities from the perspective of the twenty-first century, it is unarguable that whilst all his other artistic activities – writing, acting, speaking, public readings – had their critics at the time, nobody ever had a bad word to say about Dickens as a conjurer.

# Chapter Four Supplement

## Solving the Mystery of the French Conjurer

Most of the pertinent information known about Alfred de Caston is contained in the main chapter. However some early biographical information can be fleshed out. He was born François Léon Antoine Aurifeuille in Toulouse on 9th March, 1822; the name Aurifeuille does not appear though in the Register of Births so it is possible that he was illegitimate. Later he called himself Vicomte Alfred de Caston and claimed at times to be a native of America – hence his English must have been excellent.

His mother's name was Jeanne Andrée Aurifeuille and he attended the prestigious L'Ecole Polytechnique in Paris: however he left after only one year. He became a teacher of mathematics at a grammar school in Toulouse which today specialises in that subject. Presumably it was here that he came up with the aurifeuillian factorization theorem. De Caston died in 1882 having authored at least nine books, become the Editor in Chief of a Turkish journal, and been accepted as a member of the French La Société des Gens de Lettres.

Given that de Caston was such a pioneer in the field of mind reading and mental magic, it is rather a travesty that there is so little information on any of his shows. The main reason is probably that he was working in the type of places – French salons, private parties, hotels – where journalists did not write newspaper reviews. As is true now, if you want your act to be publicised you need to be playing a 'proper venue', normally a theatre. De Caston also gives the impression of someone who 'dabbled' in conjuring; and that might have counted against him as far as contemporary reporters taking him seriously.

Another problem, in terms of magic history, is that de Caston is completely over-shadowed by Robert-Houdin, who bestrode the French conjuring scene in the same period. The reviewer in the French Magazine, *Voleur* might well have written that de Caston was a successful rival to Robert-Houdin ('le rival heureux des Robert-Houdin') but you certainly would not know that from the history books. Magic historians such as Milbourne Christopher, David Price, HR Evans, Harry Houdini and Thomas Frost all fail to even name de Caston, whilst Clarke only wrote that he 'specialised in card and memory feats and was even more famous as an author than as a conjurer.'[1]

It did not seem that de Caston and Robert-Houdin perceived each other as rivals. De Caston, in his most famous work *Les Marchands de Miracles*, published in 1864, wrote that Robert-Houdin was the 'greatest conjurer-mechanic of our time...in creating the anti-mesmeric double sight'. Whilst Robert-Houdin

---

[1] John Randall Brown, considered by Barry H. Wiley to be the first 'thought-reading act', called himself 'The Celebrated Mind Reader'on a poster dated around 1875: [Wiley] p. 35. The quotation about de Caston never been remembered comes from [Findlay] p. 15. His date of birth of 1822 ([Whaley, Who's Who] p. 92 has it a year earlier in 1821) is from the records of Bibliothèque centrale de l'Ecole Polytechnique, which he entered in 1841. This was cited on www.numericana.com/answer/numbers.htm, compiled by Dr Gérard P. Michon – where also can be found information about his mathematics, biographical facts and the year of his death. Other information can be found in the French magic journal *L'Escamoteur* March - April, No. 45, 1954, pp. 702-7 and [Whaley, Who's Who] p. 92. The 1886 playbill of a certain A. De Caston is reproduced in [Dawson] p. 153 and [Fechner, Vol. 2] p. 81. Neither writer points out the oddity of someone's playbill appearing four years after their death. The likelihood was that an unscrupulous magician copied his name – the absence of either 'Alfred' or 'Vicomte' in the wording is perhaps of significance – in order to pass themselves off as the deceased de Caston. The quotations in this paragraph come from *Voleur*, No. 127, 8 April, 1859 and [Clarke] p. 287.

repaid the compliment in naming de Caston as the only example of the exponent of Mental Conjuring in his analysis of the six branches of magic: 'the kind of tricks performed by M. Alfred de Caston: a control acquired over the will of the spectator; secret thoughts read by an ingenious system of diagnosis, and sometimes compelled to take a particular direction by certain subtle artifices.'[2]

It did not help de Caston's legacy that his most famous audience member failed to give him a name check; if he had, perhaps magic historians would have investigated him a little more. There was much speculation in the magic press, before Staff's article appeared in 1931, as to the identity of Dickens's French army-camp conjurer. Most of the names bandied around (including Robert-Houdin himself) were rejected by their own proposers; but one person was put forward as a serious contender by Clarke when he wrote it 'has been suggested with some plausibility that Eugene Bosco was the conjurer who so impressed Charles Dickens by his performance at Boulogne.' Clarke hedged his bets by also saying that the 'conjurer has never really been identified' suggesting that he was far from certain that he had got the right man.[3]

---

[2] De Caston on R-H: cited in [Fechner, Vol. 1] p. 289. The 'anti-mesmeric double sight' is a reference to Robert-Houdin's 'Second Sight' routine. He performed it with his son, who was blindfolded, revealing information about items held by audience members. R-H on de Caston: [Robert-Houdin, Secrets] p. 30. The other branches are Feats of Dexterity, Experiments in Natural Magic, Pretended Mesmerism, The Medium Business and all others that 'cannot be classified'.

[3] Staff in his 'Charles Dickens and Magic', FS, [Magic Circular], April 1929, Vol. 23, pp. 106-8 put forward, and then rejected, in quick succession Robert-Houdin, Philippe Talon and Ramo Samee as possible candidates. [Clarke] p. 198; originally published in The Magic Wand, No. XIV, October/November, 1925, p. 143. [Sharpe] p 32: suggested that the 'brilliant French conjurer may quite likely have been Robert-Houdin himself.' But he also noted Patric Playfair's suggestion of de Caston, referred to below.

Long after it has been accepted that de Caston is the correct man, Bosco has made a comeback as the mystery conjurer, most recently in Simon Callow's 2012 *Charles Dickens and the Great Theatre of the World*. Callow wrote that Dickens 'saw the best conjuror he had ever seen, performing mind-boggling feats of mentalism. His name was Giovanni Bartolomeo Bosco, he was corpulent and sleazy in appearance...' Giovanni Bosco was the father of Eugene.[4]

Although it is not known where Clarke got the idea of his 'Bosco' from, it is known how Callow obtained his. It came from Heathcote Williams's booklet *What Larks! Charles Dickens, Conjuror* in which he wrote that the magician that Dickens had seen in Boulogne 'has been identified as Giovanni Bartolomeo Bosco': he described him as 'that distasteful fat old Italian'. Bizarrely, Heathcote Williams's provenance was from the same source as where Alfred de Caston was eventually established as the mystery conjurer – Henry Chorley.[5]

Chorley had written, before going on to sing the praises of de Caston, 'What do our keenest powers of observation avail, when they are brought to bear on the legerdemain of a Robert Houdin, a Bosco (that distasteful, fat old Italian, who executed his wonders by the aid of hands ending arms naked to the shoulder)?' Chorley did not say which Bosco he was referring to – so Williams assumed it was Giovanni Bosco. That both Clarke and Williams opted for a 'Bosco', albeit father and son, would seem to be coincidental.[6]

Leaving aside such red herrings, the details of how de Caston's identity was finally uncovered also has its own twists. It began in 1911 when Douglas Dexter wrote an article in *The Magic Circular*

[4] [Callow] p. 236. Giovanni Bosco (1793-1863); Eugene Bosco (1823-1891): dates from [Whaley, Who's Who] p. 51.
[5] [Williams] p. 7. It would seem that Williams had somehow, in transcribing his notes to the written page, confused de Caston with Bosco.
[6] [Chorley, Vol. 2] p. 221.

called 'Charles Dickens, Magician'. He was the first person to draw attention to fellow magicians of Dickens's description of de Caston's performance by reproducing the relevant passage from Forster's biography. At the end, Dexter wrote 'it would be interesting to know who this exceptionally clever performer was.'[7]

One man took the bait, although it was another fourteen years before he announced that he had. Frank Staff, former Librarian of The Magic Circle and a member of The Dickensian Fellowship, wrote in 1929 that 'no stone has been left unturned' since reading Dexter's article in trying to identify 'the most consummate master of legerdemain'; he rather half-heartedly suggested, and then rejected, some possible candidates. And he finished by writing that his identity 'is a mystery to me, and is as unlikely to be solved at this date, as the identification of Datchery in the unfinished novel, *The Mystery of Edwin Drood*.'[8]

And yet two years later, Frank Staff had cracked it. He wrote up the results in *The Magic Circular* in 'Dickens and Conjuring' in 1931. This was reproduced in *The Dickensian* magazine, although not until twelve years later: clearly he thought magicians would be more interested in his findings than Dickensians! However Frank Staff was not the first to come up with the correct answer. There is an intriguing sentence that crops up in Clarke's *Annals of Conjuring* which predated the original Staff article by some four years: 'Mr Patric Playfair makes the interesting suggestion that it was de Caston who excited the admiration of Charles Dickens in 1854'.[9]

---

[7] 'Charles Dickens, Magician', Douglas Dexter, [Magic Circular] Vol. 5, May 1911, pp. 147-152.

[8] 'Charles Dickens and Magic', FS, [Magic Circular] Vol. 23, April 1929, pp. 107-8. Information about Staff comes from his obituary in [Magic Circular] July 1952, pp. 270-1, written by Arthur Ivy – Staff died 25 May, 1952.

[9] The two articles by Staff are [Staff] and 'Dickens The Conjuror, and a Mystery

As was noted above, Clarke had also written earlier that it had been 'suggested with some plausibility that Eugene Bosco was the conjurer who so impressed Charles Dickens': presumably, with the mixed messages given, Patric Playfair's 'interesting suggestion' was never followed up by anyone. Certainly Staff, in his articles, did not refer to it at all.

In any event proof, rather than speculation, should always take precedent; so it is right that it is Staff who receives the credit for the discovery. He had unearthed a book on the writings of Henry Chorley in which an extract mentioned a conjurer called Chevalier de Caston who was described as 'the only Professor of his art who succeeded in puzzling Charles Dickens'. The only slightly perplexing part of Staff's article, as was pointed out by Peter Warlock in *Abracadabra*, was that he wrote that Henry Chorley was 'writing in or about the year 1853'; whereas it is known Dickens did not see de Caston until 1854.[10]

It is unclear how Staff came up with the year 1853, because the book from which the relevant citation appeared was published in 1873 (maybe he got confused by the 18'5'3 and the 18'7'3). It was called *Henry Fothergill Chorley, Autobiography, Memoir and*

Solved', Frank Staff, [Dickensian] Vol. 39, No. 266, Spring, 1943, p.61. [Clarke] p. 287; it was originally published in *Magic Wand*, Vol. 16, March 1927, p. 39. Patric Playfair was a professional magician who contributed many articles to the *Magic Wand*. However he never mentioned de Caston in one of these, so one must conclude that it was through a private chat or correspondence that he passed on his thoughts to Clarke. On a side note to Playfair, it was revealed that a soldier watching one of his shows recovered speech and hearing after the trauma of shell-shock. *British Theatre in the Great War: A Revaluation*, Gordon Williams, Continuum, London, 2003, p. 103.

[10] [Staff] p. 93; 'A Writer and his Magic', Peter Warlock, *Abracadabra*, 27 Dec, 1975, Vol. 61, No. 1561, p. 13. Warlock 'solved' the problem by suggesting Dickens saw de Caston a year earlier – but this was not so.

*Letters* and was assembled by Henry G Hewlett. Henry Chorley was a music critic and general reviewer. Ackroyd described him as a 'mild, broken-down, sad bachelor in late middle-age' with a 'thin voice, a shuffling gait, and a depressive temperament which he never could quite quench with drink. Yet Dickens understood him, liked him.'[11]

The book, as the title suggested, was a compilation by the editor of Chorley's various papers which were found after his death in 1872. The editor, in his Introduction, explained that a 'considerable portion of these volumes will consist of selections from an unfinished autobiography and a series of journals which were found among his MSS'. His job was the 'arrangement of these extracts, and the insertion in fit order of such letters as he has retained from the most eminent of his deceased correspondents'. Perhaps partly because of the rather haphazard nature of the project, it is not possible to date many of the events in the book.[12]

The section about Chevalier de Caston was in Chapter 12 of the second volume and was introduced by the editor as stating that Chorley had very strong opinions on 'the tenets of spiritualism' and 'how rigidly, both by word and deed, he was wont to protest against their theory and practice.' Because of this the editor, 'in deference to the earnestness of [Chorley's] feeling' even though he considered that the 'interest of the question has so long been exhausted', rather apologetically decided to include an 'extract' from 'a chapter of reminiscence.' It was fortunate that Hewlett overcame his reservations.[13]

Chorley praised de Caston to show what could be achieved by conjurers before ridiculing a couple of so-called spiritualists whom he had seen. In doing so he described part of de Caston's repertoire and concluded with 'I can only say that I am satisfied I have

[11] [Ackroyd] p. 961.
[12] [Chorley, Vol. 1] pp. 3-4.
[13] [Chorley, Vol. 2] pp. 220-1.

recounted it accurately.*' The asterisk referred to a note at the bottom of the page which read: 'This Chevalier de Caston, by the way, was the only professor of his art who succeeded in puzzling Charles Dickens, himself a consummate and experienced conjurer'. As the annotation was in quotation marks, in the same way that the selection from the reminiscences was punctuated, the assumption is that these were Chorley's own words, rather than added by the editor.[14]

(In passing, it is ironic how important footnotes are when it comes to finding out about Dickens and conjuring. Without Forster's footnote, Dickens's performance as Rhia Rhama Rhoos would have been lost; and without this Chorley footnote, de Caston might not have been tracked down as the mystery conjurer Dickens saw. It shows how peripheral conjuring is considered to be by most writers.)

It was this footnote, along with some important similarities in the tricks described by Dickens and Chorley on viewing their respective conjurers, which led to the conclusion that they were one and the same person. The only part missing was that it was not possible to date when Chorley saw de Caston: was it before or after Dickens did?[15] The relative timing is perhaps only of interest to magicians – the reason is that Chorley described a slightly different way of performing one of the tricks he saw than Dickens did. This raises

[14] [Chorley, Vol. 2] p. 223.

[15] [Dawson] p. 151 who gave a comprehensive account of the Dexter and Staff articles leading to de Caston's discovery, wrote that 'Chorley's experience with de Caston was clearly after Dickens in 1854 saw the performer'. This seemed to be based on the fact that Chorley and CD did not become friends until 1858, which is questionable. According to Chorley's editor writing in [Chorley, Vol. 2] p. 22, CD and Chorley 'did not become intimate until 1854' but 'their acquaintance has been referred to as dating from an earlier period'. However there does not seem to be any particular relevance of when CD and Chorley first met to the dates of their respective viewing of de Caston.

the question of whether it was another trick altogether; or whether de Caston had changed his way of doing it over the years; or, indeed, whether either Dickens or Chorley had misremembered parts of the presentation.

Further confirmation that it was de Caston who Dickens saw is provided in a book called *Mental Suggestion* by Dr Julian Ochorowicz which was published in 1885. He wrote about 'an "extraordinary" exhibition given by a certain "Vicomte de Caston," who performed feats of memory and prestidigitation, improvised verses, read without the aid of eyes, and divined thoughts. The séance was highly interesting to the psychologist.' Ochorowicz concentrated on one particular aspect of de Caston's repertoire, that had enough in common with part of what Dickens described to link the two. This will be considered below in the section on an 'Analysis of Psychological Forces'.[16]

## Introduction to de Caston's Tricks

In this section a detailed analysis of de Caston's three tricks, as described by Dickens, is attempted. It is assumed, in doing this, that Dickens had accurately recalled what he saw. This might not be so. The reasons for this were well set out in an article called 'How and What to Observe in Relation to Slate-Writing Phenomena'. It was written by Professor Hoffmann, real name Angelo Lewis, the author of *Modern Magic*, the first comprehensive book revealing the conjuring secrets of professional magicians.[17]

---

[16] [Ochorowicz] p 17. I am indebted to David Britland for bringing this book to my attention. It could well be that there are other references to de Caston in French journals and books. One suspects that if a French-speaking researcher decided to investigate de Caston thoroughly, much more would be discovered about this intriguing man.

[17] [Hoffmann, Slates] p. 362

In 1886 Hoffmann was asked to investigate the claims by a certain Mr Eglinton that writing which appeared on slates was produced by spirits. 'Commonly, Eglinton placed a piece of chalk between two slates provided by the sitter. These were then held tightly clamped under a table by both Eglinton and the sitter. After the sound of writing was heard, perhaps twenty lines of writing appeared on the inner surface.'[18] Despite attending twelve sessions with Mr Eglinton, Hoffmann was none the wiser – but only because the medium was unable to produce any results with the well-known conjurer in the room. So Hoffmann was forced to rely on the testimonials of people who had participated in séances where the spirit writing had succeeded. It is worth quoting at some length Hoffmann's preamble to trying to work out Eglinton's possible methods of achieving these spiritual manifestations.

> I am asked to say whether, and to what extent, the phenomena described are consistent with trickery, and to indicate any points wherein the observation of the witnesses is likely to have been defective or misdirected.
>
> It seems to me, however, that a paper confined strictly within the above lines would be too speculative to be of much practical value. Upon the hypothesis of trickery, these accounts must be taken to represent (as do all descriptions of conjuring effects by uninitiated persons) not what the witnesses actually saw, but what they believe they saw, which is a very different matter. The main outlines of each narrative are probably correct; but if the description could be compared with the reality, it would be found that there was a little omission here, a little inaccuracy there; here a circumstance that was not noticed, there another that has been forgotten.
>
> I am not seeking to disparage either the good faith or the general acuteness of the witnesses, but merely stating a defect which is

---

[18] 'Lessons written with a Small Gimmick', Loren Pankratz, [Gibecière] Vol. 3, No. 2, Summer 2008, p. 130.

inseparable from all descriptions of conjuring tricks of which the secret is not known to the describer. I myself claim no exemption from the rule.

For the last quarter of a century I have taken every available opportunity of witnessing conjuring performances, and have made a practice of immediately afterwards taking a careful note of any novel combination or effect. In so doing I frequently find the greatest possible difficulty (even where the general working of the tricks has been clear to me) in recalling *exactly* what was done – the precise sequence of given movements, and the like. Very often a second visit has shown that my first impression was wrong in material particulars.

If such is the experience of a person practically familiar with conjuring, and able to make a pretty close guess at the *modus operandi* of the trick, what chance has an outsider, however acute, of giving a precisely accurate description.

Hoffmann then went on to state how best to work out the exact method of a trick.

In the first place, in order to have a fair chance of detecting the *modus operandi* of a conjuring trick, it is necessary to see it several times repeated. The keenest expert will often be puzzled by a new trick, the first time of seeing it. But on a second visit he will note that some slight and apparently accidental movement, say the mere dropping of a handkerchief or slate, or the turning aside to a table to pick up some object, which occurred (and attracted no particular notice) on the first occasion, is again repeated. It is a reasonable inference that this supposed accident is in reality of the essence of the trick. Having got thus far, his next inquiry will be, What is the object of this particular movement?

It may take two or three more visits satisfactorily to answer this question, but at each additional visit a little more of the veil will be lifted, the inferences drawn will be more certain and more precise, till at last the whole process becomes clear to the patient observer.

The conclusion is that even someone like Dickens, who was

undoubtedly an above-average observer of detail with a far more acute and perceptive eye than most eyewitnesses, is still likely to have missed out some crucial detail in his re-enactment. Of course that is the job of the trickster, again to quote Hoffmann, 'it being the main aim and art of the conjurer to lead the attention of the spectator away from material points, and to direct it upon unimportant matters.'[19]

Nevertheless it is note-worthy that in Dickens's description of de Caston's act, unlike most non-magicians who attempt to remember the details of a trick, he has given sufficient information to give an informed opinion as to possible methods; in addition Dickens had quite an extensive knowledge of conjuring, both from watching conjurers and performing himself. All this renders his observations more trustworthy than your 'average person'. The decision has therefore been made, in attempting to unravel how de Caston's fooled Dickens, to assume that Dickens's transcript was broadly accurate and reliable.[20]

For ease of following the reasoning leading to a possible solution for each trick, the description of each part, as reported by Dickens, has been repeated. There are three: in order they have been named Psychological Forces, the Slate Trick and the Blindfold Act.

---

[19] [Hoffmann, Slates] pp. 362-3. Paragraph breaks have been added from the original text.

[20] The clue to CD apparently reproducing verbatim what de Caston said might lie in Forster writing that 'Another attraction of the camp was a conjuror, who had been called to exhibit *twice* before the imperial party'. [my italics] [Pilgrim, Vol. 7] pp. 433-4. This suggests that maybe CD saw de Caston more than once. It seems unlikely CD would have seen the same repertoire; but perhaps he took care to take particular note of what he was watching the second time around.

## Analysis of Psychological Forces

> You are to observe that he [de Caston] was *with the company*, not in
> the least removed from them; and that we occupied the front row. He
> brought in some writing paper with him when he entered, and a
> black-lead pencil; and he wrote some words on half-sheets of paper.
> One of these half-sheets he folded into two, and gave to Catherine to
> hold.
>
> "Madame", he says aloud, "will you think of any class of objects?"
> "I have done so."
>
> "Of what class, Madame?" "Animals."
>
> "Will you think of a particular animal, Madame?" "I have done so."
> "Of what animal?" "The Lion."
>
> "Will you think of another class of objects, Madame?" "I have done
> so."
>
> "Of what class?" "Flowers."
>
> "The particular flower?" "The Rose."
>
> "Will you open the paper you hold in your hand?"
>
> She opened it, and there was neatly and plainly written in pencil –
> *The Lion. The Rose.* Nothing whatever had led up to these words,
> and they were the most distant conceivable from Catherine's
> thoughts when she entered the room.

The first observation is that this was de Caston's opening trick; this
is because Dickens noted that he 'entered' the room with some
writing paper. There did not seem to be much preamble. De Caston
simply wrote down some words on a piece of paper and handed it
to Dickens's wife; he asked her to name a couple of objects and
when she opened the paper, they were revealed as correctly
predicted. This is how a less conscientious reporter might have
described what happened – in which case it would have been
virtually impossible to work out how de Caston achieved such a
feat. However by including de Caston's patter, Dickens provides
some vital clues.

De Caston was using what mind readers today would recognise

as a 'psychological force'. If you ask someone to name a 'wild animal', the chances are they will name a lion; and similarly, ask someone to name a flower and a rose first comes to mind. It is not clear how de Caston persuaded Dickens's wife to choose 'Animals' and 'Flowers' as the class of objects. However asking someone to name a 'class of objects' is a confusing question; you can imagine the audience member thinking, 'what exactly do you mean by that?' So one suspects de Caston would have guided her answer by saying something like 'name a class of objects – for instance, flowers, animals...'[21]

A clue that this was precisely what de Caston did was given inadvertently by psychologist Dr Julian Ochorowicz in his book *Mental Suggestion* – which was mentioned above in the section 'Solving the Mystery of the French Conjurer'. Ochorowicz related a similar trick performed by de Caston to the one Dickens witnessed, although he described it in a rather confusing manner which makes it hard to follow the plot exactly. But at the denouement the psychologist said that de Caston enquired 'to which of the three kingdoms, mineral, vegetable or animal, the object belonged' before revealing the word written in 'a sealed letter'. This suggests that de Caston had similarly subtlety restricted the 'class of objects' that Dickens's wife could have chosen.[22]

But what if Catherine Dickens had named another animal or another flower; or indeed a different 'class of objects' – would de

---

[21] See [Banachek] pp. 14-15 for how to execute this type of psychological force.

[22] [Ochorowicz] pp. 17-18. For those wanting to question CD's recall of how de Caston did his trick, this description would certainly give them ammunition. Here de Caston seemed to have quite a number of pieces of paper in play with possible words that might be named; and he was asking a number of the participants different questions. It appeared that when he got the right answer from someone, he then drew attention to the relevant predicted word.

Caston had been stumped? Possibly not, because the ever observant Dickens stated upfront that de Caston had written words on several 'half sheets of paper' and one of these 'he folded into two, and gave to Catherine to hold'. De Caston still retained the others, perhaps containing different combinations of animals and flowers, or indeed other possible classes of objects (such as a mineral). If Catherine had come up with some different words, that matched what he had written on another sheet of paper, de Caston probably would have secretly exchanged one for another – in the act of taking it from her and giving it to someone else to open to read.

These type of 'psychological force' tricks are not one hundred per cent guaranteed. De Caston would have had what magicians refer to as 'outs' (a way of seamlessly getting around a trick that has gone wrong without the audience's knowledge); or indeed he might have labelled the trick at the outset as an 'experiment' – it still would have been impressive to his audience if he had only nailed one of the words. As it was, in this instance, it would seem that de Caston struck lucky.

It is conceivable that de Caston had some 'misses' with some of the other sheets of paper (perhaps he handed them out to other members of the audience but then conveniently forgot about them) and that Dickens only recalled the 'hit' with his wife. This is a common ruse that mediums take full advantage of, as sitters tend to forget the information which has no relevance to them, only picking up on, and remembering, that which is important to them. Even if this was the case, de Caston's presentation still must have been exemplary for Dickens to be convinced that 'nothing whatever had led up to these words' which the French conjurer predicted.

Although psychological forces were well-known to twentieth century magicians, there is no record of other nineteenth conjurers using them. It is hard to believe that de Caston somehow discovered these 'population stereotypes', as this sort of statistical bias in naming a certain class of object, when given what appears to be a huge range of possibilities, is called.[23] Nevertheless what is clear, both from Dickens's report – and with the supporting testimony of the psychologist Ochorowicz in his book *Mental Suggestion* – is that de Caston was a master at it.

## Analysis of the Slate Trick

He had several common school-slates about a foot square. He took one of these to a field-officer from the camp, decoré and what not, who sat about six from us, with a grave saturnine friend next to him.

"My General", says he, "will you write a name on this slate, after your friend has done so? Don't show it to me."

The friend wrote a name, and the General wrote a name. The conjuror took the slate rapidly from the officer, threw it violently down on the ground with its written side to the floor, and asked the officer to put his foot upon it, and keep it there: which he did.

The conjuror considered for about a minute, looking devilish hard at the General. "My General", says he, "your friend wrote Dagobert, upon the slate under your foot." The friend admits it.

"And you, my General, wrote Nicholas." General admits it, and everybody laughs and applauds.

"My General, will you excuse me, if I change that name into a name expressive of the power of a great nation, which, in happy alliance with the gallantry and spirit of France will shake that name to its centre?"

---

[23] [Marks] p. 60. [Banahek] p. 15 wrote: 'as far back as the eighteenth century mentalists used the question, *"Name a flower, a color, and a piece of furniture."* After the volunteer named one of each, the mentalist turned over the prediction that had been sitting on table and sure enough, it matched.' Following correspondence with Banachek, he admitted that he had not actually found any references to anyone performing this type of trick in the 18th or, indeed, 19th century.

"Certainly I will excuse it."

"My General, take up the slate and read." General reads: DAGOBERT, VICTORIA. The first in his friend's writing; the second in a new hand.

To help work out the method, it is easier if the effect[24] is set out. Two people secretly wrote down a name on a single slate: one Dagobert, the other Nicholas. The slate was placed on the ground, the writing downwards. De Caston revealed each name in turn. When the slate was lifted up, Nicholas had been replaced by Victoria as the name next to Dagobert.

There were two effects here; firstly, de Caston, without looking at the slate, knew what names were written down; and secondly, one of the names on the slate magically changed. It is likely that the method as to how the second effect was achieved (the name change) will provide a clue as to the method of the first effect (the revelation of the name); so it is how a name can be changed on a slate that needs to be solved.

In the 'How and What to Observe in Relation to Slate-Writing Phenomena' article, quoted from above, Hoffmann conveniently set out all possible methods for achieving the appearance of writing on a slate. They can be summarised as follows:

1. The writing may be then and there performed by the conjurer.

2. A slate, on which writing already exists, may be substituted for the one first shown.

3. The slate used may already have writing upon it, but at the outset invisible, and rendered visible...by the application of some chemical re-agent.

4. A slate may be used with a movable face, which may be discarded

---

[24] Magicians differentiate between the 'effect' – how the trick appears to the spectator; and the 'method' – how the trick is done (or what actually takes place, as opposed to what the audience perceive happens).

at pleasure, and reveal a written surface beneath it.

5. The characters may be "printed" by the medium from some prepared surface. This may be done in the act of drying the newly-sponged slate with blotting-paper.[25]

Methods three and five on Hoffmann's list can be ruled out. This is because the slate already had Dagobert and Nicholas on them before the name change took place. The application of 'some chemical re-agent' or printing on from 'some prepared surface' such as 'blotting- paper', presupposes a blank slate at the outset.

Method one suggests that the conjurer secretly writes the name on the slate. De Caston could in theory have done this by having a writing implement stuck on his finger and writing upside down, his hand underneath the slate as he held it. This was a common technique often practised by Dr Henry Slade and other spiritualists. This is very hard to do nonchalantly, especially when in full view of an audience – as de Caston would have been. Mediums would hide the secret writing by holding the slate under a table.

A couple of other problems arise; firstly, de Caston would have had to secretly rub out the name Nicholas before writing Victoria; and secondly, in order for the effect to be convincing, he would have had to somehow make the name Victoria as neatly written, and of the same approximate size of letters, as Dagobert. All in all the method is too complex and fraught with difficulties.

This leaves methods two and four. Number four is probably the most workable and practical. The slate handed out, which is bounded by a wooden edge, has an extra slate, without any such perimeter, on top of it – this is what Hoffmann called a 'moveable face'; it nestles neatly on top of the slate kept in place by the raised perimeter. Underneath the moveable face, on the genuine slate, is

---

[25] [Hoffmann, Slates] p. 364.

pre-written Dagobert and Victoria. The two helpers write out Dagobert and Nicholas on the top moveable face. At some point, in the course of dropping the slate on the floor, this moveable flap is ditched – and when the slate is picked up the names Dagobert and Victoria are revealed.

There are two possible objections to this method. The first is how did de Caston know that the name Dagobert was to be chosen, so that he could pre-write it on the genuine slate? Victoria, of course was not a problem, because he chose the name himself. The answer would have to be that he pre-arranged before the show with someone to write down Dagobert. This is known to magicians as 'pre-show' work. Is it possible that this happened here? From Dickens's description it is.

Dickens reported that de Caston took one of the slates 'to a field-officer from the camp...with a grave saturnine friend next to him. "My General", says he, "will you write a name on this slate, after your friend has done so? Don't show it to me".' Notice de Caston chose who wrote the names on the slates – there is little doubt that if it had been a genuinely random couple of people chosen, de Caston would have drawn attention to that; and Dickens would have commented on it. As it was, Dickens did not think it was especially significant; which on the surface it was not. The effect was the impossible change of name on the slate; the fact that one of the names remained the same was seemingly irrelevant.

Probably before the show de Caston had decided he wanted to particularly impress the General. So he found out who was going to sit next to him and had a secret conversation with him. He either asked him directly 'to do me a favour' and write down Dagobert; or alternatively sussed out somehow that he would write Dagobert. With that information he was able to pre-write Dagobert and Victoria on the genuine slate and put the moveable face on top. So far, so good.[26]

Unfortunately there is a second objection which cannot be quite so easily overcome; which is that the moveable face had not been invented in 1854. Why might this be? Writing slates can be found as far back as the fourteenth century and they were in common usage in schools by the beginning of the nineteenth century. The moveable face sounds such a simple concept – why would a conjurer not have come up with it as a method for changing some writing on a slate? In order to answer that, a digression is required.

In 1848 a new branch of a semi-religious belief system, which was to have a profound impact on conjuring for the rest of the nineteenth, and well into the twentieth century, began in America. It was started by a couple of teenage girls, Kate and Margaret Fox, who attracted the sound of rappings, or knockings, in their presence. It was quickly assumed that the noise came from a spirit of some sort, and by devising a simple code – one knock for 'yes', two for 'no' – together with words been spelt out by raps which were heard when the appropriate letter of the alphabet on a basic Ouija board was pointed to – conversations could be had with the deceased person.

Other manifestations of this kind had occurred before; most notably in London with the Cock Lane Ghost of nearly ninety years previously. But what made this incident different was that the populace were now receptive to the scientific possibility (in particular mesmerism had already seemed to have opened up hitherto unexplored insights into what humans were capable of experiencing), as well as the obvious emotional appeal of the ability to communicate with the departed. Added to this, there was the

---

[26] There are numerous methods for finding out secretly before a show what a spectator is going to write down, without that spectator being aware the conjurer knows it. A good starting point for anyone wanting to research this further is *13 Steps to Mentalism* by Tony Corinda.

entrepreneurial nature of an older Fox sister, Leah, who turned the playful pranks of her younger siblings into money-making séances.

Due to the fame and financial success of the Fox sisters, other mediums jumped on the bandwagon and before long Spiritualism, as it was known, became a fully-fledged quasi-religious movement, attracting not just the general populous but also many of the intelligentsia to its cause. It also spread rapidly overseas to England and mainland Europe.

Although rapping was the initial means of communicating with the spirits, other methods quickly evolved. This was partly to render the séances more exciting and partly so that individual mediums could specialise and therefore stand out in what was becoming an increasingly competitive market for potential clients. In 1852 Adin Ballou wrote a book called *Spirit Manifestations* and listed some of the numerous ways of interacting with the spirit world which had been developed since its rather crude beginnings.

These included making peculiar noises by rappings, knockings, jarrings, creakings; the movement of material substances such as tables, sofas, chairs including shaking, tipping and sliding; causing catalepsy, trance and clairvoyance; presenting apparitions of spirit arms, hands and sometimes the whole person; and writing with pens, pencils and other substances, both liquid and solid, sometimes on paper, sometimes on common slates and sometimes on the ceiling of a room.[27]

Spiritualism almost straightaway imposed a challenge to conjurers – as mediums were potentially capable of feats as mystifying as anything the ordinary trickster could come up with. Should they therefore embrace it and essentially present their own magic tricks as similarly caused by some unknown power? This was the route taken by the Davenport Brothers who, despite been tied and locked up inside a cabinet, were able to produce inexplicable

[27] [Ballou] pp. 7-8.

phenomena such as bells ringing, musical instruments playing and objects hurtling out of the top of the oversized wardrobe. Calling their place of incarceration a 'spirit cabinet' and having a spiritual lecturer to introduce them, indirectly inferred that these happenings were not caused by conventional magic trickery.

It is a dangerous game to play; as you are directly challenging your audience to catch you out in a way which does not necessarily happen if you make it clear that you are using trickery. Certainly the Davenport Brothers came up against some difficulties; an angry audience once smashed their cabinet to pieces when their ropes were bound so tightly that they were unable to escape and carry out their 'spiritual manifestations'. But the plus side is that you are liable to attract a larger and more inquisitive audience than when putting on a traditional conjuring show.[28]

The other approach, favoured by most conjurers, is to pour scorn on the spiritualists, claim that they, too, are using magic tricks – but ones that are grossly inferior to those of the professional conjurer. This was the path adopted by John Henry Anderson. In his booklet *The Fashionable Science of Parlour Magic*, which was sold from 1843 onwards right through his career, he added in around 1854 a section on Spirit Rapping which supposedly revealed the methods of spiritualists.

And yet, in an attempt to have his cake and eat it, Anderson also presented 'his own Magical Illustration of Spiritualism' which comprised 'Drums, Tables, Bells and Trumpets', which were 'magically Spiritualised'. They were 'placed in the midst of the audience' and would 'rap replies to questions addressed to them'.[29]

---

[28] [Price] pp. 444-5. The Davenport Brothers arrived in England, from America, in 1864 [Clarke] p. 297: so it is possible CD saw them. After they had completed all their tours, they had net earnings in excess of £100,000.

[29] [Toole Stott] No. 24, p. 26: 'The Magic of Spirit Rapping, first added to The Fashionable Science of Parlour Magic c. 1847'. This is too early, as it pre-dates

But what has all this got to do with the non-invention of a moveable slate face? The point is that the idea of making words appear on a slate emerged directly from the spiritualist movement. Up to that time no-one had come up with such an effect for a trick. You can understand why. Conjuring up writing would hardly seem as impressive as pulling a rabbit from a hat or producing a piece of fruit from an empty cup.

With Spiritualism came motivation – if the message was written by a deceased person that *was* impressive. The next logical stage, after hearing from a rapping spirit, was for the unworldly being to communicate by writing. It began in a rather crude manner – mediums would channel the spirit of someone departed by participating in 'automatic writing'. Whilst in a mesmeric trance or similar cataleptic state, they would pick up a pen or pencil and start frantically writing down, powerless to resist, the dead person's thoughts and observations; which usually turned out to be less than insightful.

It was soon realised that it would be better, and easier as it required less histrionics on the part of medium, to miss out the middle man, or indeed woman. And so evolved the appearance of writing without the assistance of human agencies. In the *Book of Human Nature*, Laroy Sunderland claimed that this first occurred on 28th July, 1850 when, 'letters written by spirits [were] thrown from the air in the presence of Dr Phelps, or some of his family.'[30]

---

the birth of Spiritualism: however as Anderson's pamphlets were not dated, it is not possible to know the exact date the supplement was added. The reference to spiritualists tricks is on an Anderson programme dated 23 to 27 Jan 1865, [Gibecière] Summer 2006, Vol. 1, No. 2, p. 34.

[30] [Sunderland] pp. 279-280. However [Capron] p. 155 argued that 'Spirit-writing, without visible human agency, has never been a common mode of communicating, although it was among the early occurrences at Hydesville, Rochester and Auburn. Mr Sunderland, in his "Book of Human Nature", p.

It is unlikely that third-hand spirit writing of this sort, on the say-so of rather dubious testimonials, would satisfy all spiritualists, however gullible they might seem to outside scrutiny. It would be preferable, and much more convincing, if some sort of experiment could be devised whereby people could actually directly witness the appearance of writing. Suppose the medium could start with a clearly blank canvas and then writing would somehow materialise, courtesy of a spirit?

The first mention of this is in an 1855 book called *Modern Spiritualism*, which quoted from a letter dated April 12th, 1853. The medium's client was 'directed to put paper and pencil on the drawer. I placed several sheets of unruled letter-paper, together with a wood pencil, on it. I soon heard the sound of the pencil on the paper...On being directed to look at the paper, I discovered pencil marks on each side of the outer sheet.' In another session, under similar testing conditions, an actual sentence was written purported to be in the hand of a deceased person.[31]

Doubtless it was discovered by trial and error that it was easier to manipulate a slate than a piece of paper. A hard surface could be held in one hand – or more likely hidden from view under a table – enabling the other hand to scribble some words. If the writing wanted to be rather more robust, then one slate could be exchanged for another when placed inside a drawer, or again under a table.

The man who brought slate trickery in séances to a new height was Dr Henry Slade, many of whose secrets were revealed in the book *The Bottom Facts Concerning the Science of Spiritualism*, although the author was a little sketchy in some of his explanations: these included exchanging a slate with an assistant, secretly writing

280, says this was the first of the spirit-writing, but he is in error. The author of this work was acquainted with cases of this kind long before the disturbances at Stratford.'

[31] [Capron] pp. 347 & 353-4.

whilst the slate was under a table, pretending to show both sides of four slates 'by sleight of hand', and scratching the slate with his finger to mimic the sound of writing. [32]

Henry Slade was born in 1835 and had apparently been active in his mediumistic slate trickery since around 1860. [33] It is thought that he invented the moveable face. [34] The exact date that Slade, if indeed it was him, came up with this gimmick, or flap as it is now known to magicians, will probably never be discovered. The general consensus is that it was no earlier than 1870. [35] However the earliest

---

[32] The author wrote his sundry explanations of how Slade operated here: [Truesdell] pp. 147& 291-5. But he noted: 'As to how he produced the writing when the slate was under the table, no one could explain (and indeed it still remains unaccounted for).'

[33] [Mann] pp. 971-2 stated that Slade was 'known as a medium from approximately 1860'. No evidence of Slade's slate work prior to 1870 has been found by this writer but [Barkas] p. 40 describes a séance conducted by a Mrs Marshall and her niece on 16 November, 1861 where the writing of a name appeared on a slate placed underneath a table. It would seem, from the description, that one of the two women used their foot to write with the pencil, although both the women's feet were 'covered by ordinary boots'.

[34] In [Whaley, Dictionary, Vol. 1] p. 280 it is stated that the flap slate was 'first reported by Truesdell as being used by the American pseudo-psychic Henry Slade in 1872'. In his [Whaley, Who's Who] p. 297, written two years later, it is claimed Henry Slade 'invented' the flap slate, presumably with reference again to Truesdell. In fact there is no mention of Slade when [Truesdell] pp. 318-22 gave instructions on how to construct and use the moveable face.

[35] [Goldston] p. 20: 'Several tricks slates have been invented since the loose flap which was first introduced to the public in the year 1870.' However Al Mann wrote that the 'flap and the locking flap slates was known by a small group of magicians and mediums long before 1870' [Mann] p. 982; but provided no evidence of this. As far as mediums were concerned the use of flaps would have been risky. As Peter Lamont, an expert on Victorian Spiritualism, pointed out in an email to the author, 'the problem for a medium would be that discovery of a flap would be clear evidence of fraud'. With regard to

date at which the workings of the flap is properly revealed is 1877 in Sachs's *Sleight of Hand*, where the author wrote about a slate that has 'an extra or false interior'.[36]

All of the above may be considered an unnecessarily long preamble merely to show that method four of Hoffmann's list of possible ways of de Caston executing the slate trick was not feasible; but it was necessary to prove that the slate with the moveable face definitely did not exist in 1854. Also, though, the significance of de Caston's far-reaching and groundbreaking magic is better judged and understood in the context of the fascination with Spiritualism that prevailed at the time.[37]

magicians, Sachs in his 1877 edition of [Sachs, 1st] pp. 191-2, wrote that the flap slate 'is scarcely a trick for grown audiences', (although he went on to write 'others and myself are improving the trick a great deal'), suggesting that even as late as this date, magicians were not really utilising it. In the second, enlarged edition of the same book, Sachs did elaborate a little on his improvements in using the flap - see [Sachs, 2nd] p. 387.

[36] Sachs continued: 'The answer that is to be given is written upon the genuine slate, and the false side then put on. The slate is shown casually around without leaving the performer's hands, and a question is then written upon one side of the slate, which is waved about, and an opportunity seized for allowing the false side to drop out behind the table or at any other convenient place, and the answer is then exhibited.' [Sachs, 1st] p. 192.

[37] It is also quite possible that the slates de Caston was using did not have the wooden edges enabling the interior slate to be inserted. The slates used by JN Hofzinser – in a very different trick – who was performing around the same time, had no borders to them. See [Hatch] pp. 129-33. [Mann] p. 982 wrote that there was a rumour that Hofzinser's 'German notes contain a reference to a locking flap slate'. However consultation with Magic Christian, who has thoroughly researched Hofzinser, revealed this is not so. There is also a cartoon of de Caston holding a slate [see Plate 18], clearly relating to his blindfold revelation of dates, dealt with below, which does not appear to have borders. On consultation with an expert who had done some research into slates, his conclusion was that 'references to slates are pretty generic and

Having eliminated all the other Hoffmann methods, there is only one remaining: 'A slate, on which writing already exists, may be substituted for the one first shown.' In other words the probability is that de Caston secretly exchanged the slate written on by his two helpers (one of whom was a stooge), with another slate which he had prepared before the show. Does this fit in with Dickens's description?

It does in two crucial respects. Firstly, Dickens stated upfront that de Caston 'had several common school-slates about a foot square.' So one of those could have included the prepared slate. Dickens then wrote that de Caston 'took one of these to a field-officer from the camp'. This could mean that de Caston was casually holding the others as he handed a blank slate over. No attention would have been paid to the other slates, all concentration centred on the slate given to the General and his companion.

The second clue lies in what happened once the names were written on the slate. De Caston, wrote Dickens, 'took the slate rapidly from the officer, threw it violently down on the ground with its written side to the floor, and asked the officer to put his foot upon it, and keep it there: which he did.' It was almost certainly in that rapid action and possible 'out-of-character' violent throwing down on the ground, that the exchange of slates was made. This would be akin to a move known to magicians in card magic called the 'top change'. It is where a single card held in one hand is exchanged for the top card of the deck of cards held in the other.[38]

---

wooden frames barely get a mention in the 19C, to my knowledge': email from Peter Davies, 2014. He also wrote that the reason for the wooden frame was to secure 'the edge of the slate and helped protect fingers from splinters.' From: 'Writing Slates and Schooling', *Australasian Historical Archaeology*, 23, 2005, Peter Davies p. 64.

[38] Another possible way of exchanging the slates would be for de Caston to have the prepared slate hidden inside his jacket. On turning, he could take out this

If there was no swapping of the slate at this stage, de Caston would have done everything slowly and deliberately to emphasise the fairness of placing the slate on the ground. Indeed he probably would have had the General place the slate on the ground himself. However de Caston needed to take it from him in order to execute the switch of slates. Once done, he threw it on the ground. The fact that he asked the officer to 'put his foot upon it' suggests that by now the exchange had been made. De Caston was taking the precaution of ensuring that no-one could prematurely turn the slate over and spoil the climax of his trick.

The only other piece of the puzzle is how he knew in advance what name the General had written. The answer is clear now it is postulated that de Caston traded one slate for another. Doubtless he would have moved away to one side to discard the pile of slates he was holding – which also contained the written-upon slate. It would have been easy for him at this point to secretly read the name Nicholas.

Intriguingly Professor Hoffmann himself came up with a couple of methods of performing de Caston's slate trick – but with playing cards. They were written up in his Notebook C, which is in the New York Public Library. The heading of the two relevant pages was <u>Idea suggested by trick of French conjuror described in Volume 3 of Dickens' life</u>, a clear reference to Forster's biography. Both of Hoffmann's versions involve a confederate and a secret exchange (although here, of course, of a playing card); which provides further confirmation that the method outlined above as to how de Caston did his slate trick is a reasonable guess.[39]

---

slate, whilst undetectably putting the other back under the jacket in its place.

[39] Notebooks are undated but were probably written around 1875-80. They can be found in The Manuscripts Division, Miscellaneous Subjects: Magic collection, MssCol 1836, New York Public Library. Thanks to Will Houstoun for drawing these to my attention.

When it comes to trying to work out methods of how conjurers performed tricks over one hundred and fifty years ago, inevitably there is a great deal of speculation involved. Possibly wisely, therefore, no other magician has tried to reconstruct how de Caston achieved this stunning effect. The editors of Dickens's letters do cite Henri Garenne's *The Art of Modern Conjuring* to explain 'how the trick is done'. Garenne described the flap, or moveable face, method in his explanation of a completely different trick – whereby a numbered total magically appears on a previously shown blank slate; so it cannot even be close to the solution.[40]

## Analysis of the Blindfold Act

One more. He was blinded with several table napkins, and then a great cloth was bodily thrown over them and his head too, so that his voice sounded as if he were under a bed. Perhaps half a dozen dates were written on a slate.

He takes the slate in his hand, and throws it violently down on the floor as before, remains silent a minute, seems to become agitated, and bursts out thus: "What is this I see? A great city, but of narrow streets and old–fashioned houses, many of which are of wood, resolving itself into ruins! How is it falling into ruins? Hark! I hear the crackling of a great conflagration, and, looking up, I behold a vast cloud of flame and smoke. The ground is covered with hot cinders too, and people are flying into the fields and endeavouring to save their goods. This great fire, this great wind, this roaring noise! This is

---

[40] [Garenne] 'The Spirit Slate Trick', pp. 299-302, cited by [Pilgrim, Vol. 7] p. 435, n 2. This book was notorious for having ripped off [Hoffmann, Modern Magic]. Hoffmann certainly thought so as he inscribed in his own copy of Garenne's book that it was 'a rank piracy and was suppressed accordingly': 'Inconsequentialities', *The Linking Ring*, Vol. 27, October 1947, p. 40. This is one of the rare occasions where the Pilgrim Editors have made an incorrect reference to a conjuring source – a remarkable testimony to the scholarship involved in the compilation of CD's letters.

the great fire of London, and the first date upon the slate must be one, six, six, six – the year in which it happened."

And so on with all the other dates. There!

It is instructive to compare this description of Dickens with that of Chorley witnessing his performance of de Caston.

> There were three of us sitting on an ottoman in the front room, he, as I have said, with his back to us, and thoroughly blindfolded. Two opaque porcelain slates, to all appearance entirely new, were brought. On one of these, each of the three wrote, in pencil, a question, without uttering a word. The slates were laid face to face, and bound together with a broad ribbon, thus totally clear of transparency. My question was, in French, "What was the colour of Cleopatra's hair?" I forget the other two.
>
> The Chevalier put his hands behind his chair. I placed the slates so bound in the two hands. He retained them a moment, without staring or turning, and, to my amazement, said, "Cleopatra dyed her hair, so wore all colours." The other two questions, which I have forgotten, were no less pertinently and explicitly answered. Now, even on the theory of complicity, it would be by no means easy to explain this feat. I can only say that I am satisfied that I have recounted it accurately.[41]

The principal difference is that in Dickens's account only one slate was used; whilst in Chorley's there were two. In the former, the written side of the slate was hidden by placing it on the ground; in the latter, another slate was used to cover the writing and they were tied together. In both cases de Caston would have had to contrive looking secretly at what was written on the slates.

Counterintuitively, being blindfolded does not actually make the procedure harder, indeed it makes it simpler. Despite having your

[41] [Chorley, Vol. 2] pp. 222-3.

eyes covered by various opaque objects – such as napkins – it is still possible to look down the side of your nose and secretly read information. As the audience are unaware of this, there are more opportunities to execute this clandestine 'peeking'.

The supposition is that Dickens's narrative was more accurate; he made clear that it was de Caston who took back the slate and held it in his hand, before chucking it down. It was almost certainly at this moment that the 'peek' was made. Chorley, significantly, failed to mention who actually placed the two slates together prior to the tying. If, as seems likely, this was done by de Caston himself, then that would have been the time to perform the 'peek'. It is another indication of what an excellent visual memory Dickens had for all the intricate details.

The idea of secretly obtaining information from a slate whilst blindfolded did not originate with de Caston. In 1831 the eight-year-old Louis M'Kean was discerning messages on a slate held by his father even though his eyes were covered by a handkerchief and he had his back to the audience.[42] More interestingly, though, Dickens had previously seen the exploits of someone claiming to see through a blindfold. This was Alexis Didier, a sixteen year old from France who was nicknamed the Magnetic Boy.

Dickens wrote to the Countess of Blessington on 2nd June, 1841 urging her to see him.

Have you seen the Magnetic boy? You heard of him no doubt from Count D'Orsay. If you get him to Gore House, don't, I entreat you, have more than eight people – four is a better number – to see him. He fails in a crowd, and is *marvellous* before a few.

---

[42] 'Vernon the Mesmerist', Peter Lamont [Gibecière] Summer 2008, Vol. 3, No. 2 p. 42. A bill of 'Young Master M'Kean' is reproduced in [Houdini, Conjurers' Monthly] Vol. 1, No. 6, February, 1907, p. 184.

Dickens had also lauded the 'wonders of this boy, under the effect of magnetism, producing such wonderful effects' to his actor friend, William Macready. Didier was paraded around by a man called Chauncy Hare Townshend who mesmerised him prior to each performance thereby providing the rationale for his abilities.[43]

Someone else who saw Didier, only a couple of weeks before Dickens, was Frances Kemble. She describes the experience rather more sceptically:

> The clairvoyant power of the young man consisted principally in reading passages from books presented to him while under the influence of the mesmeric sleep, into which he had been thrown by Mr. Townsend, and with which he was previously unacquainted. The results were certainly sufficiently curious, though probably neither marvellous nor unaccountable. To make sure that his eyes were really effectually closed, cotton-wool was laid over them, and a broad, tight bandage placed upon them; during another trial the hands of our chief sceptic were placed upon his eyelids, so as effectually to keep them completely closed, in spite of which he undoubtedly read out of a book held up before him above his eyes, and rather on a level with his forehead; nor can I remember any instance in which he appeared to find any great difficulty in doing so, except when a book suddenly fetched from another room was opened before him, when he hesitated and expressed incapacity, and then said, "The book is French;" which it was.

Although written retrospectively, Kemble was not impressed. Her summing up was that the 'young lad Alexis, to whom I have referred in this letter was, I think, one of the first of the long train of mesmerists, magnetizers, spiritualists, charlatans, cheats, and humbugs who subsequently appealed to the notice and practised on

[43] [Pilgrim, Vol. 2] pp. 291-2. [Macready] Vol. 2, pp. 135-6: the reference was found in [Kaplan, Mesmerism] p. 65.

the credulity of London society.'[44]

It is evident that Dickens saw a very similar repertoire as Frances Kemble as he wrote in the next paragraph in his letter to the Countess of Blessington: 'I am told that down in Devonshire there are young ladies innumerable, who read crabbed Manuscript with the palm of their hands – newspapers with their ankles – and so forth, and who are, so to speak, literary all over.' For Dickens the power of mesmerism, which he passionately believed in and practised later, convinced him that someone could read through bandages. He therefore failed to see the inherent irony in pouring scorn on anyone who might believe someone could read by merely placing the palms of their hands on top of the printed matter.

Henry Chorley had also seen Didier and wrote about him just after extolling de Caston. Like Kemble, but unlike Dickens, he did not find him convincing; and indeed carried out a ruse to entrap Didier. The mesmerist was fooled into thinking Chorley had written down a particular word on a sealed piece of paper. Chorley did this by stage-whispering the word to a friend. Didier took the bait and revealed the word he had heard, rather than the written down one.

Whether Dickens was ever similarly 'unconvinced' of Didier's ability, it is not known. In any event he failed to make any connection between the blindfold act of Didier and that of de Caston. There is though an intriguing coda to Dickens relating his experience of seeing de Caston. Having finished describing his final trick, Dickens wrote: 'There! Now, if you will take a cab and impart these mysteries to Rogers, I shall be very glad to have his opinion of them.'

Forster expanded on this by asserting that Rogers, who was Samuel Rogers the banker-poet, 'had taxed our credulity with some wonderful clairvoyant experiences of his own in Paris, to which here

[44] [Kemble] pp. 228-9.

was a parallel at last!'[45] And who was it that Samuel Rogers saw? None other than the same Alexis Didier, now a young man of twenty eight and presumably still up to some of his old tricks. It is unlikely, however, that Dickens worked out that Samuel Rogers was talking about the same man who had so impressed him some thirteen years previously; because Rogers described a somewhat different feat of Didier's to the blindfold reading.

> When I was at Paris, I went to Alexis, and desired him to describe to me my house in St. James's Place. On my word, he astonished me! He described most exactly the peculiarities of the stair case – said that not far from the window in the drawing-room there was a picture of a man in armour (the painting by Giorgione), &c. &c.
>
> Colonel Gurwood, shortly before his death, assured me that he was reminded by Alexis of some circumstances which had happened to him in Spain, and which he could not conceive how any human being, except himself, should know.
>
> Still, I cannot believe in clairvoyance – *because the thing is impossible.*[46]

Leaving Rogers to try to square his particular circle, there are other reasons why it is unsurprising that Dickens would not associate de Caston with Alexis Didier, for what de Caston clearly had, in addition to great technical ability, were wonderful presentational skills. The way he threw the slates 'violently down' on to the floor gave a focus to what he was about to do, suggesting to his audience that something strange was about to happen. It also gave the impression of somebody not entirely in control of their own behaviour – just the type of man who would be capable of revealing hidden thoughts.

Furthermore de Caston's way of revealing the date was doubly

[45] [Pilgrim, Vol. 7] p. 435, n 2.
[46] [Rogers] p. 290.

perplexing as, rather than focusing on the year 1666 which was written down, he seemed to visualise what happened in that year. He talked about a 'great city...of narrow streets and old–fashioned houses, many of which are of wood... I hear the crackling of a great conflagration...The ground is covered with hot cinders too, and people are flying into the fields and endeavouring to save their goods. This great fire, this great wind, this roaring noise!' He concluded that it could only be the Great Fire of London and therefore the year must be 1666.

De Caston's entire act is a master class in construction; he began with some psychological tests (which may, or may not, work – a sort of warm up), then on to the disclosures, and appearances, of 'thought-of' names; and concluding with impossible revelations whilst blindfolded. All of these could easily be performed by a modern day mind reader and be just as impressive and mysterious.

De Caston did not just restrict himself to mind reading stunts; when Dickens saw him, he also performed card tricks. According to Forster, de Caston 'transformed cards into very demons'. Dickens 'never saw a human hand touch them in the same way, fling them about so amazingly, or change them in his, one's own, or another's hand, with a skill so impossible to follow.' However Dickens does not go into detail as to what he did with cards, probably because that was not what truly amazed him. It is possible to at least have some sort of explanation for a skilled sleight of hand performer, but when somebody appears to be picking up your thoughts, then you do not even know where to start in untangling the solution.[47]

---

[47] [Forster, Vol. 3] Chapter IV, 'Three Summers at Boulogne'. Forster also wrote that 'the Frenchman scorned help, stood among the company without any sort of apparatus, and, by the mere force of sleight of hand and an astonishing memory, performed feats having no likeness to anything Dickens had ever seen done, and totally inexplicable to his most vigilant reflection.' The lack of apparatus must have particularly impressed CD as it was that on which he

It has been seen earlier how far ahead of his time de Caston was in producing an appearing message on a slate; but it is conceivable that he was way ahead in other respects too. Barry H Wiley in 'The Thought-Reader Craze' wrote that 'unlike most acts in the genres of magic and mentalism, the origin of the thought-reading act can be precisely identified and dated. It was created by the American, John Randall Brown. Brown was the first person to perform a one-man mental act; or more precisely, an act focused entirely on creating the illusion of mind reading, and not relying on hidden assistants or confederates, as did the second-sight acts of the time.'[48]

It is certainly arguable that de Caston's act, at least as described by Dickens, contradicts this assertion. When Brown was a mere two years old, the Frenchman very much 'focused entirely on creating the illusion of mind reading'. The only difference is that Brown specifically called himself a 'Mind Reader' in his publicity. De Caston made no such claims; indeed Dickens referred to him both at the time, and afterwards, merely as a conjurer – albeit as a rather strange and weird one.[49]

relied for his own conjuring.

[48] [Wiley] p. 21. The 'second-sight' act is what de Caston gave credit to Robert-Houdin for performing, see note 2 above.

[49] [Wiley] p. 22: Brown did his first one-man mental act on 5 August, 1873 in a Chicago drinking establishment aged 21. [Wiley] p. 35: the poster, which was previously cited in note 1 above, also proclaimed that 'He takes your Hand and Reads Your Thoughts', a reference to Brown's skill at contact mindreading – finding a hidden object whilst blindfolded and holding on to the person who hid it. As revealed in his letter to Wilkie Collins on 26 September, 1854, CD wrote 'that the great Conjuror lives at his hotel, has extra wine every day, and fares expensively. Is he the Devil?' [Pilgrim, Vol. 7] p. 425.

## Analysis of Dickens's explanation of the Sphinx Illusion

Dickens's explanation of the Sphinx to his daughter Mamie is not just interesting to magic historians as to how Dickens was deceived, but also in his actual depiction of the illusion, particularly in the way it began. The most commonly quoted depiction of the trick is in Hoffmann's *Modern Magic* and here Stodare walked on stage carrying the box which he placed on a three legged table. He opened it up and the sphinx began talking. In contrast, according to Dickens, when the curtain was raised, the box was on another table down stage (nearer the audience); it was picked up from there and placed on the three legged table. Did Dickens get some detail wrong?[50]

Hoffmann's description appears to be substantiated by an article written in 1866 by Henry Hatton in which the author similarly stated that the 'exhibitor' entered holding in his hand a 'green baize box about two feet and a half square'. He placed the box directly onto the 'small round-topped table, made with a very slight frame, and without a cloth, or anything about it, which might be used for the purpose of concealment.'[51]

---

[50] CD's letter to his daughter Mamie, was written on 14 November, 1865, [Pilgrim, Vol. 11] p. 108. [Williams] referenced this letter twice in his booklet, but in a manner that suggested there were two different letters. On p.6 he wrote that there was 'correspondence about conjuring between Dickens and his daughter Mamie, in which he explains, in considerable detail, how various tricks that have puzzled her are done (though none of them his own).' The 'various tricks' would be Colonel Stodare's Sphinx illusion and the Instantaneous Growth of Flowers. And on p. 7, he declared that Dickens described 'the working of the 'Sphinx' illusion, in a letter to his daughter'.

[51] It was reproduced in 'Lessons in Magic' in *Sphinx*, Vol. 20, October 1921, p. 274 by PH Cannon (Henry Hatton), sub-titled 'From "Our Young Folks," November, 1866'. *Sphinx* is the name of a magic journal that was issued monthly from 1902 to 1953; and has nothing to do with the illusion of the

However there was another eyewitness, a theatrical manager called Alfred Thompson, who gave a rather different account.

> On a side table near the proscenium stood a handsome plush-covered box about a foot square, or fourteen inches every way. The lid unlocked by Stodare was opened on the side facing the spectators, and in it was seen the head of the Sphinx. A life-sized head of a handsome Egyptian wearing the typical striped head piece and the same collarette round the severed neck; for there was nothing but a head on a short neck in the box. The eyes were closed and the long eye-lashes fell on the cheek, which glowed through its Pharaoh bronze with vital blood. Closing the lid for a moment, Stodare carried this box by a handle on either side from the front to the three-legged table before our eyes, and set it down in the center.[52]

This report seems to accord with what Dickens saw – although he had not mentioned the presence of the sphinx when the box was initially shown. Could both reports be right? It is possible, as Stodare could easily have changed his way of presenting the trick over the course of his long run at the Egyptian Hall. Thompson claimed he attended the first ever performance; maybe the dummy head, which must have been in the first box, did not look realistic enough to be mistaken for a human head. So later Stodare decided to go straight to the talking-head part of the illusion.[53]

same name. Confusingly, a letter appeared in *Mahatma*, also written by Henry Hatton, where he claimed 'Stodare first carried a dummy head into the audience and used ventriloquism to make it, apparently, speak.' [Mahatma] Vol. IV, April, 1901, p. 462.

[52] Taken from The *Pocahontas Record*, 5 August, 1886, Vol. 3, Issue No. 16 by Captain Alfred Thompson, although it probably first appeared in the *New York Morning Journal*. It was reproduced in *Sphinx* by HR Evans where he stated the author was 'the well-known theatrical manager and raconteur'.

[53] Towards the end of his run, which finished in June 1866, Stodare was unwell from TB. He might well have cut out parts of his act to save his strength.

Dickens's attempted explanation of the illusion, with trap doors in the stage for a confederate to come up, and traps in the table for the head of the sphinx to emerge through, demonstrated his own knowledge of both theatres and conjuring. Many tops of conjuring tables in Victorian times concealed a 'trap' – it was used to secretly drop in, and pick up, items. And trap doors on stages were of course very common. In practice, with some notable exceptions, most conjurers rarely made use of trap doors for their illusions; this was because they were itinerant performers who had to be able to perform in any venue – whether a trap door was available or not.

The presence of the first table confused Dickens in his explanation. He could not think why it should have been there on stage at all, apart from to conceal a trap door. It is presumed he had forgotten that Stodare displayed the 'dummy sphinx' before he moved the box to the upstage table. Having convinced himself that trap doors were necessary for the performance of this trick – and indeed the previous one of the Instantaneous Growth of Flowers – Dickens then came up with the rather convoluted scenario of a confederate emerging from one to assist the person playing the part of the sphinx, who was apparently concealed in the top of the table.[54]

The table itself which was used in the actual illusion, as described by various commentators, had a very thin top – Alfred Thompson wrote there was 'no room for a drawer beneath the table'; and in the illustration on the front of Modern Magic there is very little recess – certainly insufficient to conceal a person inside. However the only known photograph taken of Colonel Stodare with the Sphinx illusion (it was a publicity photo, not taken on stage, and clearly,

---

[54] Needless to say the execution of the Instantaneous Growth of Flowers did not require trapdoors either. An explanation of the possible method used by Stodare for this trick is described in 'Modern Magicians and their Tricks', HR Evans, [Mahatma] Vol. IV, Feb. 1901, p. 445.

because it has four legs, not the same table as was used in the theatre) shows a table which could well have had somebody hidden in its top (see Plate 24). So, again, Dickens's theory about where the sphinx might have been concealed is understandable.

Sadly Colonel Stodare did not reap the deserved benefits of his success. On 11th June, 1866 he had to stop performing due to the onset of tuberculosis and on 22nd October, 1866 he died aged 35.[55] The full explanation of the Sphinx, along with illustrations, can be found in Hoffmann's *Modern Magic*.[56]

## Pepper's Ghost and *The Haunted Man*

It is probably fair to say that magicians are most familiar with Charles Dickens, when it comes to magic, as the author of *The Haunted Man*: this was because it was the first story to feature 'the greatest theatrical illusion of the day, "Pepper's Ghost".'[57] *The Haunted Man*, or to give it its full title, *The Haunted Man and the Ghost's Bargain, A Fancy for Christmas-Time*, was written in 1848 and appeared on 19th December. Despite Dickens announcing it as an immense success, it fared relatively poorly, selling six thousand fewer than the previous Christmas novella, *The Battle of Life*. Many readers found the story 'confused and confusing'.[58]

Given this, it seems a surprising selection by Professor Pepper,

---

[55] Information about Stodare is primarily from [Stodare, Dawes]: birth, p. 21; name change, pp. 28ff; the anecdote with the genuine colonel, pp. 22-3; the description of the Instantaneous Flower Growth, p. 63; Anderson failing to buy the Sphinx & Stodare buying it, p. 68; the 'something like eloquence' quotation which was from *The Times*, 19 October, 1865, cited on p. 72; TB, p. 87; and death, p. 102.

[56] [Hoffmann, Modern Magic] pp. 471-5. This was also cited in [Pilgrim, Vol. 11] p. 108 n. 1

[57] [Jay, Celebrations] p. 73.

[58] [Slater] p. 281.

the very astute scientific showman, to accompany his sensational new illusion at the Polytechnic Institute in 1862. One might have thought that a preferable choice would have been a scene from the better known and more popular *A Christmas Carol*, a book with plenty of ghosts on offer. It seems though the decision to use *The Haunted Man* was made long before Pepper came on the scene.[59]

The illusion itself was invented by Henry Dircks, a civil engineer. In 1858 he presented a model of what he called his phantasmagoria to the British Association for the Advancement of Science in Leeds. In his rather bitter book telling his side of the story in the creation of Pepper's Ghost – 'bitter' because he felt he was never given credit for his invention and that its name was hijacked by Pepper – Dircks wrote: 'In 1858, offers were made through several advertisements in *The Times*, of the Optical Illusions in question for illustrating the story of *Dickens' Haunted Man*, &c.'[60]

Clearly *The Haunted Man* had a resonance to Dircks, perhaps because the anti-hero, Redlaw, was also a man of science, albeit a chemist. As his version of events showed, he was not just putting out *The Haunted Man* as an idea for a theatrical presentation of the phantasmagoria, he had ambitiously sketched how the 'very sullen and sulky' actor and ghost would interact with each other – although he did at least omit stage directions. He was convinced that the 'well-known Christmas piece of that name', alongside his invention, would 'command a double interest'.[61]

In this respect he was over ambitious. The main reason for the lack of single, yet alone double, interest amongst theatre owners was that under Dircks's initial design the concealed ghost and the actor

---

[59] The 1866 Christmas programme at the Institute did include 'a dramatic reading of Dickens' *A Christmas Carol*, during which a succession of ghosts silently walked the stage.' [Weeden] p. 80.

[60] [Weeden] pp. 73-4; [Dircks] pp. 4-5.

[61] [Dircks] p. 65.

were on the same level, which meant the audience had to watch from a balcony above. This was totally impractical for most venues, as it would mean losing seats in the stalls. When Dircks presented his idea at the Institute to Professor Pepper four years on, it was the latter who had the ingenious thought of sloping the glass so that the ghost and the illuminating light could be housed in the pit at the front of the stage. It did create some other difficulties, such as the actor having to be permanently at an angle in order to appear upright on the stage; but this was at least soluble without overhauling an entire theatre.[62]

However Dircks at least had his way in using *The Haunted Man* as the presentation. Even before Pepper did his initial performance on 24th December, 1862 to a private view of a 'number of literary and scientific friends, and my always kind supporters, the members of the press', that year's Christmas programme, which began on Boxing Day, had been advertised. Two days before it was announced that a 'New Philosophical Entertainment, by Professor J.H. Pepper, entitled "A Strange Lecture," in which the "Photodrome," by Mr Rose, of Glasgow, and an illustration of Mr. Charles Dickens's "Haunted Man" (being an optical illusion devised by Mr. Dircks), will be introduced.'[63]

The day after boxing day a review appeared in *The Morning Post* which stated that 'a remarkable illustration of Mr. Chas. Dickens's

---

[62] [Steinmeyer] pp. 32-8 is excellent on the technical details of Pepper's Ghost. See also [Brooker] and [Weeden] pp. 71-86. In the latter is reproduced the playbill [p. 84], the programme for the Polytechnic Institute for 31 August, 1863, of the three scenes incorporating the ghost illusion. This was still been presented on 6 Dec, 1863 (advertisement in *The Era* on that date). [Weeden] p. 76 also related the story of the visit by the future King Edward VII and the move of the ghost to a large theatre for the Easter programme. The constraints of the actors in the early performances of the illusion was noted by [Pepper] p. 29.

[63] [Pepper] p.3. *The Morning Post*, 22 December, 1862.

idea of the "Haunted Man" is given in the course of the lecture, and must be seen to be appreciated'. *The Times* also mentioned the *Haunted Man* in its review on the same date.[64]

What is slightly at variance is that Professor Pepper, in his own recall of the history of Pepper's Ghost, written in 1890, claimed that his Christmas Eve performance of the illusion was intended to be used for 'Bulwer's romantic and dramatic literary creation, called *A Strange Story*'. This was a popular book written by Dickens's great friend, Edward Bulwer-Lytton, which was initially serialised in *All the Year Round* in 1861 and 1862. Did Pepper really intend the illusion to accompany a completely different story from the one that was already featured in his advertisements?[65]

A cynical explanation is that Pepper was possibly trying to put his own spin on the history of the 'Dircksian Phantasmagoria'. Doubtless not best pleased with Dircks's book, which failed to mention his name at all, Pepper, as part revenge, was reluctant to give him credit for the idea of using *The Haunted Man*. Pepper wrote that 'the late Mr O'Connor, of the Haymarket, painted the first scene used, representing the laboratory of "The Haunted Man," which Christmas story the late Charles Dickens, by his special written permission, allowed me to use for the illustration of the

[64] Part of Dircks's understandable grievance was that Mr Rose's Photodrome was often credited with being the device that created the ghost, presumably coming about from a misreading of the original advertisements. So in *The Times* review of the 'most wonderful' optical illusion, dated 27 December, 1862, Mr Rose received the plaudits. [Dawson] p. 77 incorrectly stated 'The Ghost Illusion...was shown firstly in late 1863'. It should be 'late 1862'.

[65] [Pepper] p. 3. *A Strange Story* was serialised in [AYR] from 10 August 1861 to 8 March 1862, having the unenviable task of immediately following the serialisation of *Great Expectations*. As [Brooker] has pointed out, the fact that Pepper called his presentation a 'Strange Lecture' suggests a link to the book. However there is no mention of *A Strange Story* in any newspaper advertising or reviews relating to Pepper's Ghost.

Ghost illusion.' With this wording, Pepper gave the impression that it was he who had first thought of using *The Haunted Man*.[66]

However it is also uncertain one can entirely believe Dircks's interpretation of what happened. Following up on his claim about advertising in *The Times*, this was found dated 28th June, 1858:

> Inventors, Patentees etc. A professional gentleman wishes profitable EMPLOYMENT for £400 to £500 in a desirable patented or patentable invention. Apply to Mr H Dircks, British and foreign patent agency offices, 32, Moorgate-street, City.

Given that £500 was the sum Dircks accepted from Pepper for the eventual purchase of the ghost illusion, it could be that he was genuine in his statement that he had been hawking it around four years earlier; although another interpretation of the advertisement might be that he was trying to attach himself to someone else's invention. But there is no reference to *The Haunted Man*, so it is only his word, in his retrospectively published book, that he had always considered it as the perfect bedfellow for his invention.

Just to add to the confusion, the description of what happened on stage in the early reviews, do not resemble the story of *The Haunted Man*. One in February, 1863 wrote that a 'skeleton appears to the affrighted student, who, in his terror, afterwards passes a sword through, and also attempts to demolish it with a club. It vanishes, and leaves him to wonder and to resume as he may the subject of his solitary studies.' This accords with Pepper's version of events: he wrote that 'the first story I told at my Polytechnic "Strange Lecture" had a very simple plot' – and went on to describe a similar scene.[67]

---

[66] [Pepper] p. 12. There is no other record of Dickens's 'special written permission'; it is not included in the [Pilgrim] volumes. It is a letter you would have thought Pepper might have retained and reproduced in his book.

[67] *Penny Illustrated Paper*, 7 Feb, 1863, p. 91. This was cited in 'The Polytechnic

For what it is worth, perhaps the best interpretation is that Dircks did indeed want his illusion to be performed as an illustration of *The Haunted Man*, hence the reasons for mentioning it in the pre-show publicity. However what was initially seen at the lecture theatre, as presented by Pepper, bore no resemblance to the story; nevertheless the reviewers, picking up on what was advertised, assumed it was part of a scene from the book. It was only later, when Pepper's Ghost shifted to the large theatre in Easter 1863, that it was clearly staged as illustrating *The Haunted Man*.

It would seem then that Dickens deservedly takes the credit for *The Haunted Man* as the first 'proper' story to accompany the illusion. However, in truth, the text was irrelevant: audiences had come to be amazed and amused by the ghost, not to lose themselves in a dramatic piece of theatre. Although it was produced at the Adelphi Theatre, this assessment by one newspaper review probably summed up the entertainment at the Institute: *The Haunted Man* 'was never really a success, and without its new attraction [Pepper's Ghost] it certainly would not now hold the stage for a single week.'[68]

That this was one of the most successful and best remembered theatrical versions of a Dickens book – according to Pepper it 'ran for fifteen months, and helped to realise, in a very short time, the sum of twelve thousand pounds' – is rather ironic. How often can one say about a piece of work by Dickens that it succeeded in spite of, rather than because of, the story?[69]

Ghost', Jeremy Brooker, *Early Popular Visual Culture*, 5, 2007 pp. 180-206. [Pepper] p. 29. Yet *The Times* review of 27 December, 1862 wrote about the 'haunted man' walking through 'apparently solid forms'.

[68] [Dircks] p. 24. Another reviewer wrote of this same show: 'the glass screen employed – if we may be forgiven for partially betraying secrets – renders the voice of the actor in the back-ground somewhat indistinct.' *Daily News*, June 22, 1863.

[69] [Pepper] p. 12.

## Robert-Houdin

There were plenty of conjurers who came to London after 1849[70] that Dickens might well have seen perform. These included the Davenport Brothers, Alexander Herrmann and Wiljalba Frikell. However of all the conjurers that magic historians are keen to connect with Dickens, Jean Eugène Robert-Houdin undoubtedly comes out on top.[71]

Robert-Houdin is considered to be the father of modern magic; the conjurer who revolutionised the art of illusion not just with his inventive genius and his mechanical marvels but also with his style of performing and dress; the man that inspired the great escapologist to change his name from Ehrich Weiss to Harry Houdini; the eloquent wordsmith who, in *The Secrets of Conjuring and Magic*, wrote one of the greatest of all conjuring textbooks; the ambassador who quelled a revolution in the Algiers by using little-known magic principles. He was, by a long shot, the most famous French conjurer of the nineteenth century – indeed of any century; pick up any book on the history of magic and you will find pages

---

[70] Of the conjurers CD saw prior to 1849, Döbler's retirement in 1847 is in [Clarke] p. 233; Anderson's death in 1874 is p. 222 and his imitation of Robert-Houdin's repertoire on p. 247. The satirical article was 'Dobler Outdone', *Punch*, p. 194, 17 November, 1860, cited in [Claxton] and also listed in [Claxton, Punch] p. 4. The quotation that 'numerous imitators who stole [Döbler's] name and copied his tricks' is in [Clarke] p. 234.

[71] The Davenport Brothers first came to London in 1864, returning again in1868 [Clarke] p. 297 & p. 300. Hermann was at the Egyptian Hall in 1869, [Clarke] p. 288. Frikell was in London in 1857 and 1858, [Clarke] p. 256. On p. 256 is the playbill advertising Frikell performing magic 'Without the Aid of any Apparatus'. The full title of his book was *Professor Wiljalba Frikell's Lessons in Magic, or, Two Hours of Illusions without the Aid of Apparatus*, London, c 1857, cited in [Clarke] p. 450, n 371. The quotation from this was cited in [Frost] p. 296.

devoted to Robert-Houdin (see Plate 22).

It would seem fated that Dickens and Robert-Houdin should meet. Robert-Houdin's professional life was relatively brief (1845 to 1854) but much of it exactly matched up with Dickens's own years of actively performing magic (1842-1849). It is this crossover of dates between the two that presumably compelled Trevor Dawson to write on the dust jacket of his 2012 book that Dickens 'was friendly with Robert-Houdin'.[72]

Dickens would certainly have had plenty of opportunities to have seen Robert-Houdin in London. The French conjurer was at the St James's Theatre from May to August, 1848 returning for fifteen performances in December. He came back to the same theatre in March and April, 1849. He was not in England in 1850 or 1851 but he toured the provinces in 1852. His final London appearances were two short seasons, firstly at the St James's Theatre from 28th March to 28th April and then at Sadler's Wells from May 2nd to 14th, 1853.[73]

These dates have been taken from two principal sources, Sam

---

[72] 3 July, 1845 was R-H first performance of Les Soirées Fantastiques: [Sharpe] p. 21. His final professional show was in Berlin in February 1854: [Fechner, Vol. 1] p. 379. [Dawson] dust jacket: '[CD] was friendly with Robert-Houdin, Dobler and Professor Anderson.'

[73] R-H opened in London on 2 May, 1848 at St James's Theatre; the last performance in London took place on 19 August before he then appeared again in London in December: a playbill stated the shows shall continue 'Until the End of the Christmas Vacations'. He was back again in March & April, 1849. [Fechner, Vol. 1] pp. 310, 319 & 321. That there is no evidence that R-H was in England in 1850 or 1851, but toured the provinces in 1852, came from [Sharpe] pp. 29-30. R-H performed at St James's Theatre from 28 March to 28 April, 1853 [Fechner, Vol. 1] p. 376. Sadler's Wells: [Fechner, Vol. 1] p. 377 gave ending date whilst [Sharpe] p. 32 gave start and finishing date as 9-14 May. Actually R-H began on 2 May. That R-H did his final show on 14 May is confirmed by an advertisement in *The Times* for 12 May, where it stated 'positively the last 3 nights of M. Robert Houdin'.

Sharpe's *Salutations to Robert-Houdin* and Christian Fechner's monumental two volume *The Magic of Robert-Houdin, 'An Artist's Life'.* With one exception, which will be discussed below, the dates have not been independently verified in contemporary newspapers. Rather as now, newspapers such as *The Times* and *The Morning Post* had small classified advertisements of shows in town that day – and this is the most accurate way of finding exactly who was performing where on any specific date.

Apart from London, Dickens might well have seen Robert-Houdin in Paris when the maestro performed his famous Les Soirées Fantastiques in his own theatre 'on and off' from 1845 through to 1852. The problem is that it is hard to ascertain exactly when the 'on' periods were, as there is not a definitive list of dates of when Robert-Houdin was working in France.[74]

Dickens was a Francophile. He first went to Paris in July, 1844 and wrote that the city 'is the most extraordinary place in the World.' By 1846 Dickens could speak basic French and within a few years later he had mastered the language well enough for serious correspondence. However it would take him a few more years to be thoroughly conversant. It was not until after Robert-Houdin had retired from performing that Dickens wrote to Georgina Hogarth in February, 1855: 'My ear has gradually become so accustomed to French, that I understand the people at the theatres (for the first time) with perfect ease and satisfaction.'[75]

Many of the trips that Dickens made to Paris were relatively short, often in later years accompanied by Wilkie Collins, whose influence on him might not have been entirely benign. His best opportunity to have seen Robert-Houdin was when Dickens was in

---

[74] R-H's first performance was on 3 July, 1845 and his final performance was on 5 February, 1852. [Fechner, Vol. 1] pp. 245 & 371.

[75] [Tomalin] pp. 154 ( [Pilgrim, Vol. 4] pp. 166-7 is cited), 191 & 447-8 n 16. Letter to Georgina Hogarth, 16 February, 1855 was cited in [Johnson].

Paris for an extended stay – three months from mid-November 1846 to February 1847; and in particular when his good friend Forster came out for a couple of weeks in January 1847 specifically to enjoy what Paris had to offer. Robert-Houdin opened his second season of Les Soirées Fantastiques in October 1846 but there is no record of how long the run lasted – and whether therefore it coincided with Dickens's residency in Paris. Forster listed a comprehensive list of the highlights of their own outings together, including many of the theatre shows they saw; but a visit to Robert-Houdin is only noticeable by its absence.[76]

Fuelling the certainty that Dickens must have seen Robert-Houdin, was the belief that the novelist reviewed the Frenchman's autobiography, *Confidences d'un Prestidigitateur par Robert-Houdin: Une Vie D'Artiste* in his weekly journal *Household Words*. The book was published in France in 1858, whilst the first English edition, *Memoirs of Robert-Houdin – Ambassador, Author and Conjurer*, appeared in July, 1859. As all articles were published anonymously in *Household Words*, the assumption was made that 'Out-Conjuring Conjurors' (see Plate 12), was written by Dickens.[77]

Thanks to Anne Lohrli's pioneering book, which established the authorship of all *Household Words* contributions, it is now known that the review – which was published in April 1859 and therefore must have been based on the French edition of the book – was not by Dickens but by the Reverend Edmund Saul Dixon. Dixon produced a total of one hundred and forty-four articles for Dickens's journals. He also wrote books which included *The*

---

[76] [Clarke] p. 241: 'After an unsuccessful visit to Brussels, Robert-Houdin opened his second Parisian season in October...' [Fechner] gave no details of any dates. [Forster, Vol. 2] Chapter XV, '3 Months in Paris', set out what shows they saw. CD eventually left Paris in February 1847 when his son Charley contacted scarlet fever.

[77] [Fechner, Vol. 2] p. 70. English edition is [Robert-Houdin, Memoirs].

*Dovecote and the Aviary, Ornamental and Domestic Poultry* and *Pigeons and Rabbits*: unfortunately the reference to the latter four legged mammal seems to be the only, rather tenuous, connection that one can find between Dixon and conjuring.[78]

Given that Dickens often rewrote and amended quite considerably certain articles in his journals, it could be argued, knowing about his interest in magic, that this might well be one of them. Two factors count against this. Firstly, this was a long time after he had given up conjuring – and, as will be seen in Chapter Five, part of Dickens's character profile was not really to concern himself too much with matters that did not have a direct impact on him. By this stage, too, his input into articles generally was much reduced from when the journal was first launched nine years before.

Secondly, this was when Dickens was winding down *Household Words* and embarking on a new weekly journal called *All the Year Round*. In this transition, he was going to ditch Bradbury and Evans (publishers of *Household Words*) and replace them with Chapman and Hall. The change-over took place on 4th June, 1859, with the final edition of *Household Words* appearing on 28th May, 1859. His priorities therefore would have been very much focused on the replacement journal.

Furthermore it is noteworthy that the English version of Robert-Houdin's autobiography was also published by Chapman and Hall. It would seem likely that Dickens was doing a favour to his new 'old' publishers – Chapman and Hall had been responsible for his earlier books, before Dickens left them in high dudgeon many years previously – by plugging one of their forthcoming titles; rather than deliberately selecting a book he had read and liked.

In March, 1861 Robert-Houdin produced another book called

---

[78] [HW] Vol. XIX, No. 472, 9 April, 1859, pp. 433-439. Information about the authorship, and Dixon himself, came from [Lohri] which is cited on www.djo.org.uk.

*Les Tricheries des Grecs Dévoilées: L'Art de Gagner à tous les Jeux* which translates as *Card-Sharping Exposed: The Tricks of the Greeks Unveiled*. A review of this French edition, entitled 'Cheating At Cards' again anonymously, appeared in *All the Year Round* at the end of June 1861. The first English edition of the book, *The Sharper Detected and Exposed*, was not published until 1863, once more by Chapman and Hall.[79]

The probability is that 'Cheating at Cards' was also written by the Reverend Edmund Saul Dixon, as it is known from Anne Lohri that Dixon wrote for *All the Year Round*. At present it remains unattributed, as indeed do many other contributions to that journal. Trevor Dawson assumed it was definitely written by Dickens: 'In June 1861 in *All The Year Round*, in an article heading 'Cheating at Cards', Dickens reviewed the recently published, Houdin, Les Tricheries des Grecs Devoilees [sic]...'[80]

The assumption that the two men were somehow acquainted, because a review of the Robert-Houdin's autobiography appeared in Dickens's journal, was ratcheted up by the claim by Fechner that the Frenchman 'sent a copy of his memoirs to the famous novelist'. If they were indeed friends this might well have been the case. Otherwise you would expect the French publishers to send a copy to their English counterparts.[81]

With this in mind, it is instructive to note that when it came to his book on card-sharping, Robert-Houdin wrote to his French publisher on 2nd April, 1861.

[79] [Fechner] Vol. 2, p. 130. The review of the original French edition of *The Sharper Detected and Exposed*, Robert Houdin, London: Chapman & Hall, 1863 appeared in [AYR] Vol. 5, No. 114, 29 June,1861, pp. 331-6.
[80] [Lohrli] wrote: 'The A.Y.R. Letter-Book indicates that Edmund Saul Dixon contributed also to A.Y.R.' cited on www.djo.org.uk. [Dawson] p. 180.
[81] [Fechner, Vol. 2] p. 74.

You were right to write to Chapman & Hall, and preferably to Captain Lascelles Wraxall [the translator of his memoirs]. You must have noticed the latter's style. It somewhat resembles military command or reflects a great desire to express it. The same day I received his letter, I answered him that you were waiting for my book to be finished to send a copy to Chapman & Hall. [82]

Apart from being a rather intriguing insight into what Robert-Houdin thought of his translator, it is noticeable that Dickens was not mentioned. As one might have anticipated, Robert-Houdin's French publishers were corresponding directly with Chapman & Hall. Without evidence to the contrary, the assumption must be that his first book was handled in a similar manner.

The first false provenance of the authorship of the 'Out-Conjuring Conjurers' article in the magic press was by Will Goldston in his *Goldston's Magical Quarterly* in 1934. He wrote that: 'In another part of this issue we have much pleasure in printing the first portion of a little-known essay by that greatest of all English novelists, Charles Dickens. This first appeared in Dicken's [sic] own magazine, "Household Words," in April, 1859, and was inspired by the publication early in that year of Robert-Houdin's autobiography.' This was presumably picked up by the American magic magazine, *Sphinx*, and parts of the article, which was titled 'About Robert-Houdin by Charles Dickens', were reproduced in November 1938. [83]

Leaving aside publications specifically aimed at magicians [84], there

---

[82] [Fechner, Vol. 2] p. 130.

[83] 'News of Magicians', *Goldston's Magical Quarterly*, Will Goldston, Vol. 1, No. 2, Autumn issue, 1934, p. 59. The reproduction began on p. 53. *Sphinx*, Vol. 37, November, 1938, p. 220.

[84] Some books written primarily for magicians claiming CD was the author of 'Out-Conjuring Conjurors' were [Fechner, Vol. 2] p. 74: 'very promising event was the first and very laudatory English review of *Confidences d'un*

are a number of recent books, for the more general reader, which perpetuate this error of attributing the article to Dickens. In date order, there was Heathcote Williams in *What Larks!* (1995) who wrote that 'Dickens devoted an article' to the French magician. Jim Steinmeyer in *Hiding the Elephant* (2003) wrote that the 'first English translation...was reviewed by Charles Dickens'. Ricky Jay, in *Celebrations of Curious Characters* (2011), said Dickens 'lauded Robert-Houdin, the great French conjurer'. And Simon Callow, in his *Charles Dickens and the Great Theatre of the World* (2012), who researched his knowledge of Dickens and conjuring from Williams's booklet, quoted Dickens as having written that 'a man becomes a magician only by patient labour. The tree from which the enchanter's wand is culled is no other than obstinate, persevering

---

*prestidigitateur* written by Charles Dickens in his review *Household Words* of April 9, 1859'. Just to add to the misinformation, Fechner appeared to quote Peter Ackroyd in support of CD having written the article. He related a comment made by a friend of CD after his death: 'He had in his character a vein of hardness that was like an iron bar in his soul'; and stated (correctly) that he had picked that up from [Ackroyd] p. 253 (although the actual Ackroyd quotation was: CD 'had a strain of hardness in his nature which was like a rod of iron in his soul'). In the footnote Fechner gave the reference but went on to write: 'During his trips to Paris, and perhaps also in London, Charles Dickens attended shows given by Robert-Houdin and published a long and laudatory analysis of the *Memoirs of Robert-Houdin* in his periodical *Household Words*, April 9, 1859.' [Fechner, Vol. 1] pp. 22 & 61, n 27. A casual reader might assume Fechner was repeating something that Ackroyd had written. [Dawson] pp. 177-9 who quoted extracts from the article on the assumption that CD had written it. In the footnote, on p. 219, it was incorrectly stated that the article appeared in [AYR]. At one point, Dawson seemed to go further by stating that CD had been involved in 'the publication of Robert-Houdin's books' [Dawson] p. 130. And [Sharpe] p. 36, 'Charles Dickens reviewed *The Confidences of a Prestidigitator; An Artist's Life*, in his periodical *Households Words*.'

work.' These words came from the Reverend Dixon's article.[85]

Given that some of the above books deservedly enjoyed wide distribution and critical acclaim, it is somewhat ironic that the one magic historian, Steven Tigner, who first brought the attention of the magic world to the correct authorship of the Robert-Houdin article in 1979, could not really have been less generally disseminated if he had tried. It appeared in an undated supplement to *The Journal of Magic History* that only survived for six issues. Sadly the supplement does not appear to have ever been cited in any book or journal in respect of Dickens and conjuring.[86]

Putting the article to one side, it was possible of course that Dickens still attended one of Robert-Houdin's shows – and indeed might even have met him. Dawson was convinced on both counts. With regard to seeing the French maestro's show, he wrote: 'As will be appreciated from earlier references to Robert-Houdin, Dickens was a great admirer, and had seen him in London at the St James Theatre on probably innumerable occasions in 1848 and 1849 and during his lengthy stays in Paris from 1845, had attended his Salon Soires [sic] Fantasiques presentations.' Unfortunately Dawson produced no evidence to back up this bold statement.[87]

Even Dawson's statement that Dickens was a 'great admirer' is highly contentious. The 'earlier references to Robert-Houdin', as proof of Dickens's supposed esteem for the French conjurer, related to two articles that mentioned Robert-Houdin. Dawson assumed

---

[85] [Heathcote] p. 16; [Steinmeyer] p. 141; [Jay, Celebrations] p. 73; [Callow] p. 132.

[86] Dickensians, of course, would have been familiar with [Lohrli]. [Tigner] Vol. 1 Supplement gave the correct authorship of 'Out-Conjuring Conjurors'. Some of this analysis first appeared in 'The Mystery of Charles Dickens and a Review of Robert-Houdin's Autobiography', Ian Keable, *Magicol*, No. 184, January 2013, pp. 56-67.

[87] [Dawson] p. 176.

that 'Modern Magic' and 'Mediums Under Other Names', which appeared in *All the Year Round* in 1860 and 1862 respectively, were both written by Dickens; the correct attribution is Eliza Lynn Linton.[88]

When it comes to the two of them getting together, Dawson relied exclusively on Christian Fechner who, in his *The Magic of Robert-Houdin*, wrote: 'It was Robert-Houdin, who had many meetings with Charles Dickens...' Well, that is what Dawson put in quotation marks. However what Fechner actually wrote was: 'It was Robert Houdin – whose meetings with Charles Dickens we have already mentioned...' Fechner, though, despite this assertion had not previously 'mentioned' any of those 'meetings'; and indeed no evidence of any such meetings have been found.[89]

So far this supplement has concentrated on correcting errors made and perpetuated by sundry writers with regard to Robert-

---

[88] [Dawson] pp. 127 & 134. 'Modern Magic', Eliza Lynn Linton, [*AYR*] Vol. III, No. 66, 28 July, 1860, pp. 370-74; 'Mediums Under Other Names', Eliza Lynn Linton, [*AYR*] Vol. VII, No. 156, 19 April, 1862, pp. 130-37. The authorship is confirmed on www.djo.org.uk. Whether either of those articles were ones where Dickens feared Mrs Linton strayed too close to 'the sexual side of things as to be a little dangerous to us at times' [Ackroyd, p. 624], as CD once commented to his assistant editor, WH Wills, we can only hazard a guess!

[89] [Dawson] p. 177 stated the quotation came from [Fechner, Vol. 1]; it was actually [Fechner, Vol. 2] p. 74. The wrong reference, and the subtle change in the quotation from Fechner, adds to the feeling that there was an element of obscuration on Dawson's part. A check was made with the Editor of the English edition of [Fechner] to see if something had been missed in translation - nothing was; and also with the original French edition to see if any more information was contained in them - there was none. The author, Christian Fechner, died in 2008. There are two additional volumes of Fechner's work, which have yet to be published in English. However it has been confirmed that there are no references to any 'meetings' between CD and R-H in these volumes either.

Houdin and Dickens. It is time now to be more positive. The possibility of the two meeting first emerged in an article in the *Morning Telegraph*, dated 21st April, 1919.

Henry F Dickens, son of Charles Dickens, said that once his father attended a séance accompanied by Lord Lytton and Wilkie Collins. The man who gave it was the great Robert Houdin and at the end of the entertainment he proved these manifestations were simply clever tricks, but the incident did not weaken the belief in spiritualism of either Lord Lytton or Mr Collins.

Before commenting on this, there is a follow up reference, which came from *The Recollections of Sir Henry Dickens.*

The first Lord Lytton was a profound believer in occultism, as his book, *A Strange Story*, would go to show. In order to open his eyes a little, my father arranged a séance with the popular medium of the day, without disclosing the names of any of the persons who were to attend. He took with him besides Lord Lytton, Wilkie and Charles Collins and the famous conjurer, Houdin. This meeting, so far as the medium was concerned, was disastrous. Everything that the medium did was promptly "outdone" by Houdin, who really outspirited the spiritualist in all that gentleman's tricks. But, curiously enough, this did not cure Lytton of his belief and I do not think his faith in it was ever shaken.[90]

Although told rather differently, it would appear that the two stories have somehow coalesced, both relating to the same event and from the same source: the main difference is that in the first it was Robert-Houdin who apparently conducted the séance; and in the second, he allegedly attended another medium's séance. The fact

---

[90] [Dickens, Henry] pp. 63-4. This reference was cited in [Brandon] p. 57, who accepted the story at face value.

that Charles Dickens, Wilkie Collins and Lord Lytton participated in both very much suggests that only one séance took place. The problem is that neither of them quite add up.

Taking the newspaper article first, it is highly improbable that Robert-Houdin would have conducted a private séance and then revealed his methods; this would have involved exposing his own tricks – something which magicians are very averse to doing. Robert-Houdin might have been happy to give away the methods of spiritualists generally; but there is no evidence that he ever publicly demonstrated, and then exposed, any of his own tricks. Adding to the general lack of faith in the article is the inference that Wilkie Collins was a believer in Spiritualism. Lord Lytton most certainly was – but nothing is known which suggests Collins shared his view.[91]

It is far more likely, as the book extract implied, that Robert-Houdin would have attended a medium's séance and then revealed the methods. This was a popular way amongst conjurers to garner publicity: Harry Houdini most famously used it to great effect. An article was published in *All the Year Round* in which John Henry Anderson attempted unsuccessfully to expose the spiritualist DD Home as a charlatan. It is quite possible that Robert-Houdin might have tried something similar.[92]

Where the story breaks down is when Henry Dickens wrote that his father 'arranged a séance'. This is extremely implausible. In the

[91] CD's and Collins's shared scepticism was shown by CD writing to his great friend on 22 April, 1863: 'The stupendous absurdity of Howitt's book is inconceivable. Home's is clearly (to me) the book of a scoundrel without shame.' [Pilgrim, Vol. 10] p. 239. Both these books, devoted to Spiritualism, were reviewed in a derisory manner by CD in [AYR]. R-H gave away the secrets of many of the tricks of spiritualists, including the Davenport Brothers, in *The Secrets of Stage Conjuring*, translated by Professor Hoffmann, George Routledge and Sons, London, 1881.

[92] [AYR] 'At Home with the Spirits', WH Wills, Vol. XV, No. 358, 3 March, 1866, pp. 180-4.

next chapter there is a separate supplement on 'Dickens and Spiritualism' which considers his rather ambivalent attitude towards it. However given that Dickens wrote many letters turning down invitations to séances, and appreciating how much he despised mediums, the thought of Dickens organising, and therefore paying for, a profession he had such antipathy towards, is not persuasive.[93]

A final problem with the two anecdotes is the timescale. It is known that Robert-Houdin's last performance in London was in May 1853, after which he never returned. It was actually in this same month that there is evidence of Dickens dabbling – admittedly in a light-hearted manner – with Spiritualism. On 23rd May he wrote to his friend and illustrator, John Leech: 'We spun a table in the most extraordinary manner last night...The Pembroke table in the study gamboled like an insane elephant (with a prodigious creaking) all around the room!!!' His cynicism, and therefore the likelihood of getting involved in organising, or being part of, a debunking séance, was to come later – long after Robert-Houdin

---

[93] There is evidence of CD participating in séances but none of him actually 'booking' a medium. The following are examples of letters from CD turning down invitations to séances and his antipathy towards mediums. Letter to Mrs Trollope, 19 June, 1855: 'I cannot have the pleasure of seeing the famous 'Medium' tonight, for I have some Theatricals at home. But I fear I should not in any case be a good subject for the purpose, as I altogether want faith in the thing. I have not the least belief in the awful unseen World being available for evening parties at so much per night.' [Pilgrim, Vol. 7] p. 651-2. Letter to Miss Marion Ely, 25 April, 1860: 'I must excuse myself from accepting the proposal you convey to me. My reasons for doing so, I need not enter into; they are well considered and strong.' [Pilgrim, Vol. 9] p. 242. Letter to Mrs Nichols, 1 April, 1864: 'You do not understand me – I dare say it is my fault – on the subject of your 'Test Medium'? I do not desire to see him, and indeed altogether decline to see any person making those pretensions.' [Pilgrim, Vol. 10] p. 378.

had departed.[94]

So where did Henry Dickens get his information from; or was he perhaps confusing it with another séance? He certainly could not have been aware of it when the séance supposedly took place. He was born in January, 1849, which would have made him only four years old when Robert-Houdin left England for good; the source therefore must have been second hand.

The most plausible answer is provided by an article published in 1862 in *All the Year Round*. The anonymous author of that piece wrote about attending a séance where the medium failed in his endeavours whilst 'attentively watched by five persons seated in his own room at his own table: of which five persons the writer was one, the Conductor of this journal another, and M. ROBIN of the Egyptian Hall a very dangerous third' [caps in article].[95]

The author of the article is unknown; but the Conductor clearly related to Dickens, as that was his byline used under the title heading of the *All the Year Round* journal. M. ROBIN referred to the French conjurer, Henri Robin (see Plate 28) who first came over to London in December, 1850 and performed through to October, 1851. He started a second season in December, 1851 which lasted until July the following year. It was not until 1861 that Robin would return again to London: he opened at the Egyptian Hall on November, 1861 and remained there through to October 1862,

---

[94] For R-H leaving London, see [Sharpe] p. 32. CD letter to John Leech: [Pilgrim, Vol. 7] p. 92.

[95] 'Small-Beer Chronicles' [AYR] Vol. VII, No. 176, 6 Sept, 1862, p. 608. [Tigner] p. 102 drew attention to this article and included an illustration of Robin at the Egyptian Hall, with the caption underneath of 'Robin, with whom Dickens investigated a medium in 1862'. It was almost certainly through a misreading of this that Ricky Jay wrote that CD 'assisted the Frenchman Robin on the stage at London's Egyptian Hall': [Jay, Celebrations] p. 73.

notching up a total of three hundred and six performances.[96]

It was sometime during this last season that Henri Robin would have attended the séance. This fits in with the date when the article was published (September, 1862) and the period when Dickens was most vehemently against mediums generally. What seems likely is that Henry Dickens confused Robert-Houdin with Henri Robin. This is plausible not just because their names are similar. But also, by the time the newspaper article appeared, and certainly by when Henry Dickens wrote his book, Robert-Houdin was the best-known French conjurer of the Victorian era. So it is unsurprising that Henry Dickens would have 'recalled' his name instead of Robin.

Which just leaves the question of whether Dickens might have seen Robert-Houdin perform. On 3rd May, 1853, he wrote the following letter to his friend, Frank Stone, an artist who did some drawings for the cheap editions of *Nicholas Nickleby* and *Martin Chuzzlewit*, as well as for his fifth Christmas book, *The Haunted Man*.

> My dear Stone. I think Houdin the conjurer is at Sadlers Wells. If you should happen by any chance not to be in the Vortex, and would like to wind up this glorious day in a suitable manner, I am to be heard of as above. Ever affecy. CD.[97]

On coming across this letter it was first necessary to discover if Robert-Houdin was indeed at Sadler's Wells on 3rd May. According

---

[96] [Dawes, Robin] pp. 7, 21, 31, 34, 37 & 39 for various London dates. His final show was on 4 Oct, 1862.

[97] [Pilgrim, Vol. 7] p. 76. It would seem that by 'Vortex', CD was not referring to any particular place but rather using it in the meaning of 'a constant round of excitement or pleasure'. This definition was taken from *The Oxford English Edition*, Second Edition, Clarendon Press, Oxford, JA Simpson and ESC Weiner, Vol. XIX, 2001. The dictionary gave an example of such a usage in 1877. Mrs Forrester, *Mignon I.* 191: 'She and her husband lived in a vortex of gaiety.'

to Sam Sharpe, the conjurer was only there for one week, from 9<sup>th</sup> May to 14<sup>th</sup>.[98] However a review of the classified advertisements in *The Times* for the relevant dates came up with the following:

THEATRE ROYAL, SADLER'S WELLS. – The Management have the pleasure to announce that they have entered into an engagement for a limited number of nights with M ROBERT-HOUDIN (whose extraordinary performances have been three times honoured by the express command of Her Most Gracious Majesty the Queen), who will THIS EVENING (Monday), May 2 and every evening during the week give (for the first time in England at the preset prices) his extraordinary SEANCES FANTASTIQUES. The doors will be opened at a quarter-past 7 o'clock.

So here was direct confirmation that Dickens could indeed have gone to see Robert-Houdin on 3<sup>rd</sup> May; but unfortunately no positive verification that Frank Stone took up the invitation and the two went along. Maybe his friend was indeed in the 'Vortex' and Dickens decided to stay at home instead. An impasse was reached until, that is, this book was found. It was *Familiar Letters from Europe* and was written by Cornelius Felton, the great friend of Dickens; they had first met in America in 1842. It was of course his letter to Felton which announced Dickens's interest in conjuring.

In April, 1853 Felton came over for a visit to England and Europe and wrote a series of letters about his trip to friends and relatives back home. After docking at Liverpool, Felton travelled to Leamington, then Stratford-upon-Avon, on to Oxford and finally arrived in London. The following day, after a few errands, he went to renew his acquaintance with his old friend, Charles Dickens, and met Forster in person for the first time. They had a meal together. And then Felton wrote:

---

[98] [Sharpe] p. 32.

> In the evening we went to see Mons. Houdin, the French conjurer, and were much entertained by his admirable sleight of hand.

The letter was dated 18th May – so from this information alone it was not possible to ascertain when they saw the show. However there was a later telling extract, dated 20th May, in which Felton wrote that: 'I have been now two weeks and a half in this great capital.' Two and a half weeks is seventeen or eighteen days; assuming the latter that would mean Felton arrived in London on the 2nd May. It was the evening after his arrival that Felton saw Robert Houdin, which would tie in exactly with the 3rd May – the same date of Dickens's letter to Frank Stone inviting him along to see the French conjurer.[99]

With two such pieces of strong evidence gelling together, it can be safely concluded that Dickens did attend Robert-Houdin's show on 3rd May, 1853; the tricks he almost certainly would have seen are listed in the playbill depicted in Plate 23. This was Dickens's last opportunity to see Robert-Houdin perform in London. As noted earlier, his final show was on 14th May and, after a short tour of the provinces in June, the French conjurer never again returned to England and retired permanently from magic in 1854.[100]

Felton clearly admired Robert-Houdin; was Dickens similarly impressed? An unanswerable question. But it is noteworthy that, if this was indeed the first time Dickens had seen him, the Frenchman was right at the end of his career when other conjurers, such as John Henry Anderson and Henri Robin, had copied his tricks and presentation. If Dickens had attended any of the shows of his rivals before he saw Robert-Houdin, he might have concluded that the latter was not particularly innovative.

---

[99] [Felton] pp. 24-5.

[100] A slightly different playbill to Plate 23, but relating to the same show, can be seen here: [Houdin, Unmasking] p. 44.

More significantly, though, only a year and a half later Dickens would be calling his 'rival', Alfred de Caston, 'the most consummate master of legerdemain he had seen'; with Robert-Houdin apparently long forgotten. It has already been emphasised, though, that de Caston had the great advantage of performing a new form of magic – mind reading – that Dickens had not before encountered; so it is probably unfair, tempting though it may be, to make a comparison between the two men.

What is gratifying, though, is that after so many false leads, red herrings and misattributions, it is now proven that the greatest novelist of the nineteenth century did indeed see the greatest conjurer of the same era.[101]

---

[101] For this writer the discovery that CD saw R-H is his personal highlight of this book; it would be hard to find two men, in their respective professions of literature and magic, who have been so well researched. And to find there is a genuine, proven link between the two, which had not previously been known about, is as surprising, as it is rewarding. It is really the Pilgrim editors who should take the credit; it was a footnote, in CD's explanation of the Sphinx illusion to his daughter Mamie, that referred back to CD's invitation to Stone to see R-H, in an earlier volume. Felton's book was mentioned in another Pilgrim footnote to a letter from CD telling John Leech about some fun with spiritualistic table turning. The book was checked for this reference, so it was a totally unexpected 'eureka' moment when the passage about going to see R-H leapt out from the page. It is not 100% clear from this passage that CD accompanied Felton to see R-H (although the use of the term 'we', just after he had written about dining with CD and Forster, certainly gives that inference. Also, in the following sentence, starting a new paragraph, Felton wrote 'Next morning breakfasted with Forster alone', contrasting with the 'we' went to see Mons. Houdin'): but the tie-in to the Stone letter, in which CD clearly had every intention of going to see R-H, gives the necessary confirmation. Of course neither the Felton book, nor the Pilgrim letters, are exactly obscure publications, particularly for Dickensian scholars. But such a finding would not have been of interest to them, which is why the link had not previously been made.

# CHAPTER FIVE

# The Man

The last four chapters have considered Dickens's career as a conjurer. Who initially inspired him, when he first began, what tricks he did, the sort of shows he specialised in, where he performed, how his audience assessed him, why he gave up and other conjurers he saw. What has not yet been examined is whether any of this sheds any new light on him as a person.

Dickens's apparently rather sudden conversion to conjuring in 1842 – given that his only writing on the subject to date had been his disparaging portrait of Sweet William in *The Old Curiosity Shop* – is not unexpected. He was the type of personality who, once he had decided on a course of action, completely immersed himself in it. 'The intense pursuit of any idea that takes complete possession of me', he wrote to his wife, 'is one of the qualities that makes me different'. An obvious parallel was his immersion into mesmerism: soon after he became interested in this pseudo-science, he was conducting a series of sittings with a patient with the sophistication that you might expect from a professional counsellor rather than an amateur dabbler.

On a relatively superficial level, Dickens's interest in conjuring is easy to understand. He enjoyed playing a role, he enjoyed being the centre of attention and he enjoyed dressing up. It could be said that all those needs can also be met by acting, another pastime for him; so what did conjuring add to the mix? The difference with being a conjurer is that the performer breaks down the fourth wall between himself and his audience, and thus actively engages and interacts with them. In that sense, conjuring gives an artistic fulfilment that is not necessarily provided by a conventional theatrical role.

Conjuring also provides something else not available to the actor: knowledge which those to whom you are performing do not possess. You know how the trick works: your audience, if you do the job right, have no idea. Dickens liked to know how things were done; he was incessantly curious and inquisitive about almost everything – it was part of what made him a great writer. It is quite possible that part of Dickens's motivation in going down to Hamleys and spending his money on the 'stock in trade of a conjurer' was that he simply wanted to know how Döbler did some of his tricks.

With knowledge comes power. And having the need for power – in particular control over the emotion of others – is another characteristic facet of Dickens. On reading aloud his latest Christmas Book, *The Chimes*, he wrote to his wife Catherine: 'If you had seen Macready last night – undisguisedly sobbing, and crying on the sofa, as I read – you would have felt (as I did) what a thing it is to have Power.' When he was admonished for portraying his wife's chiropodist as Miss Mowcher in *David Copperfield*, he admitted to John Forster that 'there is no doubt one is wrong in being tempted to such a use of power'.

The most obvious example of his use of power was, once again, in his mesmerism and his treatment of his patient Madame De la Rue. As a biographer wrote: 'What is perhaps most remarkable about this whole episode is the extent to which Dickens trusted his powers; here was a woman in an extremity of mental anguish, but he possessed such self-confidence that he believed he could cure her.'

Perhaps not so remarkable when one considers how much self-belief Dickens had in himself. Having supposedly successfully magnetised John Leech out of his fever, when his friend was knocked out by a wave on the Isle of Wight, he wrote to Forster: 'What do you think of my setting up in the magnetic line with a huge brass plate? "Terms, twenty-five guineas per nap".' On a different occasion he wrote to another friend about an article he had just written: 'You want an egotistical reply from me, and you shall have it.'

It is noteworthy, though, that Dickens refused to allow himself to be mesmerised: 'it was part of his need to control, to dominate, to manipulate'. The modern day equivalent of mesmerism is hypnosis; and the crossover between conjuring and stage hypnosis is often seen in performers of today. It was natural that Dickens should be attracted to both. It was in America in early 1842 that he first practised magnetism on his wife; the fact that he should take up conjuring in the same year was maybe not just coincidental.

The corollary of possessing knowledge, linked with power, is that you need to prove continually that you are better than those around you. Dickens certainly wanted to be pre-eminent at whatever he attempted. Leaving his writing ability to one side, he was the leading actor in his productions, he walked further than anyone else on his nocturnal treks, he gave the most admired speeches at public dinners, he hosted the best parties, he mastered shorthand in a mere three months and he raised more money for charity and did more good works than his contemporaries.

Having plunged into conjuring, it was natural that Dickens wanted to excel in that too. It is hard to tell if he wholly succeeded. But what is important is that Dickens convinced himself that he had. This can be seen in his own comparisons with Ludwig Döbler. 'It is better than the Northern Wizard and as good as Doebler', he wrote about a trick, less than a couple of months after he had done his first show. And later on: 'I have made a tremendous hit with a conjuring apparatus, which includes some of Doëbler's best tricks'.

Why Döbler? Because he was the one who inspired him to take up magic. Of all the conjurers he saw, Döbler was the only one in his letters who gets the consistent name check. Even de Caston, who by Dickens's own admission completely flummoxed him, was just known as 'the Conjuror'. In his attempts to describe how the Sphinx illusion worked, there was only one reference to 'the conjuror'; the actual performer, Colonel Stodare, was not mentioned at all.

When it came to his other writings, the only conjurer that Dickens ever named was Ramo Samee; and that was five years after his death. For one who found names so crucial in his fiction writing – his one imagined conjurer was of course given the name Sweet William – Dickens was remarkably lax about recalling the names of real-life conjurers. This seems consistent with Dickens's character. When it comes to other writers Dickens 'did not care' about them, 'except on those occasions when they were involved with his life or with his activities'. The same was true of most of his fellow conjurers.

Dickens did care about Döbler, because he was the one who first inspired him and created in him his initial wonderment. Döbler therefore became the measuring rod for Dickens's own conjuring skills. Once he had proved in his own mind that he was as good as Döbler, he knew he must have mastered his art; and that requisite acquisition of skills and experience came, in Dickens's opinion, remarkably fast.

This must have been further boosted by his immense self-confidence. Dickens was clearly someone who did not suffer from nerves. An acquaintance of his called George Hodder was informed by Thackeray, the author of *Vanity Fair*, before a public speech: 'They little think how nervous I am and Dickens doesn't know the meaning of the word.' Hodder went on to write:

> In confirmation of this remark I observed that I once asked Mr Dickens if he ever felt nervous on public occasions when called upon to speak; and his instant reply was, "Not in the least. The first time I took the chair at a public dinner I felt just as much confidence as if I had done the same thing a hundred times before".

It is likely Dickens was similarly sanguine when conjuring.

All of this suggests an element of self-delusion on Dickens's part.

There are indications that he had not wholly honed his craft. His lack of ability at sleight of hand would always count against him. The chopping and changing of costume for each performance indicates that he had not yet found his performing character. Right to the end he had the mindset of an actor in his conjuring shows: he needed to play a role – fluctuating over the course of a year between a Chinese and Indian conjurer.

There is no reason to conclude that Dickens was not a competent conjurer. But there is a difference between a good amateur, entertaining friends and family (as Dickens did) and a consummate professional, filling theatres (as Döbler did). Dickens certainly understood the distinction when it came to writing – he was very disparaging about amateur writers, and those who thought that writing was somehow easy and did not require much work. But it is doubtful if he applied the same critical criteria when it came to conjuring and measuring himself against the likes of Döbler and Anderson.

Dickens's belief in his own talent can also be seen in his use of the term the 'Unparalleled Necromancer' on his Isle of Wight playbill. It is accepted there was self-mockery in the title; but it also probably partly encapsulated how good he thought he was. A Victorian playbill by Professor Hoffmann, who was almost certainly a more accomplished amateur conjurer, makes an interesting comparison – his made up insertions are more self-deprecating in tone: 'Visitors to the Cattle Show should not fail to see Professor Hoffmann. He is, unquestionably, the fattest conjuror at present before the public' - *Live Stock Gazette*.

Those close to Dickens, when it came to his conjuring, would have fuelled his ego. Jane Carlyle suggested he could make a good living at the profession if he wanted to; whilst the reaction of his children, given how fondly they recalled his performances in their subsequent memoirs, would have vindicated the undoubted efforts he put into his shows. He also had a tendency to exaggerate: 'he was very fond of superlative expressions, and he had an innate taste for excessiveness'. So his own letters, praising his conjuring prowess, doubtless had an element of hyperbole in them.

Having been brought up witnessing her father's successful shows, it is not surprising that his now grown-up daughter, Mamie, would expect him to know the secret of the Sphinx illusion. Furthermore the fact that Dickens confidently embarked on a solution is absolutely what one would anticipate. For him to turn around and admit 'I've got no idea' would somehow diminish, in his daughter's, and his own, eyes, his aptitude as a conjurer. So he gets embroiled in a rather convoluted explanation that presumably convinced her.

Dickens surely believed he was right. He thought he was, even when – as for instance in his treatment of his wife Catherine after falling in love with the young actress Ellen Ternan – he was clearly at odds with the opinion of most of his friends. 'Nobody in the world is readier to acknowledge himself in the wrong than I', he once declared; 'only – I am never wrong.'

It is pertinent that he repeated Anderson's catch phrase a couple of times in his letters – the rhetorical question 'Am I right?' The most revealing use of it was in a situation where, again, most of his friends considered Dickens was acting recklessly: his continual insistence in talking publicly about the vexed subject of international copyright whilst touring America in 1842. His retort to Forster was unequivocal: 'Am I right? quoth the conjurer. Yes! from gallery, pit, and boxes.'

Having decided to uphold his reputation as a conjurer, by coming up with a solution to a trick that had, in many respects, mystified him, Dickens took the route that most would have done: he fell back on what he was familiar with. Dickens knew about 'traps', because they were used in the legitimate theatre as well as for magic shows; and he knew about 'confederates', because he had appropriated them in his own performances; and he knew about 'slides', as some of his props would have had similar mechanical moving parts. It was a combination of these three that he shoehorned together in exposing the supposed workings of the

Sphinx.

It could be thought, given the above, that Dickens might have similarly attempted an exposition of how Alfred de Caston performed his mind reading tricks. And yet here he was more than willing to admit defeat. The answer to that has already been touched upon in an earlier chapter. Here was a realm of conjuring that Dickens had had no experience of whatsoever; it was almost beyond conjuring. Dickens had no notion of psychological forcing, cold reading and pre-show work. As such, he had no starting point for an explanation.

There are two ways to go when you are as badly taken in as Dickens was. He could have whinged about the conditions under which he saw the conjurer, complained that he could not see or hear properly; claimed that if the tricks had been done on him, rather than his wife or the General, he would have worked them out.

Or, you take the route Dickens went: which was to declare the conjurer must be an 'original genius'. Of course that must be so! How could anyone of Dickens's brilliance and intelligence and know-how be tricked by anyone who was not a genius? Dickens declared himself fooled; but also made it clear that everybody else would be deceived too. His final rider to Forster was for him to 'impart these mysteries to Rogers' who had recently regaled Dickens with the expertise of a medium he had seen. And although he wrote with tongue in cheek to Wilkie Collins, 'Is he the Devil?' part of him probably wanted to believe it.

It so happens that in this particular case, Dickens was right: de Caston does appear, at least in the sphere of conjuring, to be an 'original genius'. But that does not prevent the episode also saying something about Dickens and his confidence in his own cleverness. He was always very aware, even from a young age, that he did possess an exceptional talent; he was mindful of how posterity would treat him. Calling yourself 'the inimitable' does not suggest much in the way of false modesty.

The evidence suggests that Dickens stopped performing in 1849.

It was almost as if that was a part of his life which he could now put to one side and embark on new challenges. This was another characteristic of Dickens; having thrown himself wholeheartedly into a cause he was liable to lose interest after a time. The issue of international copyright, referred to earlier, again demonstrated this. He was totally absorbed by it on his visit to America in 1842. But then, 'a few years later, he had for all practical purposes lost interest in the subject'.

Some magic historians are perplexed at the lack of conjuring references in Dickens's writings. But Dickens was too good a writer to let his interests somehow dictate his creative instincts. By far the best depiction of a theatrical touring troupe by Dickens was in *Nicholas Nickleby*, which was written a long time before he started acting seriously. Similarly no mesmerists or spiritualists made an appearance in any of his novels; so the absence of conjurers, far from being somehow an anomaly, is predictable.

It was not just in his fictional writing that Dickens ignored the topic of conjuring. It was true as well of his factual articles, in particular those published in the two weekly journals he edited, *Household Words* and *All the Year Round*. But in these it was even less likely that magic references should feature, given that when he began them, in 1850, his conjuring days were over. So, despite attempts to attribute conjuring related articles to Dickens, it is no more unexpected that it turns out he was not the author of any of them, than the paucity of conjuring books found in his library at his death.

Here, it must be remembered, was a man who decided to burn all his correspondence. So deleting from his memory bank his experiences as a conjurer would be a minor matter. Perhaps it was seeing de Caston that finally decided it for him. The realisation that here was an aspect of conjuring which went beyond not just his skill set, but also his powers of comprehension. Best, in those circumstances, to bow out gracefully.

In conclusion, the elements of his personality that emerge from his experiences as a conjurer seem to support what has previously been known about Dickens from all his other myriad activities. His impulsiveness, capacity for work, inquisitiveness, yearning for power, complete self-belief, comfort in being the centre of attention, love of playing a role, reluctance to admit his ignorance, courage in trying out something new, ruthlessness in 'moving on' and, most importantly, his sheer joy in life and giving pleasure to others, are all mirrored in his short-lived fascination with conjuring.

# Chapter Five Supplement

## Personality of Dickens

Much of the character assessment of Dickens in this chapter has relied on the initial profiling by Peter Ackroyd in his monumental work, of over one thousand pages, called simply *Dickens*. The unattributed quotations, along with supporting examples, can be found here in Ackroyd.

| | |
|---|---|
| Desire of power. | pp. 470 & 608 |
| Taking up mesmerism. | p. 257 |
| Refusing to be mesmerised. | p. 259 |
| Link between mesmerism and magic. | p. 260 |
| Fondness for superlatives. | p. 314 |
| Loss of interest in international copyright. | p. 395 |
| On naming fictional characters. | p. 411 |
| Mesmerising & treatment of Madame de la Rue. | pp. 472-6 |
| Not caring about other writers. | p. 550 |
| I am never wrong. | p. 875 |

The references to Dickens's letters in this chapter are as follows:

What a thing it is to have Power, CD to his wife.
[Pilgrim, Vol. 4] p. 235          2/12/1844
Setting up the magnetic line, CD to John Forster.
[Pilgrim, Vol. 5] p. 615          26/9/1849
Tempted to such a use of power, CD to John Forster.
[Pilgrim, Vol. 5] p. 676          18/12/1849
Intense pursuit of any idea, CD to his wife.
[Pilgrim, Vol. 7] p. 224          5/12/1853
You want an egotistical reply, CD to Mrs Watson.
[Pilgrim, Vol. 8] p. 487          7/12/1857

The self-confident public speaking anecdote was related in a book published in 1870 that also includes possibly my all-time favourite anecdote about Dickens. When Thackeray had just read the death of Paul Dombey in *Dombey and Son,* he burst into the offices of *Punch* magazine and exclaimed to the editor Mark Lemon: 'There's no writing against such power as this – one has no chance! Read that chapter describing young Paul's death : it is unsurpassed – it is stupendous !'[1]

## Dickens and Spiritualism

There has traditionally been a strong link between conjurers and their antipathy towards Spiritualism. The reason is that conjurers perceive spiritualists employing exactly the same tools that they use to legitimately trick their audience. And usually in conditions – for instance low lighting and ensuring that the sitters are carefully positioned – which make it relatively easy to execute manoeuvres like tipping and spinning tables, producing ghostly apparitions and rapping out messages. Conjurers therefore conclude that that they can bring their knowledge to bear on such proceedings, disclose how the manifestations work and expose the mediums as fraudulent.

The most famous example is Harry Houdini who pursued a relentless crusade against spiritualists, both in publications and also by attending séances purposefully to debunk them. It was on this that he and ardent spiritualist, Arthur Conan Doyle, eventually fell out; the final straw for the escapologist was the creator of Sherlock Holmes's deluded conviction that Houdini somehow dematerialised himself in order to escape from his locked boxes.

---

[1] [Hodder] pp. 277 & 279. The extract from Professor Hoffmann's playbill was dated 24 Dec, 1883 and is found in *Programmes of Magicians,* JF Burrows, L Davenport & Co., London, c. 1945, p. 6.

Houdini's exploits post-date Dickens but even contemporary conjurers, such as John Henry Anderson, generated plenty of publicity by attacking spiritualists and explaining their secrets.

Given that Dickens was also very sceptical about Spiritualism, it is instructive to consider whether his antagonistic stance towards it and its principal proponents was partly motivated by his knowledge of conjuring.

Dickens's attitude to Spiritualism is in marked contrast to his position on what one might think is a similar subject matter, that of ghosts. His thoughts on these were clarified in an article he wrote in 1848 in *The Examiner* critiquing a book by Mrs Catherine Crowe called *The Night Side of Nature; or Ghosts and Ghost Seers*. The book recounted tales of various supernatural happenings from many sources: it was written before the Fox sisters had started the craze of table rappers, so, although Mrs Crowe later became a convert, it did not cover any examples of Spiritualism.

Dickens began the article: 'We propose, in the present notice of this very curious book, to glance at a few obvious heads of objection that may be ranged against the ghosts; and, resuming the subject next week, to sum up what may be said in their favour.' Unfortunately the second article was never written; but the fact that Dickens was even contemplating putting forward arguments that might support the existence of ghosts is significant – he was never prepared to tolerate a contrary viewpoint when it came to Spiritualism.

Dickens went on to explain his personal reasons for being unconvinced by the existence of ghosts. Firstly, just because people are presupposed to perceive them in certain circumstances (in the dead of night, when in a somnambulistic state or whilst contemplating the existence of an after-life) does not mean that they do exist. Secondly, that ghosts are always rather elusive: 'their alleged appearances have been, in all ages, marvellous, exceptional, and resting on imperfect grounds of proof.' And finally, he observed, that when it comes to relating ghostly sightings, 'it is the peculiarity of almost all ghost stories, as contradistinguished from all other kinds of narratives purporting to be true, to depend, *as* ghost stories, on some one little link in the chain of evidence, and that supposing that link to be destructible, the whole supernatural character is gone.'

To support his last point he quoted a story from Mrs Crowe's book about a supposed sighting of a ghost. In Dickens's view, the only justification for believing that a ghost was really seen lies in the antics of a terrified dog – 'an animal of high courage' – who scampered away from the apparition. 'Take away the dog, or the implied occasion of the dog's terror, and, as a ghost story, the whole tumbles down like a house of cards.' Everything else ghost-like about the incident can be explained away by applying common sense.[2]

Dickens was using an analytical and logical approach to support his scepticism. In this he could well have been influenced by his reading of Walter Scott's *Letters on Demonology and Witchcraft*, in which the author gave rational reasons for people's belief in witchcraft and ghosts.[3] This outlook was shared by some of Dickens's favourite writers of the previous century, such as Fielding, Smollett and Goldsmith, all of whom displayed a sceptical stance on ghosts and similar unexplained phenomena.[4]

[2] *The Examiner*, 26th Feb, 1848, pp. 131-3.

[3] It is known that CD must have read *Letters on Demonology* as it is referenced in 'Shabby-Genteel People', *Sketches by Boz*, chapter 20: 'The man of whom Sir Walter Scott speaks in his *Demonology*, did not suffer half the persecution from his imaginary gentleman-usher in black velvet, that we sustained from our friend in quondam black cloth.' Dickens had a copy of *Demonology* in his library at his death: 'Charles Dickens and his Library', Edwin A. Dawes, [Magic Circular] Vol. 60, February 1966, p. 91.

[4] Writers enjoyed by CD are discussed in the chapter 'Dickens Reading' in [Smith, Grahame] pp. 40-59. Some examples from authors: *The Expedition of Humphry Clinker* by Tobias Smollett. One of the characters had a vision that

When it comes to Spiritualism, Dickens's tone changed. It was almost as if he did not consider the subject to be worthy of proper consideration. Whereas with believers in ghosts he seemed conciliatory and understanding of their reasons for holding such a view, he was openly sceptical of those who put their faith in Spiritualism. Certainly none of Dickens's articles on the subject in his two journals display the forensic analysis that he applied to Mrs Crowe's book. Instead he resorted to quoting from spiritualist newspapers and books, ridiculing both the writers and those participating in the practice.[5]

an old friend was going to come to dinner unannounced, which turned out to be true. Matt Bramble, a narrator, wrote as follows: 'The incident we all owned to be remarkable, and I endeavoured to account for it by natural means. I observed, that as the gentleman was of a visionary turn, the casual idea, or remembrance of his old friend, might suggest those circumstances, which accident had for once realized; but that in all probability he had seen many visions of the same kind, which were never verified. None of the company directly dissented from my opinion; but from the objections that were hinted, I could plainly perceive that the majority were persuaded there was something more extraordinary in the case.' From *Joseph Andrews* by Henry Fielding. 'But, as it happens to persons who have in their infancy been thoroughly frightened with certain no-persons called ghosts, that they retain their dread of those beings after they are convinced that there are no such things.' And from Oliver Goldsmith, 'On Deceit and Falsehood' in *A Collection of Essays* no. 8, (Saturday 24 November 1759). 'We have a *wondering quality* within us, which finds huge gratification when we see strange feats done, and cannot at the same time see the doer, or the cause. Such actions are sure to be attributed to some witch or demon; for if we come to find they are slily performed by artists of our own species and by causes purely natural, our delight dies with our amazement. It is, therefore, one of the most unthankful offices in the world, to go about to expose the mistaken notions of witchcraft and spirits, it is robbing mankind of a valuable imagination, and of the privilege of being deceived.'

[5] CD's failure to wholly discount the existence of ghosts may well be because he

In one article he recounted three incidents of a spiritualist nature that happened to him, which are clearly fictitious, to demonstrate the absurdity of the 'genuine' spiritualist experience. In another, he implied that those who experience spiritual manifestations are a little deranged. In a third, he chastised the manager of a medium for suggesting that he had attended one of her séances, having already equated her attempts to communicate with the spirits through 'rappings', with the Cock Lane Ghost hoax of the previous century.[6]

He took a similar, rather mocking, stance when it came to requests for him to attend séances. He wrote to one woman:

> I have not the least belief in the awful unseen World being available for evening parties at so much per night. And although I should be ready to receive enlightenment from any source, I must say that I have very little hope of it from the Spirits who express themselves through Mediums, as I have never yet observed them to talk anything but Nonsense.[7]

To another he commented that 'it is not at all in accordance with my reverence for the great mystery of Death and the existence beyond the grave, to put them myself through the interposition of any human creature.' However in this same letter his conciliatory

---

depicted them in several short stories. The most famous is *A Christmas Carol* but other examples are *The Haunted Man and the Ghost's Bargain* and *The Signal-Man*. Elizabeth Browning summed him up well when she said that CD was 'fond of ghost-stories, as long as they are impossible!' For Browning, 'possible' ghosts referred to Spiritualism – the quotation comes from [Burton] p. 143.

[6] The three articles are: 'Well-Authenticated Rappings', [HW] Vol. XVII, No. 413, 20 Feb, 1858, pp. 217-220; 'The Spirit Business', [HW] Vol. VII, No. 163, 7 May, 1853, pp. 217-220; and 'The Ghost of the Cock Lane Ghost Wrong Again', [HW] Vol. VI, No. 147, 15 Jan, 1853, p. 420.

[7] [Pilgrim, Vol. 7] p. 652.

mask seemed to slip and you sense his true feelings are expressed: 'I do not desire to see [the medium], and indeed altogether decline to see any person making those pretensions.'[8]

That is not to say that Dickens refused to attend any séances: indeed he was clearly caught up in the initial fascination with Spiritualism like many others. His American friend, Cornelius Felton, visited London in May, 1853 and wrote:

> Table-turning and spirit-rapping occupy the minds of the London people, I might almost say, more than any other subject. I have not entered a house without hearing it discussed or seeing experiments. The handsomest women and the gravest men are full of wonder at the marvels they themselves accomplish; and I have had several rather warm debates with ladies and gentlemen who persisted in seeing a mysterious law of nature in what was evidently the work of their own fingers.
>
> At -----'s a circle was formed each night I was there, and the table went around. Nothing could be plainer, in all the cases that I saw, than that the people around the table, after getting somewhat impatient, gave it a push; and when the pushing became strong and general enough to over the resistance, then the table went round, *and not before.* But they protested one and all, and believed, that they did nothing, except to hold their hands and *will.*
>
> We tried it at Dickens's and at Forster's, with a fixed determination to give the experiment a perfectly fair chance; and the consequence was, in three or four long trials, that neither table, nor hat, nor anything else, moved a hair's breadth.[9]

Felton's matter-of-fact description rather contradicted Dickens's own depiction of what happened at a table turning party. In a letter to John Leech dated 23rd May, 1853, he wrote: 'We spun a table in the most extraordinary manner last night...The Pembroke table in

[8] [Pilgrim, Vol. 10] p. 378.
[9] [Felton] pp. 31-2.

the study gamboled like an insane elephant (with a prodigious creaking) all around the room!!!' One suspects that this might well have been Dickens orchestrating the spinning to entertain the other participants, who included his wife and children.[10]

However a year later cynicism had set in. Attending a party given by his good friend, godfather to his son and convinced spiritualist, Edward Bulwer-Lytton, Dickens wrote that, despite attempts by his host to raise a count from the dead, nothing occurred. 'I stayed till the ghostly hour, but the rumour was unfounded, for neither count nor plebeian came up to the spiritual scratch.' He concluded: 'It is really inexplicable to me that a man of his calibre can be run away with by such small beer.' From now on, Dickens would take a much harder line. Clearly something about those experiences reinforced, or perhaps brought about, a deep contempt for mediums generally.[11]

There was one in particular for whom Dickens reserved genuine ire. This was Daniel Dunglas Home, who inveigled his way into the houses, and occasionally hearts, of Victorian high society; paying his way for food and lodgings by conducting séances. It was possible that Dickens tasted blood in his publication of the article 'The Ghost of the Cock Lane Ghost' (the follow up article to this was mentioned above). The original piece was a description of a séance conducted by one of the first spiritualists to make an impact in Victorian London, Mrs Hayden, who came over from America in 1852 with her husband and Mr Stone, her manager. Her technique was very basic. She essentially communicated with spirits by spelling out words on a crude Ouija board: as the appropriate letter was pointed to, a rapping sound was heard.

The article was written by Henry Morley who visited her with a colleague. However it was Dickens who drew attention to the

---

[10] [Pilgrim, Vol. 7] p. 92.
[11] [Pilgrim, Vol. 7] pp. 286.

similarity between the medium's rappings and the Cock Lane Ghost: and he who came up with the title.[12] Mrs Hayden was singularly unsuccessful in her rappings, claiming at one point to be talking to a spirit of someone who was still alive and at another time predicting that one of the sitters would have one hundred and thirty six children. It was said that Morley's article was partly responsible for Mrs Hayden's early departure back to America.[13]

Dickens's first exposure to Home appeared to be in turning down a request to attend one of his séances; this was soon after Home arrived in England from America in 1855. Presumably, not knowing much about him at this stage, Dickens wrote courteously: 'I cannot have the pleasure of seeing the famous "Medium" tonight, for I have some Theatricals at home.'[14]

Five years later he refused another invitation a good deal more

---

[12] 'The Ghost of the Cock Lane Ghost' [HW] Vol. V1, No.139, 20 November, 1852, pp. 217 - 223. On 5 November, 1852 CD wrote to Wills, his sub-editor: 'In the matter of the Rappings, I think a good name for the paper would be *The Ghost of the Cock Lane Ghost*...the two spirits are greatly alike.' [Pilgrim, Vol. 6], p. 799. For more information about the link between the Cock Lane Ghost and CD, see 'Dickens, Spiritualism and The Cock Lane Ghost', Ian Keable, *Dickens 200 – Text and Beyond*, Pécs University, Hungary, (written in 2012, awaiting publication).

[13] Having achieved some success in London, between June and September, 1853, the Haydens went to France and Ireland; but they were not that well received. Mr Hayden admitted that 'the stupid and silly article which appeared in Dickens's *Household Words* almost a year since, has done much to set their minds against it.' On 12 October, 1853 the Haydens gave up in Europe and sailed back to the US. The quotation from Mr Hayden comes from a letter to the publishers in Vol. II, p. 403 of *The Spiritual Telegraph*, cited in: 'Rapping the Rappers, More Grist for the Biographers' Mill', NC Peyrouton, [Dickensian] Vol. 55, 1 January, 1959, p. 28.

[14] DD Home arrived in England in March, 1855. [Pilgrim, Vol. 7] p. 651-2; the letter was written on 19 June, 1855.

abruptly, giving no excuse other than his 'reasons for doing so, I need not enter into; they are well considered and strong.' In a later letter that same year he wrote that he took 'the liberty of regarding' Home 'as an Impostor'. Six years after that, in July, 1866, he boasted about preventing Home coming out as an actor and also noted that he failed to make an appearance at a London theatre despite been announced on 'an appropriately dirty little rag of a bill'. Dickens was confident that the public had 'found out the scoundrel'.[15]

DD Home was also sharply attacked in two articles in Dickens's journal. In the first, which was written by his assistant editor, WH Wills, a description was given of a spiritualist lecture that Home gave. Wills showed his own incredulity at some of the stories Home related ('He also asserted that he had been lifted up to the ceiling of a brightly-lighted room, in the presence of several spectators.') but confessed that he, along with the conjurer John Henry Anderson who was also there, were very much in the minority. Indeed when Anderson tried to rain on Home's parade by making his own speech at the end disputing what the medium had said, he was drowned out by jeers and hisses from the rest of the audience.[16]

The second article was written by Dickens and was a review of DD Home's autobiography, *Incidents in my Life*. It mostly comprised extracts from the book, leaving the reader to pass their own judgement on the absurdity of the author's claims. Dickens does though call it 'an odious book' and expressed great surprise and regret that the prestigious publishers Longman and Company should be involved in its publication.[17]

DD Home seems to have needled Dickens for over a decade. And certainly if Dickens's object was to send Home packing, in a similar way to how he had got rid of Mrs Hayden, his strategy could hardly

---

[15] [Pilgrim, Vol. 9] p. 242; [Pilgrim, Vol. 9] p. 311 and [Pilgrim, Vol. 11] p. 227.
[16] 'At Home with the Spirits' [AYR] Vol. XV, No. 358, 3 March, 1866 pp. 180-4.
[17] 'The Martyr Medium' [AYR] Vol. IX, No. 206, 4 April, 1863, pp. 133-6.

deemed to be successful. Despite Dickens's confident assertion that 'the public had found out the scoundrel', Home continued to flourish in England after the writer's death in 1870. And as the only medium who was never actually caught out in any fraudulent activity, Home remains to this day much heralded by spiritualists.

It is not entirely clear why Dickens had so much hatred for Home whom, as far as it is known, he never saw or met. Part of the reason might be that many of his trusted friends were taken in by him. Elizabeth Browning, who was married to the poet Robert Browning, in particular was a devotee of Home: the medium was said to be the only subject that husband and wife fell out over. Another, even closer to home, was the aforementioned Edward Bulwer-Lytton.[18]

Dickens set out clearly in one letter why he did not want to get involved in discussing the truth, or otherwise, of spiritual manifestations.

> Firstly, because the conditions under which such enquiries take place – as I know in the recent case of two friends of mine, with whom I discussed them – are preposterously wanting in the commonest securities against deceit or mistake. Secondly, because the people lie so very hard, both concerning what did take place, and what impression it made at the time on the enquirer.[19]

A way of tackling both of these would have been for Dickens to have attended more séances, insisting on stringent test conditions and

---

[18] 'Another time, when he was a guest at Knebworth, Lytton cornered [CD] to ask if he would not at least investigate the *worth-while* mediums? Such as whom, Dickens asked with a slightly hunted air. Such as Mr Home, Lytton replied imperturbably.' [Burton] p. 142. [Lamont] argued persuasively that Dickens never saw Home: '... he never took the opportunity to see Daniel for himself, p. 125.

[19] [Pilgrim, Vol. 9] p. 311.

using his own perceptive eye as testimony. So there is the unanswered question of why he seemed to go out of his way to avoid several invitations – and in particular why he refused any opportunity, of which he clearly had some, to observe Home at work.

One possible explanation is that Dickens was concerned that he might be persuaded by the mediums into believing that some of their manifestations were genuine. He clearly had a predilection towards such matters. His participation in at least some séances suggested it; he believed in some of the unlikely powers of mesmerism[20] – such as those under the influence being able to read whilst blindfolded – and he had a slight ambiguity towards ghosts. Most revealing of all came from the man who perhaps knew him best, his great friend John Forster. He wrote about Dickens: 'such was his interest generally in things supernatural that, but for the strong restraining power of his common sense, he might have fallen into the follies of spiritualism.'[21]

Dickens's vehement attacks on Spiritualism do not in any way detract from this theory. It is accepted that those who take the hardest line against a cause, occasionally have an element of

[20] 'I don't want to champion homeopathy (in which I don't believe), or mesmerism (in which I do).' Letter to Henry Morley, 9 Jan, 1863 [Pilgrim, Vol. 10] pp. 192-3. CD's belief in magnetism was further confirmed by the recovery of his friend John Leech, after he was hit on the head by a wave at Bonchurch on the Isle of Wight. Having successfully magnetised him into recovery, as related in a letter to John Forster on 26 September, 1849 [Pilgrim, Vol. 5] p. 615, CD went on to explain in another letter to F Evans, dated the next day, how magnetism might have an impact on how you sleep at night, depending which way you face. [Pilgrim, Vol. 5] p. 617 & n 4.

[21] [Forster, Vol. 3] Chapter XIX, Personal Characteristics. There is evidence too that CD was still attending the occasional séance after his scepticism was at its height. 'Small-Beer Chronicles' [AYR] Vol. VII, No. 176, 6 September, 1862, p. 608, related how CD was at one with the conjurer Henri Robin.

ambivalence towards it. The most famous person who investigated, and uncovered, the fraudulent nature of the Cock Lane Ghost was Samuel Johnson. And he was persuaded to get involved in what turned out to be a fairly clumsy hoax, precisely because he was desperate to prove the existence of an afterlife.[22]

Dickens would also be anxious that he would not be able to discern exactly how some of the mediums pulled off their spiritualistic stunts. He had already confessed his failure to understand both the exploits of the magnetic boy, Alexis Didier, and the conjurer de Caston; maybe he would be similarly taken in by one or two mediums. This would be especially true of DD Home who was, by all accounts, so convincing in what he did.[23] It was much easier for Dickens to ridicule and mock from the safe environment of the writing desk than to face awkward questions in a real-world setting when interrogated by the believers. It is hard to retain the moral high ground if you cannot provide convincing answers.

Significantly, the most obvious link between Spiritualism and conjuring was never made by Dickens; he never explicitly stated that the mediumistic stunts were just magic tricks in another guise. The closest he came to it is in his review of DD Home's book where he compared the belief in the gullible contending that they witnessed the sprouting of a sprig of geranium in somebody's hand

---

[22] For Johnson the existence of ghosts was proof of an after-life. As he put it on 25 June, 1763 in *The Life of Samuel Johnson*, James Boswell, 1791: 'If a form should appear, and a voice should tell me that a particular man had died at a particular place, and a particular hour, a fact which I had no apprehension of, nor any means of knowing, and this fact, with all its circumstances, should afterwards be unquestionably proved, I should, in that case, be persuaded that I had supernatural intelligence imparted to me.'

[23] It also helped that DD Home did not charge for any of his sittings – it is far harder to be sceptical about someone who seems to be doing you a favour. For the full story on Home, check out [Lamont].

to similarly believing that

> the conjuror's half-crowns really did become invisible and in that state fly, because he afterwards cuts them out of a real orange; or as if the conjuror's pigeon, being after the discharge of his gun, a real live pigeon fluttering on the target, must therefore conclusively be a pigeon, fired, whole, living and unshattered, out of the gun!

The reason for this is that Dickens did not see any connection between the two; at least not when it came to a comparison with the type of apparatus-based conjuring that he used to perform. It was unlikely he saw any of the shows put on by the likes of John Henry Anderson who attempted to re-create what the spiritualists did in a theatre environment.[24] Ironically Dickens saw the conjurer who perhaps got closest to replicating the stunts of the spiritualists – the mind reader Alfred de Caston; but once again Dickens failed to join the dots.

Dickens therefore did not apply the logic of his own conjuring experiences. He would have known how audiences can be fooled by the simplest of tricks. Applying that same reasoning to the séance, where the medium has an additional benefit which is not available to the conjurer – the desperation of the sitters to believe in an afterlife – he similarly should have known how easily those attending séances can potentially be duped.

The conclusion must be that, for Dickens, the subject of, and experience with, conjuring and Spiritualism were separate areas of interest. There is no evidence that he sensed any crossover. Ackroyd wrote that his 'half-humorous interest in the occult' is naturally to be linked with 'his liking for magical tricks'. Such a link is

---

[24] Spirit Rapping was first introduced into Anderson's programme in the Christmas season at Edinburgh opening on 24 December, 1853; and was from then on a regular part of his repertoire: [Dawes, Anderson].

questionable. Dickens's conjuring would appear to have far more in common with his acting, speaking and public readings from his books (in other words the unadulterated enjoyment of entertaining) than it ever did with Spiritualism.

# CHAPTER SIX

# The Writer

## Conjuring References in Dickens's Writing

Dickens's foray into conjuring has never been considered of much consequence by those writing about him. This has principally been because it does not appear to have had much of an influence on his writing. This was very much highlighted in Paul Schlicke's excellent book *Dickens and Popular Entertainment*, which covered in great detail many aspects of broad entertainment – the theatre, circus, street entertainers, travelling shows – and how they are dealt with in Dickens's novels such as *Nicholas Nickleby*, *The Old Curiosity Shop* and *Hard Times*; but hardly gives conjuring a mention.

One suggested exception to the perceived lack of conjuring impact was made in Charles Forstye's *The Decoding of Edwin Drood*. He argued that Dickens applied the art of misdirection, which he had learnt from his own experiences as a conjurer, in *Dombey and Son*. He did this when he took readers by surprise in killing off Paul Dombey, the 'son' of the title, and focusing instead on the daughter. However it does not necessarily require a knowledge of conjuring to apply that type of twist in a book's plot; so it is a difficult theory to sustain.

It is broadly true that most of the references to conjuring which do occur in Dickens are rather inconsequential; they principally relate to an odd phrase here, a metaphor here, that it is arguable another writer, without Dickens's knowledge of conjuring, would not have created. Nevertheless even such trivia has its own fascination; and a greater understanding of anything written by Dickens can only enhance an enjoyment of reading him.

Leaving aside the conjurer Sweet William, whose name, occupation and repertoire have been considered in some depth in Chapter One, there is one other intriguing conjuring reference in *The Old Curiosity Shop* – this time to a better known character. This is the irrepressible and engaging Dick Swiveller, who lightened up the law office where he was working 'with scraps of song and merriment, conjuring with inkstands and boxes of wafers, catching three oranges in one hand, balancing stools upon his chin and penknives on his nose, and constantly performing a hundred other feats with equal ingenuity'.

On first reading this passage, it appears that Dickens was using the word 'conjuring' in the sense of 'mucking around with', particularly as wafers and inkstands are hardly obvious conjuring props. In Victorian times, though, a 'wafer' was not a thin biscuit, but a stationery product. A large pancake-type substance was made from wheat flour mixed with water. It was then cut into circular pieces, stacked in boxes and used, after it was moistened with water, to stick two bits of paper together.

In the 1843 Crambrook catalogue, in which some of Dickens's own purchased tricks were listed, there was an item for sale called 'The Wonderful Wafers'. As well as wafers the buyer required a palette knife and, utilising what magicians recognise today as the 'paddle move', it was possible to make the wafers vanish and reappear on the knife. Similarly, in the Novra catalogue, there was a trick called The Vase of Ink, in which ink turned into clear water. So it is possible that Dickens was genuinely referencing a couple of actual magic tricks that Swiveller could have performed with these unusual implements.

Later on in *The Old Curiosity Shop*, the word conjurer is used in a slightly different context. A gentleman was trying to elicit some information from the evil Quilp without success and eventually exasperatingly said: 'don't you know with what object I have come here, and if you do know, can you throw no light upon it?' "You think I'm a conjuror, sir," replied Quilp, shrugging up his shoulders.

"If I was, I should tell my own fortune – and make it".'

Here Quilp is using the word in the sense of having magic powers of some sort. This is the way that any writer might employ the word, as indeed it was used in this context later on in the same book: 'poor Kit was looking earnestly out of the window, observant of nothing, – when all at once, as though it had been conjured up by magic, he became aware of the face of Quilp.'

Where conjuring crops up in other books, most of the instances are of a similar generalised kind as these. In *David Copperfield*, the eponymous hero said to his future wife Agnes: 'If I had had a conjuror's cap, there is no one I should have wished for but you!' before blushingly having to admit, 'Well! Perhaps Dora first' – a reference to his present wife. In *Our Mutual Friend*, when the devious Bradley Headstone made an unexpected visit to see Lizzie Hexam, Jenny Wren called him 'quite a conjuror'.

In *Dombey and Son*, the colourful character of Toots sidled around a church in order to get a good view of what was happening inside: 'Mr. Toots's movements in the churchyard were so eccentric, that he seemed generally to defeat all calculation, and to appear, like the conjuror's figure, where he was least expected'. In *Bleak House* Dickens seemed keen to give the police detective, Mr Bucket, almost magical qualities. Esther Summerson related how he made one of his appearances. 'When we had all arrived here, the physician stopped, and taking off his hat, appeared to vanish by magic and to leave another and quite a different man in his place.' And later on: 'Mr Bucket lost no time in transferring this paper [a stolen will], with the dexterity of a conjuror, from Mr Smallweed to Mr Jarndyce.'

Dickens's references to thimble-rigging in *Sketches by* Boz and *Nicholas Nickelby*, before he took up conjuring, have already been considered. The term cropped up again in *Martin Chuzzlewit* when Tom Pinch, on being forced to leave the house of Pecksniff, avoided falling into the trap of 'ring-droppers, pea and thimble-riggers, duffers, touters, or any of those bloodless sharpers, who are, perhaps, a little better known to the Police.' A 'ring-dropper' was when a hustler 'unexpectedly' found a valuable ring on the ground, generously allowing a passer-by to buy it for less than its imagined, but far more than its actual, value.

Dickens demonstrated his knowledge of another type of swindle in *Great Expectations*. He had Pip saying 'An obliging stranger, under pretence of compactly folding up my bank-notes for security's sake, abstracts the notes and gives me nutshells'. This was a well-documented swindle which Dickens was likely to have read about, rather than witnessed.

There are, though, three rather more interesting similes that Dickens uses which bring more of his direct magic knowledge into play. In *David Copperfield*, Miss Mowcher, the under-sized hair dresser, said: 'You'd have betted a hundred pound to five, now, that you wouldn't have seen me here, wouldn't you? Bless you, man alive, I'm everywhere. I'm here, and there, and where not, like the conjurer's half crown in the lady's handkercher.'

Making a coin magically appear in a handkerchief was a trick that had been around for many years. It is quite possible that Dickens purchased it. In the Crambrook catalogue there was listed: 'The Flying Coin. A penny, half-crown, and lady's handkerchief are borrowed; the penny given to a gentleman to retain in his possession; the half-crown and handkerchief to a lady; at command, both coins are in the lady's handkerchief.'

In *Little Dorrit*, Mrs Gowan was convinced that her son had married beneath him in wedding the daughter of Mr and Mrs Meagles and subtly made that clear with the 'same feint, with the same polite dexterity, she foisted on Mrs Meagles, as a conjuror might have forced a card on that innocent lady.' The use of the word 'forced' is noticeable – it is a very particular term used by conjurers. 'Forcing a card' is shorthand for inducing a spectator to take a specific card that the conjurer wants them to take.

Finally, in *Bleak House* there is a reference to a trick that Dickens was very familiar with. Early on Dickens introduced the all-knowing lawyer, Tulkinghorn, who was later to wreck the life of his client Sir Leicester Dedlock, by bringing about the disgrace, and subsequent death, of his wife, Lady Dedlock. Tulkinghorn's power was to snuffle out the hidden secrets of his clients which he used to his own advantage. Here his first appearance is described:

> And at her house in town, upon this muddy, murky afternoon, presents himself an old-fashioned old gentleman, attorney-at-law and eke solicitor of the High Court of Chancery, who has the honour of acting as legal adviser of the Dedlocks and has as many cast-iron boxes in his office with that name outside as if the present baronet were the coin of the conjuror's trick and were constantly being juggled through the whole set.

This conjuring reference was a direct allusion to Dickens's The Pyramid Wonder which he performed on the Isle of Wight. The trick was described by Dickens in his playbill: 'A shilling being lent to the Necromancer by any gentleman...will disappear from within a brazen box at the word of command, and pass through the hearts of an infinity of boxes, which will afterwards build themselves into pyramids and sink into a small mahogany box, at the Necromancer's bidding.' In other words, a borrowed coin vanished from one box and ended up in the bottom-most box in a separate nest of boxes.

This was a great metaphor by Dickens as he was suggesting, by introducing the concept of a conjuring trick, not only that Lord Dedlock's name cropped up everywhere in his locked boxes but also that the baronet, similar to the coin, could be easily manipulated. Of course it was part of Dickens's genius that even if you are not familiar with the trick, the meaning is quite clear; but it certainly adds to the pleasure of reading the words to know the provenance.

## A Christmas Carol

A mere handful of conjuring allusions are unlikely to bring about a revisionist approach to the writings of Dickens. But there is one book in which perhaps conjuring had a greater influence than was previously thought; and is especially relevant as it is arguably his most famous work of all, *A Christmas Carol.*

*A Christmas Carol* was written in the last three months of 1843 and published in December of that year. This was the same year that Dickens 'came out' as a conjurer; the year it is known he did his largest number of shows; the year he provided evidence of working on his act; the year he compared himself favourably with Döbler; the year he received the most compliments from those who saw him. All in all, it is the year where you would anticipate there might be some overflow of his interest in conjuring into his fictional writings – and what better book than the magical *A Christmas Carol.*

One such seepage was signposted in *Oliver Twist.* Fagin said to Noah Claypole, when he persuaded him to follow Nancy and let him know what she was up to; 'Some conjurers say that number three is the magic number, and some say number seven. It's neither, my friend, neither. It's number one.' This, of course, was very much Fagin's creed; and could be said to be, before his redemption, Scrooge's too.

It is true that conjurers instinctively gravitate towards the numbers three and seven. Three phases is considered to be the ideal number in a routine. Often the first effect will take place; it will be repeated; and then for the finale, something extra will happen. Any more than three occurrences of the same magical happening and the audience tend to lose interest. Perhaps the most famous trick in magic, the Cups and Balls, comprises three cups and three balls; three thimbles are used in thimble-rigging and three cards, obviously, in the three card trick. 'The rule of three', which is common in speech making and comedy, is equally applicable to magic.

Seven is less obviously a 'magic number' but is certainly traditionally a lucky number, perhaps going back to the seven days required to create the world. The chances are that when Dickens performed his trick The Pyramid Wonder, in which the vanished coin was found in the innermost, he would have used a total of seven boxes. The name of the trick sold around this time was called The Nest of Seven Boxes.

Mind readers make use of the fact that the numbers three and seven are recalled most often. If you ask someone to name a number between one and five, there is a statistically better chance that they will go for three, before two and four. Similarly, ask them to name a number between one and ten, and number seven is the most popular response. A slightly more complex version is to ask for an odd number between ten and fifty, both digits to be different: the likely reply is thirty-seven (three and seven). A poll in 2014 amongst 30,000 people concluded that the most popular number was seven followed by three.

It is surely no coincidence, therefore, that Dickens chose the numbers three and seven to play a role in *A Christmas Carol*. Most obviously there were three spectres who came to visit Scrooge; the Ghosts of Christmas Past, Present and Christmas Yet to Come. It has been argued that the final ghost is rather superfluous, in that the ghastly state of the phantom of his deceased partner Marley had already foretold the fate that awaited Scrooge if he did not change his miserly ways. But Dickens would have instinctively realised the importance of having the psychologically satisfying requisite third ethereal being.

Equally significant is that Marley made his appearance to foretell the coming of the ghosts seven years after he had died. As Scrooge said early on in the book, after he was confronted by two gentlemen asking for charitable contributions: 'Mr Marley has been dead these seven years...He died seven years ago this very night.' The number is stressed again when Scrooge discerned his door knocker morphing into Marley's face, someone he had 'not bestowed one thought on...since his last mention of his seven years' dead partner that afternoon.'

Where Dickens's conjuring and *A Christmas Carol* truly came together was in the Cratchit's Christmas dinner which was witnessed by Scrooge, alongside the Ghost of Christmas Present. The finale of the meal was the pudding. Brought in by Mrs Cratchit it was a pudding

> like a speckled cannon-ball, so hard and firm, blazing in half of half-a-quartern of ignited brandy, and bedlight with Christmas holly stuck into the top.
> Oh, a wonderful pudding! Bob Cratchit said.

Dickens's own conjuring show always concluded with The Pudding Wonder, baked in a hat and cut up and dispensed, in his own words, 'in portions to the whole company, for their consumption then and there.' The one, the climax of the meal, the other, the climax of a show; the one a 'wonderful pudding', the other the 'pudding wonder'. It is not known for sure whether Dickens was performing the trick before he wrote this passage; but it seems very likely that the two were strongly linked in his mind.

The final possible conjuring reference was first suggested by Brian Sibley in *A Christmas Carol, The Unsung Story*. He had noted the similarity between the vanishing of the Ghost of Christmas Past with an illusion known as the Extinguisher Trick.

The Ghost of Christmas Past is hard to picture from Dickens's description (indeed most illustrators have not attempted it). It was a strange, ethereal, some might say magical, spectre constantly in a state of flux. 'What was light one instant, at another time was dark, so the figure itself fluctuated in its distinctness: being now a thing with one arm, now with one leg, now with twenty legs, now a pair of legs without a head, now a head without a body'. Its most distinctive feature was that 'from the crown of its head there sprung a bright clear jet of light' and it also had 'a great extinguisher for a cap, which it now held under its arm'.

It was this cap which Scrooge focused on, when he was begging the ghost not to haunt him any more at the end of the second stave of the book. Taking matters into his own hands,

> Scrooge observed that its light was burning high and bright; and dimly connecting that with its influence over him, he seized the extinguisher-cap, and by a sudden action pressed it down upon its head.
>
> The Spirit dropped beneath it, so that the extinguisher covered its whole form; but though Scrooge pressed it down with all his force, he could not hide the light: which streamed from under it, in an unbroken flood upon the ground.

The vanish was one of the eight illustrations that John Leech drew for the first edition of *A Christmas Carol* (see Plate 26). In it, Scrooge can be seen pressing down with two hands on the top of a giant cone, underneath of which light is spreading out. Leech was a great friend of Dickens and also played his assistant in his conjuring show. So one can be very confident that the image had the approval of Dickens and, quite possibly, was drawn with his guidance.

The Extinguisher Trick was one of the first illusions of a complete vanish of a living person: it was probably first performed around 1790. In the trick the conjurer's assistant stood on a table. He or she was covered by a large cone; and when the cone was lifted off, the person had disappeared. Apart from the absence of the table, John Leech's woodcut could almost be an illustration of a conjurer actually performing the trick.

It is not known for certain whether Dickens saw the Extinguisher Trick. One conjurer who definitely performed it was George Sutton in 1838 and, as noted in Chapter One, he was someone who Dickens might well have seen. However Dickens did of course attend Ludwig Döbler's show in 1842 and, as part of one of his routines, called The Miraculous Washing, the Austrian conjurer produced a washerwoman. Döbler's playbill has an illustration of this very trick and, although the cover under which the woman appeared is more basket-shaped than cone-shaped, it was clearly a variation on the Extinguisher Trick (see Plate 27).

More generally the image of vanishing someone with a large extinguisher was very much in the public domain through the medium of graphic art. A number of prints were produced in the first thirty years of the nineteenth century, usually depicting some allegorical representation of government policy or individual being snuffed out by a large cone. One of those artists was George Cruikshank who, in his early years before he turned to illustrating books, was considered to be one of the most vitriolic of satirists. He is now best known for his illustrations for *Oliver Twist*.

Whether these images were inspired by the Extinguisher Trick itself, or simply the extinguisher used to snuff out a candle or the lighted torches carried by link boys, is not known. But the fact that some of them definitely reference the vanishing of an individual – as opposed to merely dousing a flame – certainly gives them a strong connection to the conjuring illusion.

It therefore seems reasonable to assert that a combination of either seeing a conjurer perform a modification of the Extinguisher Trick, or alternatively coming across a graphic image depicting somebody disappearing under a large cone, inspired Dickens with the idea of making the Ghost of Christmas Past vanish in a similar way. The fact also that this particular Spirit had such magical qualities, certainly in comparison to the Ghosts of Christmas Present and Christmas Yet to Come, reinforces the conviction that Dickens would have had a conjuring illusion in mind when writing this sequence.

# Chapter Six Supplement

## Conjuring Quotations in Dickens's Novels

A number of references have been made to conjuring in Dickens's novels. They are as follows:

| Quotation | Book and Chapter |
|---|---|
| 'number three is the magic' | *Oliver Twist*, 43 |
| ' conjuring with inkstands' | *The Old Curiosity Shop*, 36 |
| 'You think I'm a conjuror' | *The Old Curiosity Shop*, 48 |
| 'conjured up by magic' | *The Old Curiosity Shop*, 60 |
| 'ring-droppers, pea' | *Martin Chuzzlewit*, 37 |
| 'like the conjuror's figure' | *Dombey and Son*, 56 |
| 'conjurer's half crown' | *David Copperfield*, 22 |
| 'If I had had a conjurer's cap' | *David Copperfield*, 35 |
| 'coin of the conjuror's trick' | *Bleak House*, 2 |
| 'appeared to vanish by magic' | *Bleak House*, 24 |
| 'with the dexterity of a conjurer' | *Bleak House*, 62 |
| 'forced a card' | *Little Dorrit*, 33 |
| 'gives me nutshells' | *Great Expectations* 28 |
| 'You are quite a conjuror' | *Our Mutual Friend*, Book the Second, 11 |

The poet, Henry Wadsworth Longfellow, perhaps best known for his epic poem *The Song of Hiawatha*, met Dickens on his trip to America in 1842. He described him as 'gay, free and easy character;- a fine bright face; blue eyes, long dark hair, and withal a slight dash of the Dick Swiveller in him.' Maybe in his portrayal of Swiveller performing tricks to Sally Brass in *The Old Curiosity Shop*, Dickens was somehow foreseeing himself as a future conjurer.

# CHAPTER SIX SUPPLEMENT

## Magic Tricks in Dickens's Novels[1]

### 1. Trick with Wafer

The full description of The Wonderful Wafers trick, which was in the Crambrook catalogue[2], was as follows: 'Six wafers are shewn on a large palette knife; they are afterwards removed, two at each time, and lastly appear on the knife, as in the first instance.' This is better known to magicians as the Paddle Trick, a wonderful principle that was written up in Scot's 1584 *The Discoverie of Witchcraft*, under a section called 'Of diverse petie juggling knacks'. In Scot's version he uses a flexible straw ('rish') instead of the wafer; and a flat board ('trencher') to replace the knife.[3]

Wafers would be perfect for the trick as it is necessary that they should both stick to the knife and yet be easily removable.[4]

---

[1] The connection between the passage in *Bleak House* and the Pyramid Wonder trick of Dickens was first pointed out in an insightful section on CD's conjuring in [Forsyte] pp. 36-42. It was Forstyte who argued that Dickens was applying his magical knowledge in the art of misdirection to the unexpected death of Paul in Dombey and Son: 'The title, *Dombey and Son*, was calculated to give the reader the impression that the story was largely about the relation between Mr Dombey and his son Paul, so enabling Dickens to spring the bombshell of young Paul Dombey's death in the fifth number. The question remains whether – and how – he had used the art of misdirection that he had learned as a magician when set out to mystify his wider audience on *The Mystery of Edwin Drood*.'

[2] The Flying Coin trick is also in [Crambrook] p. 11.

[3] [Scot] p. 193.

[4] There is an excellent version of this trick, using paper and a knife, described in [Sachs, 2nd] pp. 42-4.

## 2. Ink to Water

This trick was described in the Novra catalogue as: 'The Vase of Ink, a glass vase is shewn full of ink, a handkerchief thrown over the glass and the ink is transformed to clear water and goldfish, the handkerchief returned perfectly empty.' The goldfish was an optional extra: the basic trick was changing ink into water.

Unlike the wafer trick, to execute this does require quite a bit of advance preparation. The first conjurer to have performed the feat was Joseph Jacobs who appeared in London at the New Strand Theatre in February 1841 and was someone who Dickens might well have seen (see Supplement to Chapter One, 'Theatre Conjurers prior to 1842'). The only fly in the ointment, or indeed ink in the bottle, is that it was not until 1845 that Jacobs first 'performed the trick of turning ink into transparent water in which golf-fish swam'.[5]

The jury must be out therefore on whether Dickens was citing this trick, which was performed earlier than historical records seem to show; another similar trick; or indeed his reference to inkstands in a conjuring connection was purely coincidental.

## 3. Forced a Card

The expression 'forced a card' means persuading a spectator to remove from the pack a specific card which the conjurer wants them to take – without the helper being aware that they have been so deceived. It was written up, although not too helpfully in terms of the finer details of the technique required, in *Gale's Cabinet of*

---

[5] [Frost] p. 219; [Dawes, Great Illusionists] p. 99: 'Jacobs was one of the first conjurers to display the feat of changing a bowl of ink into one containing water with goldfish swimming in it; this was around 1845.' An explanation of the trick is given in [Sachs, 2nd] pp. 265-7.

*Knowledge* under the title of: 'For a Person to choose a Card, you not Supposed to know what it is'. The description began: 'This is called the Nerve trick, and is thus performed; having previously looked at a card, bid the person draw one, taking care to show that to him which you know.' And concluded: 'This is a very curious trick, and if cleanly done, is really astonishing; but may be accounted for from the nature of the nerves, which are always more retentive when any thing is attempted to be taken either by force or surprise.'[6]

One of the street conjurers interviewed in Mayhew talked about card forcing

> All card tricks are feats of great dexterity and quickness of hand. I never used a false pack of cards. There are some made for amateurs, but professionals never use trick cards. The greatest art is what is termed forcing, that is, making a party take the card you wish him to; and let him try ever so well, he will have it, though he's not conscious of it.[7]

The exact expression, 'forced a card', was used by John Henry Anderson when divulging some simple tricks for the 1849 Christmas number of *The Penny Illustrated News* – so this would have been nearly ten years before *Little Dorrit* was written. Anderson wrote in explanation of how to perform one particular trick: 'Having forced a card upon one of the company, after shuffling it up with the rest of the pack, you will know the card by feeling.' As useful, one might note in passing, as Gale, in explaining to the budding conjurer how to force a card.[8]

---

[6] [Gale] pp. 84-5.

[7] [Mayhew, Vol. 3] p. 109.

[8] 'Professor Anderson's Feats of Magic', *The Penny Illustrated News*, Vol. 1, No. 10, 29 December, 1849, p. 78. An explanation of how to properly force a card is given in [Sachs, 2nd] pp. 117-9, 'The Force'.

## 4. The Extinguisher Trick

It is not known who invented the vanishing of a person under a giant cone, otherwise known as The Extinguisher Trick. According to one source 'the earliest reported notice of this effect was by the French fairground conjurer, Bernard, at the Paris fairs in 1769.' The first conjurer who it is known performed it in the nineteenth century was Jules de Rovère. He had a brief appearance in London at the new Theatre Royal in the Haymarket, on 20th October, 1828. He intended to stay for a fortnight but he had to close after one week. One of his tricks was the Vanishing Lady, using his wife, which was, according to Sam Sharpe, the Extinguisher Trick.[9]

A conjurer who definitely did it – or at least a variation on it – was Sutton, who was mentioned in the supplement to Chapter One. He did a trick known as The Pie of Morocco which comprised 'causing a young lady to disappear and afterwards serving her up in an enormous pie'. There is an illustration of the trick on Sutton's playbill for his appearance at the New Strand Theatre in London in January 1838: similar to the depiction of the vanishing washerwoman in Döbler's playbill, the top of the cone is cut off, giving more of an impression of a basket-shape, as opposed to that of a cone.[10]

Sam Sharpe wrote that the trick was 'sometimes called The Great Escamotage' and as Döbler had that listed as one of his tricks on his

---

[9] Earliest performance is in [Whaley, Dictionary, Vol. 1] p. 322, under the heading of The Great Escamotage. [Sharpe] p. 25, wrote about Conus in his 1790 advertisement claiming he 'would convey his wife, who is five feet eight inches high, under a cup, in the same manner as he would the balls.' For information on De Rovère, see [Clarke] p. 204 and [Sharpe] p. 25.

[10] [Frost] p. 223. More about Sutton and the playbill illustration is in [Dawes, Rich] Mr George Sutton, 'The Great Magician', March, 2014, Vol. 108, 2014, pp. 70-2.

playbill, Sharpe assumed he performed it. However it was likely that was a different trick, as one cannot imagine Döbler would have produced a washerwoman in The Miraculous Washing and then vanished someone else using similar apparatus. Indeed in the contemporary newspaper reports of the time, it was only the appearing washerwoman that got a mention.[11] The *Literary Gazette* described it as follows:

> In the performance of *"the miraculous washing,"* as it is termed in the playbills, the artist borrows eight or ten handkerchiefs, puts them in a basin, and pours water on them. They become thus thoroughly wet; but he immediately returns them dry and ironed to their owners, which supersedes the services of a washerwoman, who nevertheless makes her appearance from out a huge basket, nobody being aware when or how she got into it, or that she was at all on the stage.[12]

The Extinguisher Trick did become very popular for a period, almost certainly due to Robert-Houdin resurrecting it as part of his programme in September 1846. John Henry Anderson, who copied much of what Robert-Houdin did, had added it to his show by 1851. The clearest example of a distinctive cone depicted in a playbill is for Henri Robin, who featured it in his first London season in 1851, under the title of La Disparition de Madame Robin. In the playbill Robin seems about to be vanishing two people, standing side by side. Of course all these post-date Dickens's completion of *A Christmas Carol*.[13]

---

[11] [Sharpe] p. 25. Another Döbler playbill can be seen here: [Houdini, Unmasking] p. 191. As well as looking at reviews in this country, contact was made with Magic Christian, based in Vienna, who is an authority on Döbler. He was also unable to come up with any record of Döbler performing the Extinguisher Trick.

[12] *Literary Gazette*, No. 1322, London, 21 May, 1842, p. 347.

[13] Robert Houdin: [Sharpe] p. 25. Anderson: A review in *The Era* has a

The first appearance of an extinguishing cone in a satirical print would seem to be by Isaac Cruikshank, the father of George, in 1795: it was called *The royal extinguisher or Gulliver putting out the patriots of Lilliput!!!* and shows a large Gulliver, cone in hand, hovering over a group of small people. In 1830 there was a print by Charles Jameson Grant called *Going! Going!* showing a depressed looking Duke of Wellington about to be vanished by William IV and John Bull, holding a large cone between them.[14]

description of JHA performing the Extinguisher trick at St James's Theatre in 1851: 'Then the Professor, having covered Master John Henry Anderson with a wicker extinguisher, spirited him away, first through one table, when he was found, upon the wicker covering being removed to the front of the stage, to have again mysteriously appeared beneath it; next through another table, when Master Anderson was found sitting in front of the boxes; and, thirdly, through another table, when, with a gentleman from the front of the house, he disappeared altogether.' Data from [Dawes, Anderson]. Henri Robin: [Fechner, Vol. 2] p. 156, playbill is undated. In reality the two people were vanished one at a time, as reported in the *Liverpool Mercury*, 24 Oct, 1851 cited in [Dawes, Henri Robin] p.29. Brian Sibley mentioned the name specifically of Henri Robin when flagging the possibility of Dickens basing his description on the trick. 'The Spirit of Christmas Past, carrying "a great extinguisher" – or candle-snuffer – suggests another famous illusion performed in a variety of ways by several magicians, including Henri Robin.' [Sibley] p. 40.

[14] Several images of the Extinguisher used in satirical prints can be found in the British Museum collection. The print by Isaac Cruikshank is BM Satires 8701 and the one by Grant is BM Satires 16320. George Cruikshank's print, referred to in the main chapter, is BM Satire 14145 and is called *The royal extinguisher, or the King of Brobdingnag & the Lilliputians*. Satirical prints came to an end around 1830, replaced by wood cut images in books and journals. There are plentiful images of the Extinguisher in *Punch* cartoons; but they were published after *A Christmas Carol* came out.

## Articles in *Household Words* and *All the Year Round*

It was not just Dickens's novels and short stories where conjuring references might appear – there were also his numerous articles, most notably in his two weekly journals *Household Words* (1850-59) and *All the Year Round* (1859-70). These were edited (although Dickens used the term 'conducted') by Dickens from 1850 right through to his death. All the articles were published anonymously which meant that many readers probably assumed entire issues were solely written by Dickens. Doubtless he did this deliberately, well aware of the selling power of his own name.

It is only comparatively recently that the authorship of those articles appearing in *Household Words* have been established. This was thanks to the pioneering work carried out by Anne Lohrli, who in her study of the Household Words Office Book, was able to ascertain exactly who had been paid for each contribution to the journal. The results were published in 1973, but it was not until 1979 that the book was mentioned in the magic press; this was by Steven Tigner in an undated supplement to an excellent article he had written in July 1979 called 'Charles Dickens In and About Magic, A Preliminary Sketch'[15].

When it comes to *All the Year Round*, the first issue of which was dated 30th April, 1859, there are still many articles which are unattributed; although it is thought that most of those written by Dickens have been identified. The full list of articles, and their authorship (where known) in both journals can be found on the

---

[15] [Lohri] and [Tigner]. In the original article, Tigner looked at several contributions to CD's two journals which had a magic content in them. At no point, though, did he state that any had been written by Dickens, just that they were 'ample testimony to his continuing interest in magic.' *The Journal of Magic History* did not last long and is unlikely to have been widely distributed: there were only six issues produced over two years. [Alfredson] p. 133.

Dickens Journals Online website. This also includes details about each contributor as compiled by Anne Lohrli.[16]

None of the articles which have a significant amount of conjuring content was written by Dickens. Apart from two considered in depth earlier – the review of the memoirs of Robert- Houdin called 'Out-Conjuring Conjurors'; and the article that mentioned Munito the Learned Dog called 'Performing Animals' – another two prominent articles of this nature were 'Modern Magic' and 'Something Like A Conjuror'. Both have been incorrectly attributed to Dickens.[17]

[16] Website address is: www.djo.org.uk. The project director, Professor John Drew of the Dickens Journals Online website, said in 2012 that 'he "very much doubted" that any new fiction by Dickens would be discovered in the journals, but hoped that around a dozen more articles by the author would be uncovered. "It's going to take time and we have to be cautious, though. It's always going to be relative. Computational stylistics gives a best fit but doesn't absolutely prove authorship one way or the other," he said. "While we're unlikely to find lots of new work we can attribute to Dickens it's possible that one or two pieces per year of *All the Year Round*'s publication under his editorship will show evidence of his authorship or co-authorship. So, cautiously, a dozen or more new pieces is what we might hope for".' *The Guardian*, 25 June, 2012.

[17] 'Out-Conjuring Conjurors' [HW] Vol. XIX, No. 472, 9 April, 1859, pp. 433-9: see the Chapter Four Supplement, 'Robert-Houdin'. 'Performing Animals' [AYR] Vol. XVII, No. 405, 26 January, 1867, pp. 105-6: see Chapter One Supplement, 'Munito the Learned Dog'. 'Modern Magic' [AYR] Vol. III, No. 66, 28 July, 1860, pp. 370-74 was written by Eliza Lynn Linton. *Modern Magic* [Hoffman, Modern Magic] was also the title of Professor Hoffmann's ground-breaking treatise on revealing the secrets of magic trick. [Dawson] p. 188 suggested that Hoffmann might have taken his book title from this article as 'he was bound to be conversant with Dickens's articles in *All The Year Round*' and he was convinced Dickens wrote the article ('In *All The Year Round* in 1860, Dickens wrote an article...which was headed MODERN MAGIC'). Even if Dawson did not have the means of discovering the actual

'Modern Magic', despite its title, and notwithstanding that it named three prominent conjurers in the first sentence, was an attack on Spiritualism. It was written by Eliza Lynn Linton who wrote eighty-four articles for the two journals in total. 'Something Like A Conjurer' revealed tricks of Indian conjurers. It is presently unattributed but, as Dickens never went to India, his authorship can be effectively ruled out.

By far the largest misattribution of articles to Dickens was made by Trevor Dawson in his 2012 book *Charles Dickens: Conjurer, Mesmerist and Showman*; a total of possibly nineteen in the two journals. Of the nine *Household Words* articles he contended were authored by Dickens, Dickens only wrote four; the other five were by other, known, authors. Of the sixteen *All the Year Round* contributions, two were by Dickens, a further five by other known

author, he should have been alerted to the fact that Linton had written that *The Spiritual Magazine* claimed that 'the unbelieving son of the conductor of this journal' had attended a couple of séances and therefore supported Spiritualism. This was personally rebutted by Dickens in an 'Editor's Note' where he wrote that his son 'told his father that what he had seen and heard was very absurd, and he gave his father a highly ludicrous detail of the proceedings!' The article itself began with: 'NOT the magic of Herr Wiljalba Frikell or the Wizard of the North; nothing to do with Invisible Ladies or Robert-Houdin's mighty mysteries; but magic of the true black and white sort – witchcraft, demonology, possession, and the like, revived in the modest phrase of Spiritualism.' It was on the basis of this that [Dawson] p. 134 thought CD had seen Wiljalba Frikell, stating that he had been 'impressed' by him. 'Something Like A Conjuror' [AYR] Vol. XIII, No. 303, 11 Feb, 1865 pp. 57-60: author unknown, almost certainly not CD. This was attributed to CD in *Goldston's Magical Quarterly*, Vol. 3, No. 1, Summer 1936, p. 163, with the title of 'Something Like A Conjurer', by Charles Dickens (Reprinted from "All the Year Round", February, 1865). In [Dawes, Stodare] p. 163, was written CD 'included a contribution titled "Something like a Conjurer".' This could be taken, by the less discerning, to infer that CD wrote the article.

authors and the remaining nine are unattributed.[18]

Dawson justified attributing them all to Dickens when he wrote: 'Articles were presented [in *Household Words* and *All the Year Round*] anonymously apart from the serialisation of novels by Dickens and occasionally others, but the major proportion, certainly of the subjects covered by this book, are believed to have been written by Dickens.' In Dawson's book, the 'subjects covered' included circus, theatre, tightrope walking, travelogues, ghosts, performing animals, Spiritualism, fairs, puppetry, mesmerism, books, childhood pastimes and conjuring.[19]

There is little doubt that Dickens did have a huge input into many articles – as Ackroyd wrote, 'he added, amended, revised, shortened, condensed and rewrote'. This was particularly so in the early years of his editorship but 'as the magazine grew more stable both in spirit and in circulation, he began slowly to intervene less actively himself.' More fundamentally, it would certainly be doing a great disservice to the actual writers – and these included the literary giant, Wilkie Collins; author of *Memoirs of Bartholomew Fair*, Henry Morley; Dickens's trusted editorial assistant, WH Wills; and the first female salaried journalist and author of over twenty novels,

---

[18] The four articles correctly attributed to CD in [HW] were: 'The Ghost of the Cock Lane Ghost Wrong Again', Vol. VI, No. 147, 15 Jan, 1853, p. 420; 'The Spirit Business', Vol. VII. No. 163, 7 May, 1853, pp. 217-20; 'A Haunted House', Vol. VII, No. 174, 23 July, 1853, pp. 481-3 and 'An Unsettled Neighbourhood', Vol. X, No. 242, 11 Nov, 1852, pp. 289-92. The two articles correctly attributed to Dickens in [AYR] were: 'Rather a Strong Dose', Vol. IX, No. 204, 21 March, 1863, pp. 84-87 and 'The Martyr Medium', Vol. IX, No. 206, 4 April, 1863, pp. 133-36. Dawson's attempts to attribute certain articles to Dickens were nothing if not imaginative. In an 1860 article in [AYR], called 'My Boys', which was written by Wilkie Collins, a boy called Thomas was mentioned. [Dawson] p. 89 wrote: 'Here Dickens intentionally misquotes the name of his son, as none of his sons was called Thomas.'

[19] [Dawson] p. 130.

Eliza Lynn Linton – to somehow suggest, as Dawson did, that Dickens was responsible for completely rewriting, or been mainly responsible for, their authored articles.[20]

To be fair to Dawson, with the exception of the 'Performing Animals' contribution and the review of the Robert-Houdin's autobiography already discussed, he did not draw that many conclusions from the incorrectly attributed articles; he was content, in the main, to quote extensively from them. What this does do, though, is convey an overall impression that Dickens was much more interested in the general world of conjuring than can be supported by the existing evidence; in particular Dawson assumed that Dickens must have seen conjurers such as Wiljaba Frikell, Addison, Henri Robin, Phillippe and the Davenport Brothers.[21] This book is just concentrating on conjurers but Dawson also took it for granted that Dickens saw the famous tightrope walker, Blondin and Daniel Dunglas Home, the most renowned spiritualist of the nineteenth century.[22]

---

[20] [Ackroyd] pp. 623 & 627.

[21] [Dawson] p. 134: Frikell is named in 'Modern Magic'. [Dawson] pp. 173-4: Addison is in 'At Home with the Spirits' ([AYR] Vol. XV, No. 358, 3 March, 1866 pp. 180-4). [Dawson] pp. 178-9: M Robin and Phillippe are in 'Out-Conjuring Conjurors'. [Dawson] p. 167: The Davenports are in 'Spirits on Their Last Legs' ([AYR] Vol. XIV, No. 328, 5 August, 1865, pp. 45-8). None of these articles are attributed to CD. It would seem that CD must have at least met Henri Robin, as he turns up as attending the same séance as Dickens in 'Small-Beer Chronicles' [AYR] Vol. VII, No. 176, 6 Sept, 1862, p. 608.

[22] [Dawson] p. 154 devoted an entire chapter to reproducing an article called 'Old Rome in Crystal' [AYR] Vol. V, No. 114, 29 June, 1861 pp. 324-7 stating upfront that 'Dickens gives a remarkable description of a Blondin performance he witnessed at the Crystal Palace in 1861.' In fact the article was written by Eliza Lynn Linton. [Findlay] p. 15, wrote: 'We find his taste in general entertainment was not completely Catholic for [CD] says in a letter in

Dickens began editing *Household Words* in 1850, when effectively his conjuring days were over (see Plate 11). It is therefore unsurprising that he wrote so little about conjuring. Apart from 'An Unsettled Neighbourhood', in which he brought up the name of Ramo Samee, there was not one article that Dickens penned which mentioned a conjurer in it, yet alone alluded to his own conjuring. His lack of interest in conjuring is in marked contrast to Spiritualism, on which subject he wrote five articles. Rather than personally review either of the two books written by the famous conjurer Robert-Houdin, he chose instead two books authored by spiritualists. It all points to where his priorities lay at this stage in his life.[23]

Below are listed all the *Household Words* and *All the Year*

1861 how Blondin was appearing at the Crystal Palace but that he has no intention of seeing this Show.' [Schlicke] p. 148 stated that CD did not like dangerous acts, which probably explained his reason for not wanting to see Blondin. [Dawson] p. 169: 'In February 1866, Home gave a lecture upon Spiritualism...Dickens attended this lecture and reported just over two weeks later, in *At Home with the Spirits*'. The article 'At Home with the Spirits' was written by WH Wills: [Pilgrim, Vol. 11] p, 227, n 3 and [Burton] p. 174. That CD almost certainly never saw DD Home was considered in the Supplement to Chapter Five, 'Dickens and Spiritualism'.

[23] The five articles by CD on Spiritualism were: 'The Ghost of the Cock Lane Ghost Wrong Again', 'The Spirit Business'; 'Well-Authenticated Rappings' ([HW] Vol. XVII, No. 413, 20 Feb, 1858, pp. 217-220); 'Rather a Strong Dose' and 'The Martyr Medium'. The books that CD scathingly reviewed in the latter two articles were respectively *The History of the Supernatural in all Ages and Nations* by William Howitt and *Incidents in My Life* by DD Home. As well as 'Out-Conjuring Conjurors', there was the review of Robert-Houdin's book on card cheating: 'Cheating At Cards', [AYR] Vol. V, No. 114, 29 June , 1861 pp. 331-336. For more on this, check out 'Robert-Houdin' in the Chapter Four Supplement.

*Round* articles which have been incorrectly attributed to Dickens in various sources.

## *Household Words*

'New Discoveries in Ghosts', Vol. IV, No. 95, 17 Jan, 1852, pp. 403-6. By Henry Morley. Misattribution by [Dawson] pp. 73.

'The Ghost of the Cock Lane Ghost', Vol. VI, No. 139, 20 Nov, 1852, pp. 217-23. By Henry Morley. Misattribution by [Dawson] pp. 117-8.

'Bookstalls', Vol. VII, No. 166, 28 May, 1853 pp. 289-93. By William Moy Thomas. Misattribution by [Dawson] p. 186.

'Robertson, Artist in Ghosts', Vol. X, No. 253, 27 Jan, 1855, pp. 553-8. By Henry Morley. Misattribution by [Williams] p. 15; [Jay, Celebrations] p. 73.

'Amalek Dagon', Vol. XVIII, No. 448, 23 October, 1858, pp. 444-7. By James Payn. Misattribution by [Dawson] p. 131.

'Out-Conjuring Conjurors', Vol. XIX, No. 472, 9 April, 1859, pp. 433-9. By Edmund Saul Dixon. See 'Robert-Houdin' in Chapter Four Supplement for misattribution of this.

## *All The Year Round*

'A Physician's Ghosts', Vol. I, No. 15, 6 August, 1859, pp. 346-50. Author unknown, almost certainly not Dickens. Probable misattribution by [Dawson] p. 75

'My Boys', Vol. II, No. 40, 28 Jan, 1860, pp. 326-9.By Wilkie Collins. Misattribution by [Dawson] p. 88.

'Modern Magic', Vol. III, No. 66, 28 July, 1860, pp. 370-4. By Eliza Lynn Linton. Misattribution by [Dawson] pp. 127 & 188.

'My Young Remembrance', Vol. V, No. 113, 22 June, 1861, pp. 300-4. Author unknown, almost certainly not Dickens. Probable misattribution by [Dawson] p. 25.

'Old Rome in Crystal', Vol. V, No. 114, 29 June, 1861, pp. 324-7. By Eliza Lynn Linton. Misattribution by [Dawson] p. 154.

'Cheating At Cards', Vol. V, No. 114, 29 June, 1861, pp. 331-6. Author unknown, almost certainly not Dickens. Probable misattribution by [Dawson] p. 180.

D'r Wilkin's Prophetic Dreams', Vol. V, No. 125, 14 September, 1861, pp. 582-5. Author unknown, almost certainly not Dickens. Probable misattribution by [Dawson] p. 194.

'A Little Magic', Vol. VI, No. 143, 18 January, 1862, pp. 400-3. Author unknown, almost certainly not Dickens. Probable misattribution by [Dawson] p. 189.

'Mediums Under Other Names', Vol. VII, No. 156, 19 April, 1862, pp. 130-7. By Eliza Lynn Linton. Misattribution by [Dawson] p. 134.

'Something Like A Conjuror', Vol. XIII, No. 303, 11 February, 1865 pp. 57-60. Author unknown, almost certainly not Dickens. Misattribution by *Goldston's Magical Quarterly*, Vol. 3, No. 1, Summer 1936, p. 163.

'An Unpatented Ghost', Vol. XIII, No. 322, 24 June, 1865, pp. 523-8. By Henry Spicer. Misattribution by [Dawson] p. 76.

'Spirits On Their Last Legs', Vol. XIV, No. 328, 5 August, 1865 pp. 45-8. Author unknown, almost certainly not Dickens. Probable misattribution by [Dawson] p. 167.

'London in Books', Vol. XIV, No. 338, 14 October, 1865, pp. 270-6. Author unknown, almost certainly not Dickens. Probable misattribution by [Dawson] p. 191.

'At Home with the Spirits', Vol. XV, No. 358, 3 March, 1866, pp. 180-4. By William Henry Wills. Misattribution by [Dawson] p. 169.

'Performing Animals', Vol. XVII, No. 405, 26 January, 1867, pp. 105-6. Author unknown, almost certainly not Dickens. See 'Munito the Learned Dog' in Chapter One Supplement for misattribution of this.

# Conclusion

This book has had three principal aims in mind. Firstly, to set out all the available information on Charles Dickens and conjuring, using, where possible, primary sources. Secondly, to correct the errors and misattributions relating to the subject that have occurred over the past one hundred or so years. Finally, to expand on certain topics that might be considered peripheral to Dickens but which give a fuller picture of some aspects of conjuring prevailing in the period.

If the conclusion of this book is that Dickens's own conjuring was perhaps narrower in scope than has previously been suggested, there is plenty of compensation to be gained by fleshing out what is known for certain. His portrayal of the fictional conjurer Sweet William; his own repertoire of tricks and their occasional citation in his novels; his in-depth description of Alfred de Caston's mind reading show; his personality, as reflected in his conjuring traits, mirroring his other interests and work; the prevailing style of mid-nineteenth conjuring impacting on his own performing; all these, and more, have produced a rich vein of revelations.

Even the apparent negatives throw up insights. That Dickens did not write any articles on conjuring in the two journals *Household Words* and *All the Year Round* shows his priorities in later years. That he had very little interest in Robert-Houdin, compared to others he saw such as de Caston and Döbler, demonstrates that perhaps the retrospective opinions on the abilities of the famous French conjurer should be reassessed. That there is absolutely no evidence of Dickens's conjuring outside the 1840s proves that his abandonment of it was as swift as his initial conversion. That there is so little mention of conjuring in his novels testifies to his great ability as a writer to keep true to his characters and plot and not be sidelined by literary irrelevancies dictated by his personal interests.

It is always dangerous to make any predictions for a book; and especially dangerous for a decidedly non-scholarly academic, both in the world of conjuring and Dickensian research, to expect any return outside the sheer reward and enjoyment of writing about two such fascinating topics. But I do hope that future biographers of Dickens will pay a little more attention to his conjuring in assessing, if not the works, at least the man; and I similarly hope that magic historians will appreciate that Dickens deserves greater respect both as a reporter on, and as a barometer of, mid-Victorian conjuring.

# List of Illustrations

# LIST OF ILLUSTRATIONS

All attempts have been made to obtain the requisite permission to reproduce the above images; please contact the author for any errors or omissions in the crediting which will be corrected in any subsequent editions.

# Bibliography

[Ackroyd] Ackroyd, Peter, *Dickens*, Minerva Paperback, London, 1991.

[Albo] Albo, Robert J *Classic Magic with Apparatus: Laboratories of Legerdemain, Volume XI*, Author Publication, 2005.

[Alfredson] Alfredson, James B and Daily, George L, *A Bibliography of Conjuring Periodicals in English: 1791-1983*, Magicana for Collectors, 1986.

[AYR] *All the Year Round*, weekly journal 'conducted' by Dickens from 1859 to 1870.

[Ballou] Ballou, Adin, *An Exposition of Views Respecting the Principal Facts, Causes and Peculiarities Involved in Spirit Manifestations*, Bela Marsh, Boston, 1852.

[Banachek] Banachek, *Psychological Subtleties*, Magic Inspirations, Houston, 1998.

[Barkas] Barkas, Thomas P, *Outlines of Ten Years' Investigation into the Phenomena of Modern Spiritualism*, Frederick Pitman, London, 1862.

[Bayer] Bayer, Constance Pole, *The Great Wizard of the North: John Henry Anderson*, Ray Goulet's Magic Art Book Company, Watertown, 1990.

[Bolton] Bolton, H Philip, *Dickens Dramatized*, Mansell Publishing Ltd., London, 1987.

[Brandon] Brandon, Ruth, *The Spiritualists: The Passion for the Occult in the Nineteenth and Twentieth Centuries*, Weidenfeld and Nicolson, London, 1983.

[Brooker] Brooker, Jeremy, *The Temple of Minerva, Magic and the Magic Lantern at The Royal Polytechnic Institution, London, 1837-1901*, The Magic Lantern Society, London, 2013.

[Burton] Burton, Jean, *Heyday of a Wizard: Daniel Home, the Medium*, George G Harrap, London, 1948.

[Callow] Callow, Simon, *Charles Dickens and the Great Theatre of the World*, HarperPress, London, 2012.

[Capron] Capron, E.W., *Modern Spiritualism: Its Facts and Fanaticisms, its Consistencies and Contradictions*, Bela Marsh, Boston, 1855.

# BIBLIOGRAPHY

[Carlyle] *The Collected Letters of Thomas and Jane Welsh Carlyle*, edited by Clyde de L Ryals, Kenneth J Fielding et al, Duke Univ. Press, Durham NC, 1990.

[Chorley, Vol. 1 / 2] *Henry Fothergill Chorley: Autobiography, Memoir and Letters*, compiled by Henry G Hewlett, Richard Bentley and Son, London, 1873.

[Clarke] Clarke, Sidney W, *The Annals of Conjuring*, edited by Edwin A Dawes, Todd Karr and Bob Read, The Miracle Factory, Seattle, 2001.

[Claxton] Claxton, Michael, 'Victorian Conjuring Secrets', pp. 165-178, *Victorian Secrecy: Economics of Knowledge and Concealment*, edited by Albert D Pionke & Denise Tischler Millstein, Ashgate, 2010.

[Claxton, Punch] Claxton, Michael, *Magic-Related Material in Punch (1841-1960)*, unpublished manuscript, [n/d, c. 2003].

[Crambrook] *Crambrook's Catalogue of Hermetical & Mechanical Puzzles...Second Edition Corrected and Enlarged*, T. C. Savill, London, 1843.

[Dawes, Anderson] Dawes, Edwin A and Dawes, Michael E, *John Henry Anderson: The Great Wizard of the North and his Magical Family. A Revisionary Biography*, Center for the Conjuring Arts, New York, 2014. This book was not yet published at the time of going to press – hence there are no page references when it is cited.

[Dawes, Great Illusionists] Dawes, Edwin A, *The Great Illusionists*, Chartwell Books Inc, New Jersey, 1979.

[Dawes, Rich] Dawes, Edwin A, 'A Rich Cabinet of Magical Curiosities', *The Magic Circular*, ongoing.

[Dawes, Robin] Dawes, Edwin A, *Henri Robin: Expositor of Science & Magic*, Abracadabra Press, California, 1989.

[Dawes, Stodare] Dawes, Edwin A, *Stodare The Enigma Variations*, Kaufman and Company, Washington, 1998.

[Dawson] Dawson, Trevor, *Charles Dickens: Conjurer, Mesmerist and Showman*, Author Publication, 2012.

[Dean] Dean, Henry, *The Whole Art of Legerdemain, or Hocus Pocus in Perfection*, London, 1722.

[Debar] Debar, J H Diss, 'Reminiscence of Charles Dickens' first visit to America by a fellow passenger', *Joseph Hubert Diss Debar Collection Ms 79-191.2*, West Virginia Archives & History, n/d.

# BIBLIOGRAPHY

[Dickensian] *The Dickensian*, a journal founded in 1905 and ongoing: published three times a year by the Dickens Fellowship.

[Dickens, Charley] 'Reminiscences of My Father', Charles Dickens: The Eldest Son of the Great Novelist, Supplement to *The Christmas Windsor Magazine*, December, 1934.

[Dickens, Henry] Dickens, Henry Fielding, *The Recollections of Sir Henry Dickens, KC*, William Heinemann, London, 1934.

[Dickens, Mamie, My Father] Dickens, Mamie, *My Father As I Recall Him*, The Roxburghe Press, London, 1897.

[Dickens, Mamie, Dickens with his Children] Dickens, Mamie, 'Dickens with his Children', pp. 30-47, *Some Noted Princes, Authors, and Statesmen of our Time*, ed. James Parton, T.Y. Crowell, New York, 1885.

[Dickens, Speeches] Dickens, Charles, *Speeches, Literary and Social*, Chatto and Windus, London, 1880.

[Dircks] Dircks, Henry, *The Ghost! as produced in the Spectre Drama, popularly illustrating the Marvellous Optical Illusions obtained by the apparatus called The Dircksian Phantasmagoria*, E. and F.N. Spon, London, 1863.

[Durham] Durham, Geoffrey, *Professional Secrets, A Life in Magic*, Author Publication, 2008.

[During] During, Simon, *Modern Enchantments: The Cultural Power of Secular Magic*, Harvard University Press, Cambridge, Massachusetts, 2002.

[Fechner, Vol. 1 / 2] Fechner, Christian *The Magic of Robert-Houdin: "An Artist's Life"*, translated by Stacey Dagron, edited by Todd Karr, FCF Editions, Paris, 2002.

[Felton] Felton, Cornelius Conway, *Familiar Letters from Europe*, Ticknor and Fields, Boston, 1865.

[Findlay] Findlay, JB, *Charles Dickens and his Magic*, Author Publication, Shanklin, I.W., 1962.

[Forster, Vol. 1 / 2 /3] Forster, John, *The Life of Charles Dickens*, Vol. 1, 1812-1842, Vol. 2, 1842-1852, Vol. 3, 1852-1870, Boston, 1875.

[Forsyte] Forsyte, Charles, *The Decoding of Edwin Drood*, Charles Scribner's Sons, New York, 1980.

[Frost] Frost, Thomas, *The Lives of the Conjurors*, Chatto & Windus, London, 1881.

251

[Gale] *Gale's Cabinet of Knowledge; or, Miscellaneous Recreations*, London, 1796.

[Garenne] Garenne, Henri, *The Art of Modern Conjuring, Magic and Illusions*, Ward, Lock and Co., London, [n/d, c. 1886].

[Gibecière] *Gibecière, Journal of The Conjuring Arts Research Center*, New York, first issue Winter 2005, ongoing.

[Goldston] Goldston, Will, *Tricks of the Masters*, George Routledge, London, 1942.

[Hatch] *The Magic of Johann Nepomuk Hofzinser*, compiled by Ottokar Fischer, translated by Richard Hatch, Walter B Graham, Nebraska, 1985.

[Hibbert] Hibbert, Christopher, *The Making of Charles Dickens*, Harper & Row, London, 1967.

[Hodder] Hodder, George, *Memories of my Time, including Personal Reminiscences of Eminent Men*, Tinsley Brothers, London, 1870.

[Hoffmann, Modern Magic] Hoffmann, Professor, *Modern Magic: A Practical Treatise on the Art of Conjuring*, George Routledge and Sons, London, 1876.

[Hoffmann, Slates] Lewis, Angelo J, M.A. (Professor Hoffmann), 'How and What to Observe in Relation to Slate-Writing Phenomena', *Journal of Society for Psychical Research*, August, 1886.

[Houdini, Conjurers' Monthly] *Conjurers' Monthly Magazine*, edited by Harry Houdini, Vol. I, No. 1, September, 1906 - No. 12, Vol. II, August, 1908: republished by Richard Kaufman and Alan Greenberg, USA, 1991.

[Houdini, Unmasking] Houdini, Harry, *The Unmasking of Robert-Houdin*, The Publishers Printing Co., New York, 1908.

[HW] *Household Words*, weekly journal 'conducted' by Dickens from 1850 to 1859.

[Hutchings] Hutchings, Richard J, *Dickens on an Island: A Biographical Study of Charles Dickens in the Isle of Wight*, James Brodie, Bath, 1970.

[Jay, Learned Pigs] Jay, Ricky, *Learned Pigs & Fireproof Women*, Robert Hale, London, 1987.

[Jay, Journal] Jay, Ricky, *Jay's Journal of Anomalies*, Farrar Straus and Giroux, New York, 2001.

[Jay, Celebrations] Jay, Ricky, *Celebrations of Curious Characters*, McSweeney's Books, San Francisco, 2011.

[Johnson] *The Dickens Theatrical Reader*, edited with a Prologue and Notes by Edgar and Eleanor Johnson, Victor Gollancz, London, 1964.

[Kaplan] Kaplan, F, *Dickens: A Biography*, William Morrow & Company, New York, 1988.

[Kaplan, Mesmerism] Kaplan, F, *Dickens and Mesmerism: The Hidden Springs of Fiction*, Princeton University Press, Princeton, 1975.

[Kemble] Kemble, Frances Ann, *Records of Later Life*, Henry Holt and Company, New York, 1882.

[Lamont] Lamont, Peter, *The First Psychic: The Peculiar Mystery of a Notorious Victorian Wizard*, Little, Brown, London, 2005.

[Lewis] Lewis, Hal, Student at Law from Kenny Meadows, 'The Street Conjurer', *Head of the People: or, Portraits of the English*, Vol. 1, R. Tyas, London, 1840.

[Lohrli] Lohrli, Anne, *Household Words: A Weekly Journal, 1850-1859, Conducted by Charles Dickens. Table of Contents, List of Contributors and Their Contributions, based on the Household Words Office Book in the Morris L. Parrish Collection of Victorian Novelists, Princeton University Library*, University of Toronto Press, Toronto & Buffalo, 1973.

[Mackenzie] Mackenzie, N & J, *Dickens a Life*, Oxford University Press, Oxford, 1979.

[Macready] *The Diaries of William Charles Macready*, edited by William Toynbee, Chapman and Hall, London, 1912.

[Magic Circular] *The Magic Circular*, the monthly magazine of The Magic Circle founded in 1905, ongoing.

[Mahatma] *Mahatma*, Vol. 1, No. 1, March, 1895 - Vol. IX, No. 8, February, 1906: republished by Richard Kaufman and Alan Greenberg, USA, 1994.

[Mann] Mann, Al, 'Retrospective', *The Pallbearers Review*, Karl Fulves, Volumes 9–10, L & L Publishing, Tahoma, 1993.

[Marks] Marks, David and Kammann, Richard, *The Psychology of the Psychic*, Prometheus Books, New York, 1980.

[Mayhew, Vol. 1 / 3] Mayhew, Henry, *London Labour and the London Poor*, London, 1851.

[Novra] *Catalogue of Conjuring Tricks and Puzzles, from Henry Novra's Magical Repository*, 95 Regent Street, London, [n/d, c. 1860].

[Ochorowicz] Ochorowicz, Dr Julian, *Mental Suggestion*, translated by J Fitzgerald, The Humboldt Publishing Co, New York, 1887: first published in French in 1885.

# BIBLIOGRAPHY

[Pepper] Pepper, John Henry, *The True History of Pepper's Ghost. A reprint of the 1890 edition with a new introduction by Mervyn Heard*, The Projection Box, London, 1996.

[Pilgrim, Vol. 1-12] *The Pilgrim Edition of the Letters of Charles Dickens*, edited by Kathleen Tillotson, Graham Storey and others, Oxford, 1965-2002.

[Price] Price, David, *Magic: A Pictorial History of Conjurers in the Theatre*, Cornwall Books, London, 1985.

[Robert-Houdin, Memoirs] *Memoirs of Robert-Houdin: Ambassador, Author, and Conjuror Written by Himself*, translated by Lascelles Wraxall, Chapman and Hall, London, 1859.

[Robert-Houdin, Secrets] Robert-Houdin, *The Secrets of Conjuring and Magic*, translated by Professor Hoffmann, George Routledge, London, 1878: first published in French as *Les Secrets de la Prestidigitation et de la Magic*, 1868.

[Rogers] *Recollections of the Table-Talk of Samuel Rogers*, edited by Alexander Dyce, D. Appleton and company, New York, 1856.

[Sachs, 1st] Sachs, Edwin, *Sleight of Hand: Being minute instructions by the aid of which with proper practice, the neatest and most intricate tricks of legerdemain can be successfully performed* , 'The Bazaar' Office, London [n/d, 1877].

[Sachs, 2nd] Sachs, Edwin, *Sleight of Hand: A Practical Manual of Legerdemain for Amateurs and Others*, Second, and Greatly Enlarged Edition, L Upcott Gill, London, [n/d, 1885].

[Scot] Scot, Reginald, *The Discoverie of Witchcraft*, John Rodker, 1930.

[Schlicke] Schlicke, Paul, *Dickens and Popular Entertainment*, Unwin Hyman, London, 1988.

[Servant] *The Servant Girl in London*, R. Hastings, London, 1840.

[Sharpe] Sharpe, Sam H, *Salutations to Robert-Houdin*, Micky Hades, Canada, 1983.

[Sibley] Sibley, Brian, *A Christmas Carol: The Unsung Story*, Lion Publishing, Oxford, 1994.

[Slater, Dickens] Slater, Michael, *Charles Dickens*, Yale University Press, New Haven, 2009.

[Slater, Journalism] *Dickens' Journalism, Volume 3, 'Gone Astray' and Other Papers from Household Words 1851-59*, edited by Michael Slater, J.M. Dent, London, 1998.

[Smith, Albert] Smith, Albert, *The Adventures of Mr Ledbury and his friend Jack Johnson*, Richard Bentley & Son, London, 1886.

[Smith, Charles] Smith, Charles Manby, *The Little World of London; or, Pictures in Little of London Life*, Arthur Hall, Virtue, and Co., London, 1857.

[Smith, Grahame] Smith, Grahame, *Charles Dickens: A Literary Life*, Macmillan Press, London, 1996.

[Sperber] Sperber, Burton S, *A Checklist of Conjuring Catalogs and their Dealers or Magic Shops in English from 1843-2006*, A Real Miracle, 2007.

[Staff] Staff, Frank ("F.S"), 'Dickens and Conjuring', pp. 93-4, *The Magic Circular*, Vol. 25, No. 284, March, 1931.

[Steinmeyer] Steinmeyer, Jim, *Hiding the Elephant*, Carroll & Graf, New York, 2003.

[Stordare] Stodare, Colonel, *Stodare's Fly-Notes; or, Conjuring Made Easy*, London, George Routledge & Sons, London, 1867.

[Strutt] Strutt, Joseph, *The Sports and Pastimes of the People of England*, Thomas Tegg, London, 1838.

[Sunderland] Sunderland, Laroy, *Book of Human Nature: illustrating the philosophy (new theory) of instinct, nutrition, life*, Stearns & Co., New York, 1853.

[Tigner] Tigner, Steven S, 'Charles Dickens In and About Magic: A Preliminary Sketch', pp. 88-110, *The Journal of Magic History*, Volume 1, No. 2, July 1979. Volume One Supplement, 'Charles Dickens in and about Magic', pp. 228-9, [n/d].

[Tomalin] Tomalin, Claire, *Charles Dickens, A Life*, Viking, London, 2011.

[Tomalin, Invisible] Tomalin, Claire, *The Invisible Woman*, Vintage Books, New York, 2012.

[Toole Stott] Toole Stott, Raymond, *A Bibliography of English Conjuring 1581-1876*, Harpur & Sons, Derby, 1976.

[Truesdell] Truesdell, John W, *The Bottom Facts concerning the Science of Spiritualism*, S. Low & Co., London, 1883.

[Weeden] Weeden, Brenda, *The Education of the Eye, History of the Royal Polytechnic Institute 1838-1881*, Granta Editions, Cambridge, 2008.

[Whaley, Dictionary, Vol. 1 / 2] Whaley, Bart, *The Encyclopedic Dictionary of Magic 1584-1988*, Jeff Busby Magic, California, 1989.

[Whaley, Who's Who] Whaley, Bart, *Who's Who in Magic*, Jeff Busby Magic, Idaho, 1991.

[Wiley] Wiley, Barry H, 'The Thought-Reader Craze', pp. 9-134, *Gibecière*, Vol. 4, No. 1, Winter 2009.

[Williams] Williams, Heathcote *What Larks! Charles Dickens, Conjuror*, The Box of Tricks, edited by Daniel Stashower, Redstone Press, 1995.

[Witt] Witt, Wittus, *Zauberkästen* [Magic Box], Wittus, Heinrich Hugendubel Verlag, München, 1987.

[Young] Young, Julian Charles, *A Memoir of Charles Mayne Young, Tragedian, with Extracts from his Son's Journal*, Macmillan and Co., London, 1871.

# Acknowledgements

So many have assisted with this book that it is hard to know where to start. I will begin with David Britland (as he is the only one listed here who is actively involved in pitching television programmes!) who helped me develop the slightly unusual structure of the book; and, as always, did not hold back with his pungent comments. He whipped this book into some sort of shape and saved me from some embarrassing errors.

Geoffrey Durham took up the running and made numerous suggestions to make the book read better – in the process correcting many elementary grammatical errors and clarifying what I was attempting to say. I did not think anyone could be so conscientious in reading someone else's work. That is, until Brian Lead also had a read of a draft and applied an equally forensic – and time consuming – examination of the text. If this book is considered halfway readable then it is mostly due to the generosity of these two gentlemen.

This book could never have been written without Dr Edwin (Eddie) Dawes, Professor Emeritus of Biochemistry at the University of Hull, Chairman of The Philip Larkin Society and indisputably the most renowned living magic historian. Not just for his assistance and encouragement in my own researches – which included allowing me to use data from his yet unpublished book on John Henry Anderson – but also for pointing me in the direction of how the writing of magic history should be approached, with relevant citations to back up facts and theories. It is no coincidence that his name crops up more than any other in the bibliography. A similar academic approach to magic history has been adopted by James Smith who kindly checked out – and corrected – the sections relating to historical conjuring books.

I wanted to ensure that the 'Dickensian' side of this book was as error-free as possible. So called upon the services of Dr Tony Williams, Associate Editor of *The Dickensian*; Honorary Senior Research Fellow in Humanities, University of Buckingham. As well as conscientiously reading a draft, he drew my attention to further books and articles to explore and turned up a couple of conjuring references that I would have missed. I am very grateful for him giving his time so gracefully.

My main two institutional research sources have been The British Library and The Magic Circle Library. The chief librarian of the latter is Peter Lane and both he, and his staff, have been endlessly helpful; if the library itself did not have access to some material, the chances are that it was in Peter's own collection. Equally invaluable has been the website Dickens Online Journal (www.djo.org.uk) that has the complete works of *Household Words* and *All the Year Round*.

A lot of emails have been sent by myself to sundry people asking for help on specific subjects. In particular Daniel Cudennec (Alfred de Caston), Magic Christian (Döbler and Hofzinser), Peter Lamont (Spiritualism), Jeremy Brooker (Pepper's Ghost), Peter Davies (slates), Banachek (psychological forcing), Heathcote Williams and Claire Tomalin (citations in their books), Andrew Rouse (ballads), Michael Claxon (*Punch* magazine), Lorna Gibb (ghosts), Byron Walker (Hans Wecker's book) and Geoffrey Dicks (*The Dickensian*): I am indebted for all of them for taking the time to respond. Special thanks to Tracey Earl, the Archivist at Coutts Bank, for checking out Dickens's spending at Hamleys – and to Richard Evans for pointing me in her direction and Mark Dickens for expediting it.

Other helpful parties have been Jonathan Allen who found a copy of *What Larks! Charles Dickens Conjuror* for me and also pushed me towards reading Simon During's *Modern Enchantments*; Brian Sibley for sharing my enthusiasm for Dickens, his thoughts on *A Christmas Carol* in particular and the book in general – not to mention some last minute error checking; Janet

# ACKNOWLEDGEMENTS

Clare for pointing out the difference between 'been' and 'being'; Bob Loomis for tracking down obscure references; Brian Lead (again) for tactfully reminding me that I had missed out Pepper's Ghost in the first draft; and Will Houstoun who found unexpected connections between Professor Hoffmann and Dickens. In 2012 I purchased a 'Dickens lot' owned by John Fisher at an auction: some time ago he had considered writing a book on Dickens and conjuring and these were his preliminary research papers. I am grateful for being able to access his initial work.

I cannot pretend to have even touched the surface of research into Dickens. My main knowledge of Dickens, outside his conjuring, has come from the three superb biographies, produced in the last twenty five years, by Claire Tomalin, Michael Slater and Peter Ackroyd. In particular, Chapter Five could not have been written without the insights that emerged from the latter. Two other invaluable sources have been *The Dickensian* – as a subscriber you get access to all the back copies – and the twelve volumes of wonderfully edited Dickens's letters, collectively known as the Pilgrim Edition.

Self-publishing creates its own hazards; self-typesetting (which is also what I have done) is probably a step too far. So apologies if the layout of the book does not live up to the contents (or indeed, if it comes out okay, the contents do not live up to the layout). I did have the common sense, however, to get the cover professionally designed and I am grateful for Lucy Byatt for her skill and patience in this role.

The motivation for writing this book was twofold. Firstly, I was asked to speak, as an author, at a Dickensian conference in Boston. Unfortunately I did not have a book to back up the talk – so I decided to write one. Writing with a deadline is much easier so I am grateful to Deb Benvie from the North of Boston Branch of the Dickens Fellowship for providing this.

Secondly, in 2012, Trevor Dawson brought out a book on Dickens and conjuring which, I thought, was going to be the one I had planned to write – making my task redundant. Instead it acted as a spur to write this book. Whatever my criticisms, I am grateful to him for leading me down avenues I might not have otherwise explored, which have certainly enriched my overall knowledge of the subject matter.

Any readers who feel that I have been rather harsh on this author – and indeed others – can take comfort that any errors which are discovered in this book (of which there are sure to be some) will doubtless be leapt upon with joy and quoted back at me with relish. Rest assured that all those mistakes are mine alone and I take full responsibility for any brickbats that are deservedly received.

In summing up my general thanks, I must mention a response I got from the distinguished academic Peter Davies. I asked his permission to quote something he had written to me about slates, which admittedly has rather a tenuous connection to Dickens and conjuring. 'It's nice to be asked about slates', he wrote back, 'my colleagues think I'm nuts…' It is because of so many similarly 'nutty' people that this book has emerged into the daylight.

Finally, a huge thank you to my wife Elizabeth, and for my two children George and Carly, for allowing me to skip many household chores and family outings with the excuse: 'I really need to work on this book'.

# Index

# INDEX

# INDEX